TIN CUP DREAMS

ALSO BY MICHAEL D'ANTONIO:

Fall from Grace (1990)

Heaven on Earth (1992)

Atomic Harvest (1994)

The Best Medicine (1999) (with Dr. Mike Magee)

TIN CUP

DREAMS

A LONG SHOT MAKES IT ON THE PGA TOUR

Michael D'Antonio

NEW YORK

Copyright © 2000 Michael D'Antonio

All rights reserved. No part of this book may be reproduced
in any manner whatsoever without the written permission of the Publisher.
Printed in the United States of America. For information address: Hyperion,
77 West 66th Street, New York, New York 10023-6298.

Library of Congress Cataloging-in-Publication Data

D'Antonio, Michael.
   Tin cup dreams : a long shot makes it on the PGA Tour / by Michael
D'Antonio.
      p. cm.
   ISBN 0-7868-6497-4
   1. PGA Tour (Association)   2. Golf—Tournaments—United States.
   3. Toledo, Esteban.   4. Golfers—United States—Biography.   I. Title.
   GV969.P75 D26 2000
                                      99-053824

FIRST EDITION

10 9 8 7 6 5 4 3 2 1

Book Design by Oksana Kushnir

For the rest of my foursome—Toni, Elizabeth, and Amy—and for the Toledo family.

ACKNOWLEDGMENTS

Like golfers, writers must work alone, but they thrive on support and kindness. Much kindness has been extended to me by Esteban and Colleen Toledo, their son Nicholas, and by Jon Minnis. I've been coached on matters of golf and the PGA Tour by fellow writer Curt Sampson, by David Barrett of *GOLF Magazine*, and by the PGA Tour's own Lee Patterson. And I've been supported, as always, by the members of my family who endured the absences and obsession necessary to complete this work.

CONTENTS

FOREWORD

More than any sport, golf rewards individual effort and commitment. Success is not delivered simply by the luck of the genetic lottery. It is earned through hard work, sacrifice, and faith in the possibility that every long shot has a chance to make it. The people who exemplify this ethic, often called grinders, display a kind of strength that transcends the game. Their stories offer real lessons for life.

Even in an age when pop stars have made the concept of easy, instant wealth and fame into an article of faith for the masses, golf inspires thousands of youngsters of all shapes, sizes, and colors to embrace the kind of discipline that makes victory on the course possible. Visit an inner-city public course like Brackenridge in San Antonio. In the heat of summer or the gathering darkness of winter, you'll see girls and boys pounding balls, building their dreams with second-hand irons. Whether or not they make their golf dreams come true, they are learning how to believe in themselves, set a goal, and work hard.

This is a book about one of those kids—a grinder—who had a passion for the game and the determination to succeed, which stayed with him well into adulthood and remains strong today. Esteban Toledo possesses an astonishing instinct for survival. A child of abject poverty, he suffered from a profound speech defect, witnessed the death of his father, and virtually raised himself on an isolated farm where nights were lit by candles and water was drawn from a river. Golf would eventually be his way out, but he would endure more than fifteen years of frustration before finding real success. His story is as much about the resilience of his spirit as it is about his chosen sport.

●

I came to love the game of golf when I began to work as a caddie at Wentworth-by-the-Sea Country Club in the 1960s. Built at the turn-of-the-century, the private Wentworth course hugs a small harbor in the seacoast town of Rye, New Hampshire. Marsh grass and wild roses grow at the places where the salt water reaches toward the rough. The clubhouse is white shingles, a high red roof, and green awnings; the kind of starched Victorian architecture that makes you stand a little straighter as you climb the steps.

In 1967, everything that was right about golf, and everything that was wrong with it, was on display every day at Wentworth. The club was restrictive in its membership. And some of the members could mistreat the scruffy caddies. For their $5, they expected me to carry a huge and heavy golf bag three miles, clean their clubs, track their shots like radar, and wait like a puppy leashed to a fencepost during lunch.

None of these negatives could obscure for the caddies Wentworth's saving grace: the game. Out on the course, even the more arrogant members were brought to their knees by skulled irons, pulled drives, and chunked chip shots. In the midst of their suffering, they often turned to me. Can I reach it with a six iron? Is it in the water? Do you see what I'm doing wrong? At such moments, in the just and honorable realm of golf, we were equals.

Even more grace came at dusk. While the members soothed themselves with alcohol, the caddies were allowed to play. We imitated the swings we had been on TV, and discovered that sometimes we hit solid drives or true putts. Alone on the golf course, our shadows lengthened as the sun dipped to the horizon. Every tree, shrub, and blade of grass glowed. And it all—the green fairways, the sound of the waves on the ocean holes, the buttery light—belonged to us.

My younger brother and I became so obsessed with the game that we turned our school's playground into a par-three layout, even hauling the family's lawnmower over to trim the make-believe fairways. In the dead of winter, when snow covered everything, I'd go to the beach at low tide and practice bunker shots in the sand. Thirty years later, the beach still looks like one giant bunker to me.

But it was not just the intricacies of the sport that drew me to golf. Even as a twelve-year-old boy, I could see that the human dramas played out on the PGA Tour touched on issues beyond the game. Many of the players I admired came from poor or middle-class families. They had been caddies too. And their success was built primarily on hard work, not brawn or privilege. They proved to me that the game's basic fairness was real and that it deserved my faith.

•

The story of big-time golf in America begins in 1913 with the stunning long-shot victory of Francis Ouimet at the U.S. Open. The frail child of a gardener, Ouimet had caddied for twenty-eight cents per round at The Country Club in Brookline, a suburb of Boston. But as a nonmember he was barred from playing there. When the Open came, young Francis intended to be a spectator. Instead he was recruited to fill out the field and promptly trounced Henry Vardon and rest of the world's elite. He was celebrated across America as the working class youth who wrenched the game out of the hand of the British aristocracy.

Ouimet's achievement is not unique. For decades after his success, the professional game was filled with players from modest means who beat the odds. Walter Hagen and Gene Sarazen started as caddies, as did Byron Nelson and Ben Hogan. Banned from playing the club where he worked, Hagen built his own little course in a vacant field and played with odd clubs discarded by the players he served. Sam Snead grew up on a chicken farm. He also made his own course—a four-holer—and he made some of his own wooden clubs. Among more recent stars, Lee Trevino was raised in a four-room house with no running water or electricity. Ray Floyd was an Army brat who lived on military bases.

I do not mean to say that either golf or the PGA Tour has been open to all on an equal basis. Racism was practiced more thoroughly, and far longer in golf than in other sports. And it exists to this day. But though it was stained by bigotry, the professional game has always been vulnerable to the determined outsider. The Trevinos and Sncads achieved a level of wealth comparable to members of any private club, and status that was even higher. Charlie Sifford broke the most imposing color barrier in all of sport, winning PGA Tour titles in Hartford and Los Angles. They were heroes to me and all the other caddies at the Wentworth. In their success we could see that through the game, the last could become first.

Perhaps more than any sport, golf allows for the underdog to prevail. Golf is not easy. If it were, then Michael Jordan wouldn't lose so much money on the course. But a dedicated and gifted athlete of only average size and strength can reach the top through hard work. Ben Hogan, one of the most revered players of all time, lived this truth. Undersized and self-taught, he struggled into his mid-thirties before he began to win major championships. Then he went on to become a legend of sport.

Hogan prevailed because he mastered the most difficult challenges in golf, which are not physical but psychological. No athlete is more naked than the golfer poised alone above the ball. He cannot rely on a teammate, or even react to an opponent. He is solely responsible for the swing, the flight of the ball, and the numbers on the scorecard. To make matters worse, it all looks so easy. The ball is just sitting there on the ground. How hard could it be?

The annals of the golf are filled with the all-too-human collapses of truly gifted players who proved how hard it is to train the mind as well as the body. The most infamous may be Leo Diegel, who played most of the major tournaments in the 1920s and 1930s. At the U.S. Open of 1925, Diegel led up until the last six holes. Needing only pars to win, he was struck by so much anxiety that he scored nine over and lost. A more recent example of golf's vagaries is Corey Pavin. Though he won the U.S. Open in 1995 and earned $850,000 in 1996, Pavin couldn't manage to finish in the top ten in any tournament the next year.

Anyone who had ever played golf can empathize with Pavin's plight, which did not improve significantly until 1999. The golf swing is a complicated dance of more than 100 muscle movements that take place in less than two seconds. It is fragile, and impossible to perfect. And every player who has ever mastered it for a moment has also lost it. Indeed, a lifetime of golf would involve thousands of such moments of mastery and loss. This experience, shared by the PGA Tour pro and amateur alike, explains the deep connection between the professional golfer and weekend players who form the base of the PGA Tour's audience. Even though the game is played on two distinctly different levels, we believe that we know how the best players feel, and, to an extent, we do.

•

In recent years golf has changed radically. High-tech clubs, aerodynamically perfect balls, and precision-groomed courses have made the game more forgiving. In the same time, the PGA Tour has become a very big business. Multinational corporations now sponsor a ten-month season of events that generates billions of dollars' worth of economic activity. Tour purses total more than $100 million per year. It's not unusual for first prize at a tournament to be $500,000. Inevitably, money has become almost a universal obsession among players.

With pro golf becoming ever more sophisticated and profitable, the making of a PGA Tour–caliber player has also evolved into a rarefied process. Most of today's young pros are the product of endless lessons aided by computers, trainers, consultants, and cameras. They go to college on golf scholarships and from there turn pro. The best ascend immediately to the PGA Tour with its seven-figure endorsement deals and $4 million–dollar purses. If times get tough, they turn to sports psychologists to help them handle the pressure of competition.

The irony of this era, when TV ratings are higher than ever and record numbers of amateurs have taken up the game, is that the long shot faces more obstacles than ever before. And the underdog stories that inspired me to love the game seem to be fading away. Many writers and old-time professionals have begun to worry aloud that the pro game is losing touch with golf's values. Too many players are becoming as remote as *Fortune* 500 CEOs and as spoiled as pop divas. "They think they've gotten bigger than the game they play, and bigger than the people who pay to see them," observed Arnold Palmer.

With this in mind, I set out to discover whether golf at its highest level still reflects the values of the game itself. Is it still open to all? Could a caddie still make it to the top? And if so, what would it take to get there, and stay? I found the answers to these questions in Esteban Toledo's life story. His long-shot dream, and his struggle to make it come true, suggests how we may all do the same.

Golf touches me because of all the games, it is the most forgiving of the body and most demanding of the spirit. In the end it has always rewarded—there's really no other way to put this—goodness. In golf, you don't beat the other player. You don't push him around, or shove the ball in his face. In golf you master first your self, including all your inner demons, and then endure the solitary test that each course delivers. The game reveals character, and that is its most important service to the young players who take it up. This is how it has worked from the beginning. And this is why it matters today.

Not Tiger Woods

If Ouimet, Hogan, Snead, and Trevino left a trail behind on their way to greatness, it passes through the golfing hell called Q. School. Formally named the PGA Tour Qualifying Tournament, Q. School is a six-day event. Topflight amateurs and struggling pros pay $4,000 out of their own pockets to play 108 holes. In the end, thirty-five out of 164 will win a PGA Tour Card and a chance to play for million-dollar purses every week of the coming season.

In theory, Q. School, like the game of golf itself, promises the kind of opportunity that has all but disappeared from professional sport. Anyone of any age can play his way to Q. School and, if he succeeds, instantly become a Tour pro. It's as if the New York Yankees held an open try-out every spring and guaranteed a handful of participants a spot on the team.

In late November 1997, I traveled to Grenelefe Golf and Tennis Resort in Haines City, Florida, as the first part of my quest to see if golf and the Q. School still keep their promises. I knew that while everyone else was getting ready for the holidays, the ultimate grinder, the vagabond pro who will seize his dream, would be there. I wanted to find this player, so I could follow his adventure through Q. School and a year on the PGA Tour. I knew I would have to arrive early, because he surely would.

•

It's a few minutes after 6 a.m. and the sun is just breaking the horizon as I drive into the empty parking lot at Grenelefe. Two tractor-trailers, one green, one painted the colors of the American flag, are lined up on the strip of grass that separates the lot from the golf course. The red-white-and-blue truck is loaded with computer scoring equipment. The other holds a huge power generator that is, for the moment, silent. Not a person is stirring, and the trailers are the only sign that something special is going to happen here.

A few minutes pass. Vapor rises from the coffee cup on the dashboard and condenses into a little circle of moisture on the windshield. At 6:15, a white sedan wheels into the lot. Its tires crunch over loose bits of gravel, making a sound like someone chewing ice. It stops next to the trailers. A dark-haired man, maybe thirty years old, quickly emerges from the passenger side and is at the trunk before the driver releases the latch. The lid rises and he reaches in to grab a pair of black spikes. He balances against the car and slips them on, snapping the laces tight. The driver, a white-haired, older man, gets out and pulls a golf bag out of the trunk. He slams the lid shut, and the two disappear through the space separating the trucks, heading for the golf course.

I follow them to the felt-like grass of the practice green, where I get a better look. The player is a slim but muscular man about five feet, nine inches tall and perhaps 165 pounds. He has bushy black hair and a brown face shaped by Spanish and Indian blood. His brown-black eyes are so intently focused that they almost vibrate. Without a word, he reaches into the golf bag and throws three balls on the green. He steps up to them, hunches over his putter, and draws it back. The clubface meets a dimpled Titleist with a thud. The ball sprays a little rooster tail of dew as it makes a line straight to the hole. It drops with the sound of a coin tossed into a beggar's cup. For a moment a half smile crosses his face.

The smile doesn't last long. Indeed, this man is so grimly serious that I decide that I won't even try to talk to him until he's finished playing today. But as we stand beside the green, his caddie introduces himself as Jon Minnis and whispers a bit of the Esteban Toledo story. He tells me that this year Toledo *had* a chance to earn his Tour Card a different way, by finishing among the top fifteen players in the Nike Tour, pro golf's junior league. But a late-season collapse did him in. Now he's at Q. School for the *tenth* time. He's thirty-five years old, old enough to consider quitting.

I think that a bit of luck and a bit of calculation have already brought me face to face with the true grinder I am looking for. The problem is, he's not likely to make it this time, either.

ROUND ONE

At 8:30 a.m., Esteban Toledo stands as silent and rigid as a tombstone on the tee of the first hole. His cheeks dimple as he nervously breathes in, holds his breath for a moment, and then exhales. The other player in this twosome is Chris Couch, age 24. Couch is tall, sinewy, strong, and aloof in a pair of deep black wraparound sunglasses. He has a scraggly little goatee and the slightly down-turned mouth of a piranha. He looks like a member of a Gen-X rock band.

No gallery has gathered at Grenelefe, but the players are nevertheless introduced by an elderly announcer with a baritone voice. After the old man calls—"Esteban Toledo of Mexicali, Mexico"—Toledo glares at his ball and lashes it into the sky. This may be a game, but he is not a man at play.

Eventually Toledo will tell me that he actually enjoys golf, but during Round One he seems miserable. He bolts off the first tee, leaving his caddie struggling to catch up. He silently finds his ball, pulls an iron from the bag, and slings the ball onto the green. There he hits a lag putt to within five feet. He settles over the ball again and then freezes. Back down the fairway, two old men, each carrying a stomach the size of a ninth-month pregnancy, are walking toward us and chattering in full voice. Toledo stares at them and raises his hand like a traffic cop. "Please!" Chastened, they shut their mouths. Toledo makes the putt.

On the next hole the same two men—their names are Rod and Clem—try to whisper. They are both hard of hearing and their voices rise as Toledo checks the numbers that are fixed on sprinkler heads, showing the distance in yards to the center of the green. He consults a notebook where he has recorded information about each hole. He wipes his club with a towel. He checks the wind. The routine is designed to settle the nerves as well as set up the shot. It also consumes a great deal of time. Rod and Clem decide it's ridiculous.

"He is sure fussy," says Rod.

"He looks like he's taken some punches," adds Clem. "Maybe he's not right."

Toledo growls again to silence them. He then lands a ninety-yard wedge shot safely on the green. Rod and Clem mutter about his "rabbit ears" and walk away. Toledo and his caddie march on.

●

As he churns down Grenelefe's fairways, Esteban Toledo doesn't notice the blue heron in the pond on the fifth hole or the Hispanic gardeners at work in the yards of nearby condominiums. He says but a few words to Chris Couch, and hardly looks at him at all. His mind is riveted on one thing, beating this golf course.

At 7,301 yards, Grenelefe West is longer than all but one of the courses that the PGA Tour visited last year. The other layout being used for Q. School is Grenelefe South, which is 600 yards shorter. On both, the fairways are narrow and lined with southern pine and live oak draped in Spanish moss. They look like the great lawns of plantation houses. The greens are small. Nearly every one is bounded by a multitude of grasping bunkers.

I can see right away that Toledo is a steady player who hits the ball straight, if not very far. (Later I'll learn that his driving average is about 260 yards, quite low for a professional.) He makes up for his lack of distance with consistency and creativity. On this round, the one time he gets in a jam he uses the rules to his advantage. Caught in a sloping bunker, his ball buried deep, he notices an anthill under his feet. When confronted with a live hazard, be it ants or alligators, a player can move his ball without penalty. Toledo summons a rules official, who grants him a free drop, which just happens to give him a much better shot.

"Every shot could be the one that breaks you," his caddie whispers to me. "You use everything you can."

As Toledo cruises silently, the younger and more aggressive Chris Couch mutters to himself and slams his clubs around whenever the ball goes astray. And when it does go astray, it goes a very long way. Couch has no trouble sending the ball more than 300 yards off the tee, a distance comparable to that achieved by the Tour's number one distance driver, John Daly.

But the artillery doesn't give Couch any real advantage. At the end of the morning these two very different golfers reach the same destination—seventy-one, which is one under par. Their names are posted comfortably in the middle of the scoreboard. I've managed to stay out of the way for eighteen holes, which is enough to earn an invitation to lunch from Toledo's caddie. He winks at me and says, "C'mon, let's go. It may be the only time a caddie ever buys you anything."

•

In the clubhouse coffee shop, players and caddies crowd around a dozen little tables. The little cafe is decorated in a way that is obviously intended to force cheerfulness on its occupants; bright white and yellow paint, daisies in little vases. It's the perfect place for snowbird foursomes to share BLTs after a pleasant morning on the greens. But the decor will do nothing to cheer a desperate Q. Schooler. It's not hard to imagine that by the end of the tournament someone could throw one of those little vases through the window that overlooks the practice range.

Among the competitors who are recuperating here from Round One is Michael Campbell, the onetime sensation who came out of obscurity and almost won the British Open in 1995. Campbell never realized his potential, which explains why he's at Q. School. Today he nervously chain-smoked his way around Grenelefe and after just one day is already four strokes over par.

Despite the golfers' brave efforts to ignore it, the tension of Q. School buzzes in the air. The laughter coming from Campbell's table on the other side of the room is a little too loud, a little too high-pitched. Almost everyone in this room is certain to see his dream broken here this week; forced smiles don't change that fact. As we sit down, both Jon and Esteban invite me to call them by their first names. They are friendly, but also cautious.

Gradually I discover that the man who is buying the sandwiches is no ordinary caddie. Jon Minnis is, in fact, a sixty-year-old, self-made millionaire from California who was Esteban's sponsor when he immigrated to the United States from Mexico in 1982. Tall, with a pale craggy face and bright blue eyes, Jon's appearance couldn't be any more different from Esteban's. But he is the closest thing to a father Esteban knows, and Esteban sometimes even calls him Dad. Jon's support for Esteban's golf dream has included everything from financial backing to English lessons to carrying his clubs at every Q. School.

Both men are stingy with the details of Esteban's life before he came to the United States. I figure they are either wary of me, or just plain tired. But they do tell me that Esteban grew up poor and taught himself to play on the driving range of the Mexicali Country Club, where he was a caddie. He was an amateur boxer, and even fought professionally for a brief time. Golf became his passion when appendicitis and two operations made his abdomen so vulnerable that he could not longer take a pounding in the gut. He made it all the way through Q. School once before, in 1993, but played so poorly on the tour that he lasted just one season.

Jon's own story, or at least the abridged version he offers here, is a classic example of a poor boy making it rich, losing it all, and then getting it back. In his case it was in the concrete business during California's booms and busts. Minnis had raised himself up through hard work and guile. Both men insist that for Esteban the same thing is possible in golf. "If you work hard, you have a chance," says Jon. "It is pretty fair."

It is also Darwinian. Esteban recalls Q. School 1991, when he was told that he had won his PGA Tour Card but then stood by the scoreboard and watched with dread as other players finished with surprisingly low scores. Hours passed and his gut churned. Eventually, enough remarkable rounds were posted to push him to the wrong side of thirty-fifth place. After 108 holes, he would lose by the smallest whole number: one.

That Q. School defeat was much worse than the others. For a few hours Esteban had let himself believe that ten years of grueling work had finally paid off. In that decade, he had given up everything for his dream. He had delayed dating and falling in love. He had forsaken the comfort of a real home life. He had fought against the doubts that periodically welled up inside him, against the physical strains and injuries, against the thousands of other men who wanted what he wanted. He had a right to feel elated when it seemed the card was finally his. When his name was pushed to the wrong side of thirty-fifth place, shock yielded to a feeling of overwhelming disappointment. It was all too much. He broke down in tears beside the eighteenth green, and cried more on the night flight back to California.

Q. School failure exiled Esteban to the minor league of pro golf known as the Nike Tour. The Nike is golf's version of Triple-A baseball, with a few important differences. Unlike baseball players, Nike golfers receive no salary. In fact, they are required to pay an entry fee—usually $250 per tournament—before they can even compete. They must also cover all of their own expenses. The players travel the countryside in cars or vans or campers watching both the road and their credit card limits. The Nike Corporation, which sponsors the circuit, runs TV commercials that depict the players gamely persevering down to their last $100, which, incidentally, wouldn't buy them a pair of the company's better spiked shoes.

When I ask Esteban to compare the PGA and Nike Tours, I expect him to describe the top tour as golf heaven. Instead he looks around the room at the other players, making sure they are not listening. "I've been there," he says. "It doesn't work the way you think."

Using the back of a paper place mat for notes, Esteban and Jon then describe the system that determines who actually gets a chance at the money on the Tour. It reminds me of the work rules that used to govern the printers' union jobs at newspapers back in New York City. The whole idea is to protect insiders and to make it as difficult as possible for newcomers to stick. Here's how it is done:

A typical PGA Tour event has room for between 150 and 165 players. Dozens of past champions, sponsor favorites, and lifetime members can all claim a spot. Then come the top 125 money winners from the previous year, who are admitted according to rank. Only after all of these—more than enough to fill the tournament—do a few of the Q. School graduates get a chance. At the beginning of the season they are admitted according to their Q. School scores. The number one finisher gets the first opening. Number thirty-five may not get in at all.

The challenge doesn't stop with an invitation to play. Like everyone else, the Q. Schooler grads must perform well in the first two rounds of every tournament, because then the field is reduced for the weekend to the top eighty or so. Those who are cut earn nothing for the week. (No other pro sport asks athletes to compete for zero compensation.)

Although the weekly cuts are based on scores, the overall ranking of PGA Tour players, calculated after every tournament is played, is based on earnings. This is the most important scoreboard of all, the only one that really matters at year's end, and it is rigged against the steady grinders. Indeed, a player who wins one tournament, but misses every other cut, will always rank higher than a competitor who consistently plays well enough to make the cut but finishes near the bottom. Every aspect of the grinder's game may be superior—his scoring average, putting, driving—but he will be trumped by his opponent's one big week.

The money list system becomes all the more cruel at the end of each year when only the top 125 money-winners will have their precious PGA Tour membership cards renewed. When he played his one year on the Tour—1994—Esteban was admitted to roughly half the tournaments. He survived the cut in about half of those, but earned just $66,049. He lost his card. He has spent the last three years trying to get it back.

As we finish lunch, I tell Esteban I'm looking for the pro who will succeed on Tour even though he is not Tiger Woods. If Esteban makes it through Q. School, I add, I'd like to follow him on the Tour to see if he manages to stick. Esteban is skeptical, not about his own chances for success, but about me. As he stands up from the table, he looks around the room before offering a response.

"I'm not here to cha-cha-cha with all these guys. I'm here to get my card and I will get my card. Then I'm going to the PGA Tour and I'm going to keep my card. You can come along, if you want. It doesn't bother me."

•

Outside the clubhouse restaurant, players gather around a scoreboard that is roughly forty feet long and ten feet high, and is painted a rich country club green. This is where the hopefuls measure themselves at the end of every day, by searching for their names and comparing their scores with the others. This time around, Esteban

Toledo has decided to protect himself from this one bit of Q. School torture. He will not look at the board all week.

For those who dare to look, the board shows that the day's best total is a sixty-six, shot by Scott Verplank. No surprise there. Verplank is a longtime member of the PGA Tour who played on a medical exemption in 1997 but failed to finish in the top 125. He is expected to contend for first place at Q. School from start to finish.

There is a surprise name posted in second place. Ivan Smith, of Columbus, Ohio, fired a sixty-seven. No one standing by the board seems to know Smith. According to a one-page questionnaire he completed for the Tour media office, Smith is a forty-one-year-old carpenter with no prior professional experience. At one under par seventy is another unknown named David McCampbell. He is a former pig farmer from Indiana. Like Esteban, both of these men are self-made pros and true grinders.

ROUND TWO

A TV crew from the PGA Tour is assigned to follow David McCampbell on his entire round. The Tour makes films that promote the game's mystique in order to boost TV ratings and revenues. They are effective. Last year, various television networks agreed to pay a total of $100 million for the rights to broadcast tournaments from 1999 to 2002. This is more than double the Tour's previous take for television rights. At the same time, prices for TV commercials on golf tournament broadcasts are also rising. For example, half a minute will cost $156,000 during the upcoming AT&T Pebble Beach National Pro-Am. Last time around, thirty seconds cost less than $100,000.

In McCampbell, the PGA Tour may have a story that will prove the magic of the game. What could be better than going from pig farming to golf professional? It doesn't hurt that he looks ten years younger than his age, thirty-eight, and that he bears a faint resemblance to a young Kevin Costner. To make matters even better, he is accompanied by his devoted girlfriend, a pretty young woman named Amy Jewell. The producers have attached a wireless microphone to Amy's collar. It will capture the swooshing sound of her nylon jogging suit and every word she says as she walks the eighteen holes of Grenelefe West and pulls for her man to succeed.

Though it must have seemed like a good idea before he teed off, by the time he reaches the fifth hole, I have to believe that McCampbell knows it was a mistake to let the camera crew tag along today. He has already put his ball in two bunkers and scored bogeys on three holes. This is not what he imagined would happen when he walked onto the first tee this morning.

It was not what Amy expected, either, and she has started looking away when her boyfriend approaches the ball. On the fifth tee, she puts her hand over the little microphone and leans toward me. "You know, David has never even applied for a job," she says. Aside from farming, which he hates, David has no way to make a living.

McCampbell has already given farming a good try. When he was in his twenties, he raised hogs and grain on his family's land. He was married, and then divorced by age 26. Looking ahead, he could see only endless days of hard work. His relief came at a local golf course, where he was obviously the best player.

This is how a pro golf career can begin. Other golfers at the club started to ask McCampbell why he didn't give the PGA Tour a try. He fantasized about it, but always stopped short of taking action. It was only after his father recognized his unhappiness on the farm, and granted his permission, that McCampbell decided to leave the barn for the fairway. He moved to Florida and committed himself to training. His father's blessing was a gift that McCampbell now wants to repay with success at Q. School. In winning a card, he would justify his father's faith.

At Grenelefe, McCampbell steadies himself with a birdie on the sixth hole and smiles the kind of strained-jaw smile that fighter pilots in the movies flash as they depart on a suicide mission. Unfortunately, more bogeys wait on the back nine. He misses easy putts and his frustration grows. He stops talking to the people in the small gallery. His brave smile disappears.

He is not alone in his misery. On Day Two, the sounds of frustration echo around the course. Somewhere in the distance, a ball strikes a tree and clatters from branch to branch like a Surlyn-covered squirrel. Someone cries, "Oh, fuck!" Minutes later I watch as a young man on an adjacent fairway mishits his ball and then uses his club to beat the plastic bottom of his golf bag as if it was a Florida 'gator on the attack.

By the end of Round Two, McCampbell's score of seventy-five drops him deep into the mass of players below thirty-fifth place, the Tour Card cutoff point. Meanwhile,

Esteban Toledo has made another steady, determined march around the course to score an even par seventy-two. Chris Couch does even better, with a seventy. At least two golfers are holding their own against the golf course and the pressure.

As McCampbell joins the solemn crowd around the scoreboard, he looks less like a young movie star and more like his thirty-eight years. But unlike Esteban, he is talkative and unguarded. He tells me that when he was a boy, he was good at every sport he tried. His glory days came when he was the star quarterback at Turkey Run Junior-High School. But he was too short and too slow to be a professional ballplayer. He had to let go of that dream.

Listening to him, I remember something my wife, a psychotherapist, once told me about her male patients. In therapy, each and every one of them eventually talks about a sports dream. The way they talk, you would think the Earth is populated by billions of males who came within a hair's width of sporting immortality. Most cling to an image of themselves as serious contenders undone by an injury or bad break. All mourn the end of their quest to become that modern tribal hero: the professional athlete. Of course the moment of acceptance, when a man finally realizes that he'll never play point guard for the Bulls, is often the start of adulthood. It is what Judith Viorst has termed a "necessary loss," and painful as it may be, it leads to new dreams.

For those who take it seriously, the bitter blessing of golf and the Q. School is that they prolong the male fantasy and, most likely, delay maturity. Other sports make things clear very early in life. They tell you in no uncertain terms that you are too slow, too small, too weak, or too something else to make it. But golf is different. Every avid amateur has heard of men who broke into the pro ranks at age 30 or 40. It is this evergreen sports fantasy that drives David McCampbell. He looks up at the scoreboard, where his name is now in fifty-eighth place and declares, "I still have a chance."

ROUND THREE

"Hi, I'm Billy Downes. How ya doin' this afternoon?" (Actually, it's morning.)

The older man looks at him, draws on his cigarette, and exhales both the smoke and his reply: "Smith." He looks down at the driver in his hand. He doesn't have to tell Billy Downes to shut up.

At forty-one, Ivan Smith is one of the oldest men at Q. School, and he looks it. Slightly built with a creased face, red hair, and pale freckled skin, Smith has spent the better part of his life scrambling to support himself with winnings from minor golf tournaments and odd jobs. Last winter he moved office furniture. He's come to Q. School hoping to at last put hunger and defeat and menial jobs behind him.

Though Q. School is supposed to be bright with opportunity, Smith starts the day looking edgy and depressed. He is justified. After an opening round sixty-seven, which left him in second place, he crashed with a second-day score of seventy-seven. His name was moved, down from the group clustered just below Scott Verplank, to the middle of the pack.

Bob Hyde, the PGA Tour press officer, tells me that Smith is a mystery. As far as Hyde can tell, Smith has absolutely no golf pedigree, no amateur championships, no college golf experience. But the truth is that Smith actually played the PGA Tour from 1983 to 1985. He lost his card when he didn't finish high enough on the money list.

Smith last attended the Qualifying Tournament in 1986, and began play so well that he was almost certain to go back to the Tour. Then he hit a drive into some thick underbrush, where it likely skittered out of bounds. Still on the tee, he hit a second ball, in case the first couldn't be found. Players are allowed to do this, but first they must declare that it is a "provisional" shot. Though everyone in his group understood what he was doing, Smith failed to say the required words. Another player reported the mistake, and Smith was disqualified. Enraged, he waited in the parking lot, fists clenched and assault on his mind. In the end he didn't carry out the attack. Instead, he went home and actually tried to give up golf.

Twelve years later it's Round Three of another Q. School—the first he's attended in eleven years—and I'm watching as Smith's ball lands in a greenside bunker on the first hole. He gets it out with a splash of sand and saves his par. But his face registers disgust as he gets into his golf cart. For the first time ever, carts are allowed at Q. School because a disabled player named Casey Martin filed a lawsuit to get one, and a federal judge required that the Tour allow it. In the coming months, as Martin's case proceeds, the issue will make front page headlines around the country as PGA Tour officials fight the challenge to their authority.

Here, at Q. School, the Casey Martin lawsuit means that anyone who wants a cart may use one. Smith is one of the few who takes advantage, but it doesn't seem to be helping. On the second hole, he is so hesitant and nervous that his first putt doesn't even make it halfway to the cup. After a bogey six, he gets behind the wheel of the cart and drives away, hunched over like a commuter in a ten-mile traffic jam.

As I follow Smith to the next tee, I spot Woody Austin, once the symbol of Q. School hope, on a nearby green. Austin got his card in the 1994 Q. School and in his first year won the Buick Open, $734,000 and Rookie of the Year. But he had a terrible 1997, and lost his card. (The year was so bad that during one tournament, after missing a putt, he hit himself in the head with his club and bent the shaft like a banana. Videotape of this incident has been played and replayed on sports broadcasts ever since.) As I watch Austin at this Q. School, he misses an easy putt. He manages to control himself long enough to get the ball into the hole with a second try. Then he uses his putter to whip the ground so hard that the sound of the impact carries a hundred yards.

Standing there between the slumped Ivan Smith and the flailing Woody Austin, I realize that these men may actually be addicted to their quest. If not addicted, they are certainly obsessed. This is not unique to golf or the Q. School. The entire U.S. economy is built on the compulsive pursuit of the one big achievement that will yield a lifetime of wealth. For authors, it's the big book. For drug dealers, it's the big score. In golf, it's "The Card."

In all these cases, the pursuit is set up like the classic "Skinner box" experiment. Harvard's B. F. Skinner put pigeons in boxes that were equipped with levers, which, when pecked, released grain. When the grain came on a predictable schedule, the pigeons pecked calmly, assured of their reward. And when no grain at all was delivered, they soon ceased to try. But when the reward was unpredictable, the birds worked themselves into a frenzy trying to make the magic that produced the reward. It is the similarly unpredictable quality of golf, and the Q. School, that keeps these men pecking and pecking.

As Ivan Smith struggles to no avail, I try to avoid making direct eye contact. (The code of golf, and the code of all men, call for averting the eyes in these situations.) But when slow play up ahead forces him to wait on a tee, Smith seeks me out for company. It's probably because I'm the only one around, besides him, with any gray hair. We talk about the trial of Q. School, and he confesses that his obsession with the sport frightens him. "I've been scared that it's the only thing I know how to do," he says. "But when you are on the Tour, you're a king. This is the dream of the American male, isn't it? How do I give it up?"

Fortunately, after I leave, Smith is able to pick up his game. He finishes with a seventy, which is a solid score on the West Course. With a seventy-two, David McCampbell does not improve his lot at all, but at least he maintains his position. Esteban grinds on with a seventy. He has not played a poor round yet. Chris Couch makes a sixty-eight.

ROUND FOUR

As the weekend arrives at Grenelefe, Q. School is starting to look more like a pro golf tournament. A few thousand fans, many of whom are friends and family of certain players, turn out to watch the competition. Agents and the representatives for Titleist, Nike, and other companies that sell to the golfing public show up on the driving range. They are easy to spot, because they all have impeccable haircuts, their clothes look like they just came out of the wrappers, and they all wear the same smile.

Most of the reps are looking for players whom they can pay thousands of dollars to wear their corporate logos on their caps and shirts. The investment pays off every time a TV camera focuses on a fellow who is wearing the company's name. Reps dream of coming to Q. School and finding the next superstar player and signing him to a contract. They hope he's naïve enough to sign before he has an agent.

Of course, the agents have also come to the Q. School, and they are just as eager to find a new star or two to generate commissions on endorsement deals. At 8 a.m., I stand beside the practice green and watch as one of them, Chris Clark, hovers around a lanky, long-haired young golfer named Patrick Bates. Clark works for IMG, the most powerful sports agency in the world. IMG is so big that it actually created the convoluted system for ranking the world's players.

As he talks, Clark bends at the waist, like an earnest waiter reciting today's specials. Patrick Bates struggles to remain focused on his putting. A soft-spoken, devoutly Christian young man, Bates is not about to shoo Clark away directly.

But Clark takes the hint when Bates offers grunting replies to his questions. The agent leaves the green to take a place beside me. He tells me that Bates was once IMG's client.

"And you want him back?" I ask.

"We want Pat to be happy," he replies.

Today I'll follow Chris Couch for some of the fourth round. Couch has done so well that all he has to do is keep up his current level of play and he is sure get his card. Today, he appears at the first tee wearing a black nylon warm-up suit and the same wraparound sunglasses he has worn for every round. Something about him—maybe it's just his Darth Vader fashion sense—makes him difficult to like.

On the second hole, Couch's drive lands in the trees, and he flubs a pitch shot into the rough. The best he can do is a bogey. Then, on the sixth, he lands in a greenside bunker and blasts the ball out with so much extra effort that it flies thirty feet past the cup. Another bogey. On the par three seventh hole, he hits an errant tee shot, misses the green completely, and then slams his club down so violently that the head buries in the turf. He leaves it sticking in the ground for his caddie to extract.

After nine holes, Couch's score is forty, which would mean eighty—and no card—if he plays the back nine at the same pace. He's taken off the black warm-up suit and his swagger is gone. As he walks down the tenth fairway, his caddie tells him a story about a basketball player who misses a dozen shots in a row, but sinks the last one to win the championship game. I begin to feel sorry for them both.

As I walk along, Chris Couch's fiancée and mother, two blond outdoorsy-looking women who have been following

him all day, introduce themselves. Mardi Couch tells me
that her husband, Chris's father, played minor league
baseball. He taught his four sons golf, and then taught
them to compete by conducting family tournaments and
posting the results on a scoreboard at home. By age 10,
Chris was winning every time. At age 16, he played in a
Monday qualifier and actually got into a PGA Tour event,
the Honda Classic. This feat won him a blurb in *Sports
Illustrated*, the house organ of sports fantasy. That same
year, he was named the top junior golfer in the United
States. He went on to be a star at the University of Florida
in his home town of Gainesville.

Despite his early promise, Chris Couch never
received the kind of financial support that helped make
a boy named Eldrick Woods into a young man known
by the world as Tiger. "Tiger's father was paid for years
by IMG, so he could be his coach full time," says Mardi.
"Then he got a lot of sponsor exemptions to play in
tournaments."

(Tiger's father did receive money from IMG, but the
amount had not been public knowledge. As for the sponsor exemptions—Tiger got them because his fame drew
fans to tournaments. They also allowed him to earn a card
without enduring Q. School.)

At each tournament, the main sponsor—usually a cor-
poration—is permitted to invite a handful of players to
compete even though they might otherwise not qualify.
These spots may go to famous players who draw fans or to
those who are friends of the company officials. Chris
Couch fell into neither category.

"My husband is a roofing contractor," adds Mardi. "For

years we drove Chris around the country to play, eating sandwiches in the car and watching our pennies."

To sustain himself on the Nike Tour, Chris Couch accepted the backing of some hometown businessmen. They pay for his cheap hotels and fast food. In return they get 90 percent—yes, 90 percent—of everything he earns. "I know it sounds bad, but some of the players have it worse. They give back everything they make," says Mardi.

Listening to his mother, it's easy to recognize that years and years of her time and energy and hopes have been poured into young Chris's golf career. His father has devoted himself, too, and it's not hard to imagine that the life of the entire family has revolved around this one young man's golfing fortunes.

On the course, Couch begins to look like he's carrying a couple of generations' worth of sports fantasies on his back. He presses each shot, trying to get a few extra yards out of his swing. He risks going over trees and shooting directly at flagsticks, even when the landing area is narrow and bunkers promise to seize any less-than-perfect shot. He makes some birdies, but the effort isn't enough. He finishes with a seventy-four, and drops well below thirty-fifth place. He says he is not discouraged. The look on his mother's face says that she is.

●

Back at the clubhouse, the scoreboard shows that David McCampbell has tumbled to the point where he must be reconsidering the farm life. Ivan Smith has managed to stay in the middle of the pack. And Esteban Toledo, grinder exemplar, has finished his second consecutive seventy-stroke round. If Q. School ended today, he would play next year on the PGA Tour.

ROUND FIVE

The Golf Channel has cameras in place on both courses this morning. The two remaining rounds will be broadcast live to 17 million subscribers. The production requires that several different tractor-trailer-sized electric generators be turned on, and left on. Their grumble can be heard and felt from a half mile away. The addition of a hamburger stand near the tenth tee and a growing crowd of onlookers remind me that Q. School leads to the PGA Tour, and the Tour is more than golf. It is that most precious American commodity: entertainment.

Today's list of starting times puts Chris Couch and Esteban Toledo together again, this time on the first tee of the South Course at 8:48 a.m. They are fortunate to be playing the easier of the two courses, but you can't tell this by Esteban's face. On the way to the first tee, he is so solemn that a Tour official stops him to ask if he's sick. He is not sick, just focused. In fact, he may feel better than he has ever felt at Q. School.

As he plays the fifth round, Esteban falls into a state of grace that quiets every distraction and doubt. This is the bliss of The Zone, a magical frame of mind marked by a level of intense but relaxed concentration that allows athletes to perform at the highest level.

Psychologists who have studied this state refer to it not as "The Zone" but as "flow." Flow has been documented scientifically through measurements of brain waves, respiration rate, and performance. Certain factors cause it. First you must face a challenge that is substantial, but not impossible to overcome. Then you must give yourself entirely to the task. This means letting the body and mind do what they are conditioned to do without the interference of doubts and anxieties. Gradually, the sound of the crowd disappears, focus becomes sharper, muscles perform perfectly. (The phenomenon was named and described in detail by Mihaly Csikszentmihalyi in his book entitled *Flow.*)

For golfers, flow can be as elusive as true love. Poised over a tiny ball that lies motionless on the ground, they are exquisitely vulnerable to flow-destroying thoughts. This happens all the time in golf, but not this time, not with this golfer. On hole after hole, Esteban calmly sets up beside the ball and can literally feel what he must do to land it near the flagstick. He swings and the white dot flies high into a sky that seems to be the most tranquil of blues. Before it lands, the ball curves gently toward the pin. On impact, it stops near the hole. On the green, it seems as if the hole is ten times its normal size and Esteban can simply will the putter to knock the ball in. Birdies and pars pile one upon another.

While Esteban glides along, Chris Couch desperately tries to cut every dogleg corner and flirts with every bunker that protects a pin. The result is a mix of mishaps and spectacular successes. One of the latter occurs on hole number twelve, a long par five. Here he uses a three wood to hurl his second shot over a stand of trees and onto the green. This shot is so impressive that it moves a couple of retirees watching from their back porches to come jogging out to the fairway to applaud.

Leaving Couch and Esteban for a while, I walk through some backyards and gardens to search for Ivan Smith, who needs an exceptional round if he's going to have a chance to get his card tomorrow. I find him on the fifth green as he rolls a birdie putt into the hole. He should be smiling, but his demeanor is dour. On the way to his cart he tells me that he double-bogied an easy par three, which is two holes back. He seems so grim that I promise to follow another group, so I'm not a distraction.

"Okay," says Smith. "But it's not you that's the problem. What I really need is to get out of my own way." He gets in the cart, slumps over the wheel, and presses the pedal to the floor.

Up ahead, Esteban Toledo and Chris Couch reach the eighteenth tee. Couch is on his way to a seventy; not quite the score he needs, but a good round nonetheless. He will have a reasonable chance to finish in the top thirty-five tomorrow.

Esteban is, at the moment, four strokes lower than Couch. He is playing so well that he has attracted camera crews from both the Golf Channel and a Japanese network. The camera operators and sound technicians jog down the fairway behind him, stumbling and cursing the weight of their equipment. Esteban doesn't even notice them.

The final hole is a par four with a narrow fairway that ends in an elevated green with bunkers all around. A column of live oaks wearing scarves of Spanish moss marches down the left side. Esteban lands his drive amid these trees, in a spot where he has no direct line to the hole. From here, a bogey would be a decent result.

With his lips pursed, Esteban enters the thicket and shuffles his feet on a bed of loose pine needles. As he swings, he loses his footing. The ball hits a branch and trickles ten yards into the fairway. Esteban follows the ball into the fairway where Jon puts his hand on his shoulder. Together they march off the distance to the nearest marked sprinkler head. Jon hands him a six iron, which Esteban uses to land his ball four feet from the hole. He makes the putt, saving par. His score of sixty-six is the lowest of the day among all the competitors. The Japanese pull him aside for an interview.

•

Up near the clubhouse, dusk brings out the scorekeeper. The dividing line between the top thirty-five and the rest of the field is a five-round total of 353. Esteban is four strokes ahead of this mark. He cannot recall being in a better position to start the last day of Q. School. But he refuses to discuss the possibility that he will join the PGA Tour next year. He's confident about tomorrow, but anything might happen.

As I scan the green scoreboard, Ivan Smith sidles up to me. He has a can of beer in his hand. He tells me that in the middle of his suffering today he had realized that he had been taking his eye off the ball just before impact. It's a very common mistake. Players do it when they are struggling because they are anxious to see the outcome of their shots.

Once he knew to stop looking up, Smith birdied the last three holes. He shot sixty-seven, good enough for thirty-fourth place.

As the shadows stretch across the grass, making the area around the scoreboard cold and dark, many of the agents and equipment reps turn and walk the fifty yards to the eighteenth green to watch Stiles "Big Daddy" Mitchell finish his round. Big Daddy is a 275-pound Southerner with a loud voice, a cherubic face, and a huge grin. His major achievement in golf to date is winning the 1996 Master Blaster Long Drive Championship by hitting two shots for a combined 700 yards.

Mitchell has played well enough so far that a simple par on the final hole would get him the score he needs to have a reasonable chance for a card tomorrow. But from the fairway, he hits the ball over the green and into a clutch of azalea bushes that grow beneath some tall, straight pines. He finds it trapped in the greenery. After securing his footing, he slashes at the ball. It moves just a few feet out of the thicket. Frustrated, he hitches up his pants, sets himself again, and sends the ball skittering onto the green and then off it. He needs two more strokes to finish with a double bogey worthy of a weekend hacker.

None of this seems to bother Big Daddy very much. He has probably ruined his chance to win his card, but he can still drive a golf ball 350 yards, and that's worth something to the people who make equipment. Minutes after his debacle, he stands at the concession stand with a hamburger in his hand and an agent at his elbow. Reps from equipment companies circle, the dollar signs almost visible in their eyes. Behind him, the sunset is turning the pale blue sky a blazing orange. Big Daddy is smiling like he just won the Masters.

ROUND SIX

An hour before play begins, no one dares to talk on the West Course driving range. On the practice green, players avoid making eye contact. In the men's room, a man wearing khaki pants and spiked shoes is on his knees in one of the stalls, retching.

Of the four players I have followed closely, only Ivan Smith and Esteban still have a chance. Chris Couch is pretty much destined to return to the Nike Tour, and David McCampbell might already be hearing the sounds of tractors and grunting hogs.

I start the day by walking a few holes with Ivan Smith, who seems to do poorly whenever I am around. It happens again. He bogeys the second hole and the fourth. Once again I leave, on the chance that my presence is the thing that disrupts his game.

I find Esteban on the second fairway yelling at his golf ball. "Fly, fly!" It falls into the rough just short of the green. For the first time, he seems unnerved. In a whisper, Jon Minnis tells me that Esteban's rhythm is off. He's swinging too quickly and missing with every shot. He's had to struggle just to make pars. On the eighth hole he manages to slow down enough to reestablish his swing. He lands a fifty-yard pitch shot inches from the cup where it makes a little pockmark and spins to a stop. With a tap-in, he makes his first birdie of the day.

Somewhere ahead of us, Ivan Smith is surely slumped and scowling. He's on his way to a score of seventy-five, which will drop him out of the ranks of the card winners. He will be offered full privileges on the Nike Tour, where he will join the cart-riding Casey Martin, who will also fail to win a PGA Tour Card. Chris Couch, who was in the first group to start play at 8 a.m., is even further into his own nightmare. He too will come in at seventy-five, and be invited to play in the junior circuit. David McCampbell will finish so far behind them that he won't get even this consolation prize.

Only one of the grinder hopefuls I picked at the start of the week remains in contention. With four holes to go, and his score now one over par, Esteban must at least par the remaining holes to get a card. Now he is calling after every shot he hits.

On the fifteenth, his drive—"Fly!"—drifts right and lands in some trees on the slope of a hill. He saves par with a low shot that whizzes under a tree limb and then runs all the way to the green.

On the sixteenth hole, a 208-yard par three, he hits a three iron. "Fly! Fly!" The ball does fly, to within twenty feet of the hole. Two putts. Another par.

By the time he reaches the final hole, on the final day, Esteban is still one over. Par—a score of five—would assure him a spot among the select thirty-five. A bogey could ruin him.

Esteban's drive lands in perfect position on the right side of the fairway. Ahead waits the green, surrounded by bunkers and flanked on the left and in the back by little man-made hills that resemble moguls on a ski slope. As he walks to the ball, anxiety rises through Esteban's chest. This feels nothing like flow. It is more like terror.

When he gets to the ball, Esteban is most afraid of making a big mistake—shanking, skulling, or just topping the ball. He steps up to it and then backs away. For a moment he is unable to trust all of his practice and experience. He decides to play cautiously. The result reflects his fears. A weakly hit iron goes to the right and settles under a tree that is still 100 yards away from the hole.

(Esteban doesn't know it, but 1,000 miles away at the Mexicali Country Club, his brothers and friends are watching the Golf Channel broadcast via satellite and suffering with every shot. As Esteban approaches the ball at Grenelefe, the crowd at the club's bar in Mexicali falls desperately silent. More than one of the viewers says a prayer.)

Now, instead of an easy wedge to the green, Esteban is forced to try a hard, low shot under some branches. He punches at the ball, but no amount of pleading will get it to the green. It stops in heavy grass at the base of a little slope ten yards short of the putting surface. On his walk toward the ball, where a small crowd has gathered, Esteban tries to quiet his fear of a bogey and another Q. School failure.

Wading into the rough, Esteban finds the ball and settles into his stance. His anxiety starts to rise. A breeze kicks up, hitting him squarely in the face. His eyes fill with tears and his hands start to shake. His throat is tight and his mouth is dry. And when he calms down enough to form a coherent thought, he doesn't like what he hears in his brain, the doubts, the fears. No matter how it ends, this is a moment he is going to remember for the rest of his life. And he knows for certain that if he doesn't quiet his mind, something terrible will happen.

Instead of forcing his way through the fear, like a boxer

charging in the ring, Esteban makes himself slow down. This is the difference between then and now. Now he knows how to empty his mind of emotion, how to trust his body, and his heart. He takes his stance in the tall grass and shuffles his feet until he feels good and steady. He pulls the club back, and then makes his move down and through. The bottom edge of the club face slices through the grass. The ball rises gently toward the hole. For a moment Esteban is frozen. Then he runs toward the green. Half way there, he stops to watch the ball land softly and roll five feet straight into the cup.

It went in. Esteban roars and punches the air. Jon runs to him. They embrace and Esteban says, "Thank you, Dad."

At the Mexicali Country Club, a party begins. It will go on all night.

•

At day's end the crowd around the scoreboard swells to a couple of hundred. Ivan Smith stands there, holding another can of beer and staring at the numbers. "You can't argue with them," he says. He has no regrets. He tried his best. Smith's caddie, a young man he had brought from Ohio, is a little drunk and struggling to stay composed. "It's just that he's a great guy," he says, swallowing a sob with his beer.

Because of ties at the thirty-five mark, the Q. School graduating class of 1998 will number thirty-eight. Five are older veterans who have already made more than $1 million on the Tour, somehow lost their cards, and are regaining their status. Among them is Bob Gilder, age 47, who has $2.7 million in winnings and six victories. Another is Blaine McCallister, 39, who has five championships and almost $3 million to his credit. These players and the other millionaires hardly qualify as lifelong grinders. The same is true for more than a dozen men under age 30. Richard Coughlan, a twenty-three-year-old Irishman who succeeded at his first Q. School, simply hasn't suffered enough to join the grinders guild.

When the millionaires and the youngsters are set aside, the Q. School class of '98 includes fourteen true long shots, grinders who failed before but refused to give up. Each of them is more than thirty years old and has toiled more than a decade in the purgatory of minor golf circuits. Some have made it to the Big Tour before, but not one has managed to play well enough to retain his card.

As a group, these long-shot players can claim more than 100 trips to Qualifying School and thousands of competitive rounds played in lesser-known tournaments from South Africa to Asia to South America. Besides Esteban they include:

TIM CONLEY—A pro since 1981, he has won twice on the Nike Tour, and played the Big Tour in 1993 but failed to keep his card.

BOB FRIEND—As cheerful as his name, Friend may be best known as the son of retired big league pitcher with the same name.

JEFF GALLAGHER—Part of a family of pro golfers, he played in 89 of the Nike Tour's first 90 tournaments. He had one year on the PGA Tour too, and failed.

J. P. HAYES—Having played four different PGA Tour seasons, Hayes has never managed to earn enough money to keep his card.

BRADLEY HUGHES—An Australian with a home in Orlando, Hughes was Rookie of the Year on the tour in his homeland in 1989. He's never finished above eighth place in a U.S. PGA Tour event, and this will be his first year as a full member of the tour.

STEVE JURGENSON—On last year's tour Jurgenson led the Deposit Guarantee Golf Classic on Sunday morning, but fell to fourth place. He's been no closer to glory before, or since.

TIM LOUSTALOT—After ten years as a pro, this will be Loustalot's first as a full member of the PGA Tour. He's managed to get into twenty-four Big Tour events over the years, but has survived the cut only six times and earned less than $20,000 altogether.

TOM PERNICE—A college All-American in 1981 and 1982, Pernice just missed keeping his card in 1997. He's spent more than a decade watching UCLA teammates Corey Pavin, Steve Pate, and Duffy Waldorf excel on the Big Tour.

LEE PORTER—He's been a tour member in Europe, Japan, Canada, Asia, and South America. Last year he finally made it onto the PGA Tour, but like so many others, failed to stick.

JOHN RIEGGER—Another college All-American, Riegger had one previous shot at the PGA Tour—1992—and finished 192nd on the money list.

VANCE VEAZEY—No one on the PGA Tour has a shorter resume than Veazey. At age 32, his professional career has been spent almost exclusively on mini-tours. When he finally tees off in a PGA Tour event, it will be his first ever.

MARK WURTZ—In his one previous year on the PGA Tour—1994—Wurtz distinguished himself with the fourth-best putting record. Unfortunately he finished 153rd on the money list.

LAN GOOCH—The last long shot player to make it through Q. School—in thirty-eighth place—and onto the PGA Tour deserves special mention. Lan Gooch had so little hope of actually making it that he admits to anyone that asks that he is almost shocked to be in this band that will move on to the PGA Tour. A thirty-three-year-old from Mississippi, Gooch has nursed a dream to play on the PGA Tour since he was a boy knocking around a little nine-hole public course. (He used to pretend that he was Lanny Wadkins.) Gooch didn't even play at the Nike level last year. He competed at regional tournaments where the players' entry fees make up the purse. Prior to this success he had been to eight Q. Schools in a row, failing at each one. This time he had come hoping only to finish high enough for a Nike card. Instead he won the grand prize: fifty-two weeks of PGA Tour pro status.

•

Lan Gooch's success is remarkable, but of all the new tour members, Esteban has surmounted the greatest obstacles to reach this point. As a child he was poor in a way that the others can only imagine. In order to reach his goal he has had to master not only golf, but a foreign culture and a new language. Now he basks in his moment of ascension to the Tour. He is surrounded by golf industry reps, agents, TV cameramen, and reporters.

"My dad told me, if you keep knocking on the door they will let you in," he tells the reporters. "Now I'm in."

For the rest of the day, Esteban will enjoy his success. But tomorrow morning he will awaken to the fact that Q. School is only the doorway to golf's most exclusive fraternity. Those who pass through must run a gauntlet that will determine whether they can keep their cards and take up long-term residence. Historically, only one third of Q. School grads do well enough to return for another year. To make matters even more difficult for Esteban, he begins this test knowing that he failed it once before.

2.

Less Than Zero

On the day after Q. School, Esteban flies home to suburban Los Angeles, to Colleen, his wife of just one year, to his seven-year-old stepson Nicholas, and to friends who want to celebrate as if his achievement is their own. This is the curse of the pro golfer. Everyone who has ever swung a club or watched a tournament on TV has some advice to offer. Esteban is smart enough to ignore all of it.

He has too much on his mind, anyway. First and foremost is coping with the financial facts of life for the Tour's less-wealthy citizens. A Tour golfer is an independent contractor, an entrepreneur who is responsible for his own travel, food, and shelter. Golfers do not play home games. There are no team-paid airplanes or hotels. A typical pro can easily spend $3,000 dollars per week on transportation, meals, hotels, and a caddie. He'll spend more if he brings a wife, or a lover, or a family along. Then there's the matter of taxes. Golfers pay state income taxes everywhere they play, which means filing dozens of returns per year. Finally there's the whole problem of injury and illness. There is no disabled list, sick leave, or paid vacation in pro golf.

To cover the cost of competing, players turn to sponsors, corporations that will pay thousands of dollars to put their name on the front of a prominent player's hat so that it appears on television every time he does. The payments for the very best players are high. Nike has set aside $48 million to Tiger Woods to guarantee that every time his picture is taken he's wearing the trademark swoosh on his cap, his shirt, even his shoes. Greg Norman is a successful and well-paid salesman for Chevrolet and pasta sauce. But his biggest deal, with Reebok, generates $100 million a year in clothing sales.

For the elite, the sponsor money doesn't stop even when they leave the regular Tour. Golf legend Arnold Palmer hasn't won a PGA Tour title since 1973. Nevertheless, in 1998, at age 69, he pocketed $20 million selling everything from Pennzoil to Rolexes. Stars like Palmer use great care in choosing sponsorship deals, avoiding anything that might erode the value of their names. They typically reject more offers than they accept.

Nearer the bottom of the PGA Tour, where Esteban dwells, it is the player who chases the sponsors. Though a matter of constant conversation among insiders, the details of these arrangements are generally hidden from the public. Titleist, which sells about 260 million golf balls per year, would prefer that amateurs think a player chooses its balls because they fly farther and truer than all others, rather than because he is paid $500 per week to do so. But the truth is that the money helps pro golfers choose equipment in the same way that payola helped disk jockeys pick hit records in the 1950s. If one set of irons is as good as another, you go with the company that offers you $1,000 per week to use theirs.

How much money does the average PGA Tour player receive in sponsor money and corporate bonuses linked to performance? It's safe to say they each one starts the year with enough to cover most of his expenses. If you want to estimate how much more he'll receive as the season wears on, it is typically equal to his Tour winnings. If he makes $300,000 on Tour, his sponsor money will likely total that much or more.

•

In the weeks after winning his card, Esteban lines up his sponsors for the year. Tear Drop, a putter manufacturer that had backed him on the Nike Tour, comes through with $50,000. In exchange, Esteban will wear the company name on his cap. LaMode, a sportswear manufacturer based in Los Angeles, gives him an unlimited supply of golf clothes with the maker's name displayed on the shoulder of each shirt. (Clothing companies, especially Tommy Hilfiger and Dockers, are Big Tour sponsors because they hope millions of men will want to wear the shirts and pants their sports heroes wear.)

Though LaMode and Tear Drop are quick to lend their support, Esteban receives no offers from the big-name firms—car manufacturers, financial institutions, technology companies—that invest heavily in the PGA Tour. Convinced he needs the money, and the prestige of a recognizable corporate label, he asks a car dealer at his local club to introduce him to executives at Toyota. Toyota already sponsors Mark O'Meara, Chi Chi Rodriguez, and a few others. Chi Chi leaps in the air in TV commercials for Toyota cars.

As he waits for his meeting with the Toyota execs, Esteban worries about whether they will find him appealing. Sponsors look for more than solid golf. They want players who look good, and sound good in front of TV cameras and the public. Would Esteban's accented English be a problem? Would his reputation—as a rather serious grinder—match the image Toyota wants?

Image is a valuable commodity for pro golfers, worth almost as much as a gifted touch with the putter. Chi Chi's endorsement deals come because he's the beloved course jester of golf. After making a long putt, he rarely fails to wield his club like a sword, slashing the air and returning it to an invisible scabbard. It's schlock, but it pleases the masses as well as a kickline in Vegas.

Of course, most golf pros lack Chi Chi's charisma. As a group they can seem bland and homogeneous, a long line of white men who say they like hunting and fishing and cars and speak with Southern accents. The good thing about this for Esteban is that it doesn't take much for a man to stand out in this milky sea of humanity. Peter Jacobsen does it by telling a few jokes. Along with hitting long drives, John Daly distinguishes himself with a country boy demeanor and by being open about his personal struggles with alcohol and gambling.

Over the years Esteban has given considerable thought

to his persona, beginning with his heritage. Mexican-born pros have been few and far between in American golf. Esteban saw this as an advantage, one way he could stand out from the crowd. He also knew he had to look good for the TV cameras. He long ago had his smile made perfect by braces. He always has a fresh haircut. He chooses his wardrobe carefully, and irons each outfit before putting it on. He wears cologne every day (sometimes too much, according to Colleen) and is deliberately patient with fans.

Despite all these careful choices, Esteban remains ambivalent about the most unusual aspect of his persona—his past as a boxer. He still considers boxing his first love, the sport he would have preferred to pursue. He is proud that he had the courage to enter the ring and proud that he won all of his fights but one. But he is also sensitive to the fact that he now labors in the more genteel world of golf. His boxing could distract the press and public from his golf game. He wants people talk about his knockdown shots, not his knockdown punch.

But no matter how he may try to avoid his boxer persona, his once-broken nose, and a tendency to grunt and growl at the ball always seem to betray him. And though he can't fully accept it right now, this could be a very good thing. Too many PGA Tour players are robotic pretty boys. The game desperately needs some spice, a personality who might shadowbox at a moment when Chi Chi would draw his sword.

Apparently Toyota agrees. One meeting with Esteban leads immediately to contracts and the payment of one top-of-the-line car. The Toyota name will go on all of Esteban's golf shirts, right over his heart.

Esteban's sponsor lineup is completed with deals with Titleist and Taylor Made, the company that makes the driver he hits. Titleist agrees to pay about $20,000 if he uses the company's balls, gloves, and shoes all year long. Taylor Made admits him to an unofficial competition—called a pool—for pros who use its clubs. The company divides the season into trimesters, and awards points to each player according to his tournament finishes. At the end of each trimester, the winner gets $40,000. Last place nets $8,000. Over a season the minimum each Taylor Made player could receive would be $24,000. The maximum is $120,000.

The pool provides a financial incentive for each player to do his best and thereby boost the image of Taylor Made. Most other club companies operate similar contests. Though the money involved is substantial, the companies that make golf equipment consider it a good investment. An amateur, shopping for a driver—a single club that can cost $500 or more—may well be impressed to learn that one brand is played by more pros, or has won more tournaments, than another.

The money Esteban could make from sponsors is not limited to the payments made to close a deal or the Taylor Made pool. Like all other players, his contracts also call for special bonuses to be paid if he wins a tournament, or finishes in the top five or ten. In a typical sponsorship deal, a victory at the Masters or one of the other three major tournaments can carry an additional bonus of $100,000 or more.

All this unseen money, much of it based on bonuses, creates what amounts to a sponsor-based tournament within a tournament every week. This means that when the TV announcer says that a certain putt on the last hole of a tournament is worth some enormous amount of money to a player vying for the lead, the casual fan doesn't know the half of it. If making the putt and winning first place is worth an extra $100,000 from the tournament purse, the player holding the club knows it could be worth much more to him in sponsor bonuses and future endorsements.

As he approaches the Tour season with more than $100,000 worth of guaranteed support from sponsors, Esteban can be confident that at least his travel expenses are covered. But he wants much more. He estimates that to keep his card he must win at least $230,000 in prize money. This would put him solidly in the top 125 and return him to the tour for another season.

•

Esteban should be happy. He has lined up lucrative sponsorships and will play the coming year without any financial risk. But as we talk on the phone, I notice that the excitement that was in his voice after Q. School is fading. At first I assume it's because he is worried about the upcoming golf season. Then he corrects me. He is not nervous, he insists. Everyone wants to believe he is, but he's not. Nervousness beat him the last and only other time he got his card. But he has learned to overcome that feeling and he doesn't feel nervous.

Instead, he feels uneasy because Christmas is coming. This is more than the holiday blues. As a child in Mexico, where the celebration lasts more than a week, Esteban had always watched from a distance. His family never had money for presents or a tree, or a feast. Christmas always meant envy, anger, and the guilt he felt for having these feelings.

Like so much about Esteban, his feelings about Christmas became clear to me only after many halting conversations. Most of his memories of his years in Mexicali are painful and he will not be forced to go back there, even in his mind. "You have to understand that I started not from zero, but from less than that," he tells me. "I don't like to remember it."

As an adult, Esteban's antidote for his holiday blues involves loading his car with food and clothing and driving south to Mexicali, where he will give it all away. On these December visits, the Toledos also host a barbecue and a golf outing at the Mexicali Country Club. Friends, family, and members of the club fill the crowd, but Esteban spends much of his time with the greenkeepers, maintenance men, cooks, and waitresses. On this one day, they enjoy the same privileges as the club's members.

●

The three-hour trip to Mexicali takes Esteban, Colleen, and Nicholas south to San Diego and then east, on Interstate 8, into the mountains. Here the lush green of the coast gives way to a moonscape of boulders and scrub brush. Every few miles they pass a yellow caution sign that shows a family, in silhouette, running with linked hands. The border is just yards away at some places along the road. Illegal immigrants from Mexico have been killed trying to cross the highway on foot. But for golf, and his inner drive, Esteban could be one of these migrants.

In a tiny town called Jacumba, California, the Toledos stop at a gas station. While Esteban fills the tank, a border patrol officer wheels through the parking lot in a pale green government jeep. It's forty degrees Fahrenheit, a good thirty degrees colder than it was in San Diego. A Mexican family—mother, father, two sons under age 8— shivers beside the door of a convenience market watching the border officer who stares at them as he drives by.

Outside Jacumba, the highway falls down into the heavily irrigated desert that is the Imperial Valley. After coastal plain, and barren mountains, this is the third distinct environment the Toledos have seen in the space of a hundred miles. In the distance the smokestacks of factories called *maquiladora*—manufacturing plants that export to the U.S.—fill the horizon with smoke. A turn south, on two-lane California Rte. 98, brings them to the huge farms where Mexican hands pick the winter lettuce crop. Another half hour and they are in downtown Calexico, California, sister city to Mexicali. Calexico is a splashy little carnival of a town. The signs on the little stores and restaurants are colored in bright Mexican yellow, red, and green. In a vacant lot a vendor sells *"Abolitos Navideños Desde $15."* Christmas trees less than $15.

Traffic at the border is heavy. At the Mexican customs station, police question Esteban about the bags of clothing and golf equipment he is carrying in the car. At first they refuse to believe he's an actual golf pro from the United States. Then it turns out that one of them knows the Mexicali Country Club. Esteban invites him to play in the tournament. Suddenly the issue is solved. The duty fees are waived.

As they finally drive through the checkpoint, the Tole-dos enter not just another country, but a distinctly poorer economy. Mexicali looks old, and tired. Here, the streets are crowded with people walking, and the buildings all seem to need a coat of paint, if not major repairs. Instead of neat little gas stations and fast food outlets, the road-sides here are lined by dubiously constructed tire repair shops and tamale stands.

Though some streets in the city boast comfortable, stucco homes, the vast majority of people in Mexicali occupy ramshackle houses, in makeshift neighborhoods laced by rutted dirt pathways and filled with smoke from the outdoor fires used for cooking. Dogs and children run wild. Running water is a luxury. As often as not, electric power is pirated from nearby transmission towers and dis-tributed by a jury-rigging of stolen wires.

Anyone who makes the border crossing from Calexico to Mexicali notices that he has entered a different world. Esteban feels this shift, and something more. He is enter-ing another time, as well. As he follows the highway to the unmarked road that leads to the country club, he is visit-ing his past.

•

Though he returns to the Mexicali Country Club as a member of the PGA Tour, Esteban is also remembered here as a barefoot boy in ragged clothes who scavenged in the water hazards and underbrush for lost balls and sold them at the edge of the fairways. The only things the club members and staff knew about him then was that he lived on the other side of the canal that bordered the club, and that he swam across almost every day. He showed no sign that he harbored special talent or drive. In fact, he seemed so dull-witted that most people took for granted that he was destined to be a menial laborer or, at best, a subsistence farmer. Perhaps he would ride a bus every day to work on one of the huge farms in the Imperial Valley. Maybe he would join the river of migrants that flows north with the seasons, to pick fruits and vegetables.

What the country club golfers couldn't appreciate was that life had already brought Esteban enough tragedy and loss to drive a grown man to his knees. The tenth of ten children who were raised in a home with neither running water nor electricity, Esteban was a surprise baby, a hungry addendum who arrived when all of his siblings were already in their school years.

When he first told me about his childhood, Esteban confessed to being nicknamed "*Perico*," the Spanish word for "parrot." In his original explanation, he said only that he was "a little baby who squawked like a parrot." It would take almost a year, but eventually he would offer me a more complete and disturbing explanation.

Perico may have been a cute name, even a term of affection, but it also recalled a terrible affliction. At the age when most children learn to speak, Esteban found it impossible to get beyond babbling a few syllables. His family, with no money, and no idea that such help existed, did nothing to help him. Today he believes that they just figured that in the isolated little world they inhabited, such a disability actually mattered little. Life was work, and little else. He didn't need to talk much, and if he didn't learn how, he wouldn't suffer.

At an early age, Esteban could see that life was indeed work. Every morning, his father tended a few cows and chickens before leaving to labor on nearby farms. Sometimes his father would walk for hours just to find work, and return well after dark. On more desperate days, he would trek into town and search for edible produce in the trash behind fruit and vegetable markets. Sometimes Perico went along, happily picking up pieces of fruit and eating around the spoiled spots.

Young Esteban felt no shame in this. His parents were simply fixed in the routines of a traditional way of life that Esteban now calls "Indian ways." Even today, his mother knows almost nothing of the world outside. She has trouble distinguishing the PGA Tour from the Mexicali Country Club, and she has no idea where her son is from week to week.

As soon as he could walk, Esteban was sent out every morning to search the weeds for the eggs that the family's chickens had laid. As a boy, he climbed fig trees to collect fruit and waded in the canal that ran by his home to draw water for his family and to catch crayfish for dinner. By age five, Esteban was traveling off the farm with his brothers and sister to pick tomatoes and cotton. One of his earliest memories is of resting on a bag of cotton that his sister was filling. He rode along as she dragged the sack, and eventually fell asleep as she worked down the rows.

Hard work formed the routine for days that flowed one after another. What little play he was allowed required ingenuity and imagination, because he was never actually given a toy. Once, when he was about six or seven, he spotted a toy tractor in a neighbor's yard. It was there every day as he walked to school. Finally, after a week, he went to the yard when no one was around, grabbed the tractor, and ran. He felt some guilt, but mostly joy, every time he pushed it through the dirt. It was the only toy he ever had.

But even without toys, Esteban often managed to have fun. He and his brothers would prowl the countryside and the river. They salvaged hooks and leaders that recreational fishermen had lost on logs and rocks and fastened them to sticks. They used worms and crayfish for bait and caught catfish and small bass. The Toledo boys were ingenious fishermen and soon figured out that they could hang more than a dozen hooks from a line, anchor one end on the shore and swim across to tie the other end to a tree. In an hour or two they would return, yank up the line, and harvest enough fish for the family's dinner.

One of the most exciting moments of young Esteban's life came on a morning after he and his brother had forgotten the line they had laid out the day before. When they got to the riverbank, fish hung from every hook. At the center of the line, in the deepest part of the stream, the water churned and boiled like a hot spring. Excited and frightened at the same time, Esteban and his brother paddled a little boat to the whirlpool and began pulling on the line. Up came an angry and exhausted catfish. It was the biggest fish they had ever seen. It frightened them, but it excited them more. They tugged on it for half an hour before they wrestled it into the boat. A few whacks on the head and the giant *bagre* was subdued for the little row to shore. Once on dry land, they carried it home as both a trophy and a feast.

Often a playground, the river was also the site of the first tragedy in Esteban's young life. It happened when he was just four, and one of his teenage brothers failed to come home one night. The family searched the neighborhood and the nearby woods. Days passed with no sign of the boy until the howls of the family dog brought Esteban to the river. There he saw the body. His brother had been beaten and thrown in the water, where he had drowned. Years later, Esteban would guess that his brother, who may have been mildly retarded, had witnessed drug smuggling along the river and was killed as a matter of criminal routine.

A year after the murder, Esteban's father died of a sudden heart attack. Again the little boy was there to witness death. This second tragedy broke the family into pieces. In the months that followed, his older brothers and sisters each moved off the farm and into a barrio of tumbledown houses on the edge of the city. His mother descended into chronic depression and grief. Left to raise himself, Esteban was, for all purposes, an orphan. He took over much of the work on the farm. He hunted quail, which he seasoned with salt and pepper and roasted on sticks over an open wood fire. He chased away the coyotes that threatened the livestock, and tried to patch the holes that let the wind blow through his house.

Though life at home was hard, school brought a whole new kind of distress. All of a sudden he was confronted with an astounding variety of new people and experiences. Here he saw books, pictures, and, for the first time, television. All of this was difficult to take in, but the worst came when he tried to speak.

"I think a lot of the kids thought I was retarded. I definitely wasn't, but to them I was really strange," recalls Esteban. "I got beat up almost every day. They would get me down and kick me in the head. I was like an animal then, making noises and trying to defend myself. It was pretty bad. It happened almost every day. I know now they did it because I was different. Maybe they were afraid of me. But I still remember this one kid, he told me he was going to beat me up every day, and he did."

The beatings stopped only after Esteban went to a gym with his older brother Mario and learned how to box. "He taught me to keep my head up, to look at the other guy, and to punch," he recalls. "After about six weeks I was good enough to take on that kid and beat him good. Then I did it to him every day for about a month. The teachers saw it but they didn't stop it. I think they were glad for me, a little bit. After that, nobody bothered me like that again."

Boxing changed Esteban's life in many ways. No longer afraid, or humiliated, his confidence grew steadily. At the same time, his speech problems receded. By age 10, or 11, he could make himself understood in any situation. A few years later, he spoke as well as any boy his age. Today, he cannot explain this improvement. Perhaps it came simply from learning to protect himself and, therefore, relaxing enough to listen to conversation at school. Or maybe it was, as he suspects, God's hand.

God's hand may have been at work again when Esteban first swam across the section of river that separated his house from the Mexicali Country Club. He had often stood on his side of the stream, watching the golfers lose balls in the water and underbrush. Eventually he got the courage to cross the water, scavenge for the lost balls, and offer them to the golfers for a few pesos apiece. Soon this was a daily routine. He also collected the clubs that enraged players sometimes threw into the river or ponds on the course. These he kept for himself. Late in the evening, when the members had deserted the club, he would take his clubs out of their hiding place, and try to imitate their shots.

Young Esteban never gave a thought to becoming a professional golfer, if he even knew there was such an occupation. He never imagined that across North America, thousands of young boys and girls were being groomed to be golfing machines. They were being instructed by doting adults and possessed all the proper equipment—matched sets of clubs, spiked shoes, soft leather gloves. They competed in local junior tournaments and, if they were good enough, traveled far to play competitions against equally talented kids. Esteban had none of this.

"Sometimes my brothers went with me," he recalls. "We didn't know anything about golf except that you were supposed to hit the ball into the hole. Sometimes we would chip in. We got very excited because we knew it was good. But we didn't know what to call it."

The golf course was primarily a place to make money, and play always came after work. When he was big enough to carry a bag, Esteban graduated from ball-scavenger to caddie. He cleaned shoes and swept the clubhouse. On weekends he would wait in the dark until 2 a.m. so he could clean up after a party or wedding reception.

But the golf course was not the only place to make money. When work at the club was slow, Esteban would hop on city buses and start singing for coins. He would do almost anything to feed himself. Once he went into the city, sat down in a restaurant, and ordered a meal he knew he could not afford. When the bill came he rose without a word, walked into the kitchen, and began washing dishes.

In this time, golf was one thing that freed young Esteban from the struggle of everyday life. It's not hard to imagine why he was attracted to it. In a chaotic life, golf was an escape, a neatly groomed, cool green holiday. This is a key part of golf's allure. It is not just a sport. It is an environment. When he walked the course, or hit one ball after another on the range, he would lose himself in the landscape and the challenge of game.

Through trial and error, Esteban discovered how to make the ball fly. Repetition ingrained the series of commands his brain would fire at his muscles to make thousands of little movements, in just the right order. Young players schooled by instructors are simply given this information, and led, by the hand, to make a textbook version of the swing their own. Self-taught boys and girls literally create their own unique templates. This is what it means to be a 'feel' player. Feel players experience an exquisite sense of harmony when their bodies are following the internal template, and they produce good shots with swings that can seem unorthodox. When that harmony is lost, it can be recaptured mainly through practice, not instruction. Indeed, an insensitive instructor who tries to fix a feel player can make things much worse.

As Esteban learned more about the game, he organized tournaments for neighborhood boys. Tin cans the size of one-gallon buckets would be planted in different corners of a dirt lot. Circles were drawn in the dirt around the cans to represent putting greens. Each boy would throw a few pesos into a kitty for the champion. There was no prize for second place.

The pretend tournaments fed a competitive drive in Esteban that was already well developed. Confronted with so many adult-sized obstacles, Esteban had learned early to depend on his innate aggressiveness to survive. In sports, this translated into a fierce desire to compete. He would badger his older brothers to let him play golf with them. Most of the time they sent him away. They were much better players. *"Perico"* only slowed them down. But when they did let him play, he burned with the desire to beat them.

Like poor boys everywhere, Esteban prayed that sports would be his salvation. But the sport he pinned his hopes in was boxing. Boxing was his first true love in sport, and he spent as much time in the gym hitting a heavy bag as he spent at the golf course hitting little white balls. At age 15, he was five feet, nine inches tall, but still weighed less than 130 pounds, which made him an unusually tall bantamweight. Quick on his feet and armed with a powerful left hook, he attracted the attention of a local trainer, who groomed him. By age 16 he was fighting in gyms all over northern Mexico, using his height and long reach to advantage. As one win piled on top of another, he was noticed by local sports reporters. While still in high school, he turned professional.

In boxing, Esteban found another release from everyday life. When he climbed into the ring to face another fighter, his punches were a furious expression of his will to climb out of the life he had been born to. In the ring, he could be brave, strong, and fearless, and he could win.

Long after he took off the gloves for the last time, Esteban could clearly recall how it felt. "The focus is so intense," he explains. "You don't hear the crowd, you don't feel any pain if you get hit. There's no fear. It's just you and the other boxer and you are determined to make him go down."

There was only one time when Esteban failed to send his opponent to the canvas. It happened in Ensenada, just south of Tijuana. "In boxing, you take it like a man. That's what I did. I went down once, but I got up," recalls Esteban. "After that, I put my hands up, probably threw a few punches, but my head was messed up. The referee stopped the fight." Asked why he lost, Esteban has a simple, honest reply. "The other guy was stronger than me."

Like so many poor Mexican boys, Esteban saw boxing as a noble way out of a dismal existence. Boxing has always been a poor boy's sport. Who else would be desperate enough—some might say primitive enough—to take the physical punishment, and dish it out? Boxing requires a depth of anger, even rage, that may be best acquired, one day at a time, in a *barrio* or ghetto. In the ring, that emotion, combined with intense pride, makes a young man courageous. Esteban had this courage, and he had the physical traits—a long reach, quickness, endurance—to go far.

Esteban compiled a 12–1 pro record before coming down with acute appendicitis. He had an emergency appendectomy at a local hospital. Infection and a second operation followed, leaving him with a scarred and permanently weakened abdomen. He would never be fit to box again.

In truth, Esteban had never considered becoming anything but a boxer. His grades at school had been middling. He was not interested in a trade, or in going to college. Boxing was everything to him. It had rescued him from humiliation at the hands of the bullies in the schoolyard. It may have even given him the presence of mind to learn to speak. Leaving the gym, with its smells, sounds, and the sweet, satisfied exhaustion he felt when a workout was over, was one of the most difficult things Esteban would ever do. He gave away the trophies he had won. He put away the clippings from the sports pages. He would never enter the ring again, except in dreams.

With his boxing career ended, Esteban returned to the one place where he had always been able to earn a few pesos—the Mexicali Country Club. He cleaned shoes and poured drinks in the clubhouse bar. And he mourned the loss of his boxing dream. After a few months passed, his will to succeed returned. In between jobs, he began to devote the energy he once spent in the gym into his golf swing.

Most of this work was done on the same driving range—a patch of dirt, really—where Esteban was sometimes required to pick up the balls hit by members. (This work was done by hand, not machine.) At the time, he still wasn't thinking about becoming a touring pro. He just loved the game and wanted to discover how good he could be.

Though he hit the ball well, Esteban got precious little encouragement from the club's members. Then and today, golf in Mexico is the domain of the wealthy, fair-skinned, "Spanish" minority. At the Mexicali Country Club, many of the members ridiculed Esteban's efforts to develop as a golfer. Others went further, as he once explained to me:

"I can tell you a story about what it was like at the country club back home when I first got really serious about golf. I was seventeen years old, I think. I was working at the club doing a lot of things, including being a bartender. When I wasn't working I played a lot, but I wouldn't say that I thought at that time I would be a professional golfer. My own brothers beat me all the time.

"Then one day I saw this poster in the locker room about a tournament they were having near Mazatlán. It's a long way from Mexicali. I asked the man who worked in the locker room what it was all about. He went to the bar and the people there all put some pesos in a hat. He collected enough—about a thousand pesos—so that I would have the money to go. I called the number on the poster. I said, 'My name is Esteban Toledo and I'm a four-handi-capper. Can I play in your tournament?' They had one place left in the tournament and they let me have it. I took my golf clubs and got on the bus. I rode for more than a day.

"When I got there I was the last one to show up. The pro there invited me to play a practice round and I beat him. I didn't have any golf shoes and I was playing with all these different clubs. Some of them didn't even have grips that stayed on. But I beat him. He was pretty surprised.

"They had a Calcutta bet organized for the tournament. The rich people would each claim a player and put up some money. If your player wins, you get the money. The pro, after we played, told this friend of his to buy me. He was a doctor, I remember that. I was the last one picked. That doctor told me, 'You win and I'll take care of you.' And then he followed me for the whole tournament.

"I made eagle on the sixteenth hole and birdie on the seventeenth. I won the tournament. The guy won a lot of money. I mean a lot, like $15,000, because the odds were against me. Nobody knew who I was. He was so happy he gave me $500 and he bought me a plane ticket home. It was the first time I was ever in an airplane. I went on that plane holding the trophy.

"The next year, I was the defending champion and I went down there in a car with my brother to play. When I got there the people running the tournament came to us pretty upset. They said that someone from the club in Mexicali had called down there and said we didn't really represent the club. We were caddies, they said. 'Don't let them play.' The tournament was for players who were members of the clubs. They said we couldn't play. I couldn't defend the championship.

"I found out who it was who called. Some people told me. I thought he liked me. He was one of those who put some money in to help me the first time. But he thought I was going to fail. When I won, he didn't like it. So when he got the chance, he did that to me. I went back and con-fronted him, but he denied it. That's the way some of them are. To them, I will always be the poor kid who worked for them as a caddie, nothing more."

The members were not the only ones who undermined Esteban's efforts. The club pro in Mexicali, unimpressed by this brown-skinned boy's game, aggressively policed his use of the golf course. Once, when he caught Esteban chipping balls onto the practice green against club rules, he prohibited him from playing for a month. Many years later it would be a memory that still pained Esteban.

Despite all that might have discouraged him, Esteban was nevertheless a determined young man. This is what Jon Minnis and his wife Rita—who speaks fluent Spanish—saw when they came to Mexicali in 1982 and stopped at the country club to play golf. They came back every day for a week, and no matter when they arrived, Esteban was there practicing. Minnis is a millionaire whose charity is deliberately personal. He doesn't donate large sums to organizations. He helps individual people. A conversation with Esteban led to an immediate friendship. Then the Minnises made an astounding suggestion: Come live with us and we'll support your development as a professional golfer.

At first, Esteban was confused. Were the Minnises to be trusted? Why did they choose him? In accepting the offer, would he betray and abandon his family?

Jon Minnis made it clear that he had chosen Esteban for his work ethic, his sincerity, and his intelligence. Esteban talked to his sister and his mother. When both gave their blessing, he went.

It was not an easy transition. In Milpitas, Jon and Rita Minnis lived in the grandest home in a gated, mountainside community that overlooked most of the valley south of San Francisco. A golf course occupied the hillside below, waiting for Esteban to play. A short par seventy-two, Summit Pointe challenges players with plenty of water hazards and rough. It is so hilly that Esteban, accustomed to the perfectly flat terrain of Mexicali, felt like an ant climbing a camel's back. Still, it wasn't long before he set the course record.

Inside the Minnis home, hired help took care of the cleaning and maintenance. A fleet of luxury cars, with chauffeur, waited to take the family to expensive dinners or down to a second home in Carmel-by-the-Sea.

The luxury of this life in America was almost too much for Esteban to accept. He was dazzled even by the ordinary aspects of life in Milpitas. Everything—the buildings, the gardens, even the streets—was so clean and well-maintained in comparison with dusty Mexicali. In his eyes even the colors of the grass, the flowers, the buildings, and the cars were impossibly vivid, like a cartoon. He couldn't quite believe that this was where he would remake himself.

In exchange for this opportunity, Esteban was required to work at his golf and learn English. Though it may sound like an easy bargain, Esteban struggled with it. After all, he was hundreds of miles from home, surrounded by English speakers, and completely unfamiliar with his surroundings. Even the idea that someone might embrace him as the Minnis family had was difficult to fathom. He felt confused, isolated, and lonely, and for the first few months rarely left the house. He spent many long nights trying to complete his English homework with Rita's help. He often cried with frustration, but here were light moments, too. Jon Minnis recalls the time he found Esteban in the garage, sitting on top of a car, pointing to an animal that had him cornered. That was when he learned the word "skunk."

The torture of learning English should have been relieved when Esteban went to the golf course. After all, a good many of the workers there were Mexican-born, too. They could have been his friends. But these workers wouldn't accept him. They regarded him as a rich man's pet, someone who had been given an extraordinary opportunity for no apparent reason. They were jealous and resentful, and probably even a little frightened of his connections to Jon Minnis.

At times Esteban couldn't blame the Mexican workers for rejecting him. *He* was uncomfortable with the situation. He couldn't help thinking that it was only yesterday that he was sweeping floors and polishing other mens' shoes so that he could feed himself. Now he was riding in expensive cars and wearing new clothes, and he didn't have to worry about where his next job, or his next meal, might come from.

All of the inner conflict and confusion came to a head after he was in Milpitas for a few months. Alone in the big house, unable even to understand what he heard on the television, he was overwhelmed by homesickness. He packed a bag and fled, returning by bus to Mexicali and familiar faces and surroundings. He stayed there for a few weeks, but eventually his older sister told him he was being foolish.

"What chance do you have here?" she asked him. "Stay in Mexico and maybe you'll never get out. Take this chance and who knows how far you can go?"

He went back to California to stay, but he would never feel like it was truly home. He held onto his name—Esteban—instead of changing it to the English version, Steven. In his heart he began to cultivate dreams beyond golf. He wanted a wife and children. And he wanted to buy a home, maybe a big home in Mexicali, that would be entirely his. Not given, but earned.

•

Once Esteban's game was in shape, Jon Minnis agreed to support him as he traveled around the country to play minor tournaments. Over the years, many pros have developed under similar patronage. Often a small group of wealthy men will pool their money to back a player. In other cases, a newcomer will sell dozens or even hundreds of shares in his future, promising to pay investors back, with interest, if he ever succeeds. Esteban accepted Jon Minnis's help, but he was never comfortable accepting the money. So he stayed in the worst motels, ate almost exclusively at cheap buffets, and spent whatever he won on his expenses, so that he wouldn't have to call on Jon for money. Of course, just knowing that his sponsor's help was there if he needed it made it possible for him to stay focused on golf.

Though he was obviously a gifted athlete, Esteban did not impress everyone who saw him swing a club. When the top pro at Summit Pointe first saw Esteban play, she told Jon Minnis that Esteban should develop some other skill, and get an education, because she was certain he would never make it to the PGA Tour. He was inconsistent, especially on the greens. And he just didn't hit the ball far enough. He might be able to conquer little Summit Pointe, she said, but the PGA Tour was beyond him.

Esteban was also remarkably ignorant of almost every-thing about golf outside of his own game. When he came the United States he had never heard of the Masters, the U.S. Open, or even the Ryder Cup. He did not understand much about the PGA Tour, and the only prominent golfers he could name were Greg Norman and Jack Nick-laus. The greats from bygone days—Bobby Jones, Byon Nelson, Sam Snead—may as well have been the great chefs of Europe, for all he knew.

If he had known more, Esteban might have been heart-ened to discover just how much he had in common with perhaps the greatest of them all—Hogan. Like Esteban, Hogan had witnessed his father's death at a very early age. Both men practically raised themselves in poverty condi-tions, working long days at whatever menial work was available. Boiling with unresolved grief, insecurity, and a fear of inferiority, Hogan was a fighter too, though his fists were used in back alleys, not in the ring. Like Hogan, Esteban is a self-taught golfer who believes that a punish-ing practice routine is the only way to succeed. And like Hogan, he is almost pathologically competitive.

After turning professional in 1986, Esteban played in minor tournaments in Mexico and California. He spent one season in Asia, where he discovered the limitations of his game and the unexpected challenges of international golf. In Bangladesh, he putted on greens laced with tree roots. As he flew out of Pakistan, he looked down and saw his suitcase and golf clubs on the runway. In South Korea, an opponent spent seventeen holes talking as Esteban played, ignoring Esteban's pleas that he quiet down. On the eighteenth hole, Esteban, who had by this point missed the cut, lost his patience. He walked over to the other player, threw a left hook, and knocked him unconscious. The following year, Korean officials tried to ban him from the tournament. He talked his way in by claiming the knockout artist was his brother.

"When I went to Asia I really didn't know what to expect. All I knew was that I could beat my brothers and the people I played with in Mexicali and California. I figured that I could beat those guys too, no problem.

"Let me tell you, when I got there I was in for some kind of surprise. These guys could hit it higher, land it softer, do anything with the ball. I only made one cut, in India. I came home from Asia ready to quit. It was Jon who said I should keep going a couple more years."

Throughout Esteban's adult life, Jon Minnis would be a teacher, mentor, and friend. A child of the depression who grew up in poverty-stricken rural Pennsylvania, Minnis had himself endured much hard work as a child. When he was a small child, his father took him into the fields to learn how to work a horse and plow. By the time he was eight or nine, Jon was behind the horse by himself.

"I think Jon probably understood that a big part of the problem had nothing to do with golf," says Esteban. "I mean, just a little while before I met him I was riding a bike around Mexicali. I didn't know anything about the rest of the world. This may sound strange to you but we didn't even have toothbrushes in my house. I didn't know what that was. So it was very hard for me to just go straight into playing golf all over the world. I was very lonely a lot of the time, and I didn't really feel comfortable except when I went back to Mexicali. But I knew I couldn't stay there. There was really nothing for me to do in Mexicali, no job or anything. I had to keep trying."

After rebuilding his confidence in Mexico and at smaller U.S. tournaments, Esteban joined the Nike Tour (then called the Hogan Tour) in 1990. The Nike Tour is supposed to be a bridge to the big time. The top fifteen players each year are promoted to the PGA Tour without having to suffer through Q. School. Esteban was never able to earn enough money on the Nike circuit to graduate. In his first year, he played thirty events and barely cleared $11,000. In 1992, 1993, 1995, and 1996 he would average less than $30,000 a year. He came close to winning tournaments twice, but lost the 1991 Reno Open in a playoff and then missed winning the 1993 White Rose Classic by a single stroke. He made national headlines once, though, when he fought off three muggers who attacked him as he was using a gas station pay phone in the middle of the night in Knoxville, Tennessee. Other than that one notice, he toiled in obscurity.

During all of his years in pro golf, Esteban had attended every single PGA Tour Qualifying School. Before 1997, he succeeded at only one other, in 1993. The following year, he joined the PGA Tour. He started off well for a no-name rookie, tying for nineteenth at Pebble Beach and earning more than $60,000 in the first half of the year.

Looking back on 1993 with the wisdom of a few years, Esteban would say that he had been undone by personal problems. Before he got his card, he had met a young woman and fallen in love for the first time. But having never even seen a romantic relationship up close, he didn't know the first thing about maintaining the connection. As he took to the road to play tournaments, this relationship devolved into a drawn-out series of long-distance misunderstandings and arguments.

"I didn't do things like buy gifts, send flowers, or write letters. I didn't know about those things," he would later say. "And she became very demanding, wanting to be almost like a groupie. It was very distracting, very upsetting to me. I couldn't give her what she wanted. Sometimes I couldn't even tell what that would be."

Esteban wasn't then, and isn't now, the kind of person who spends much time reflecting on his relationships or talking about his feelings. He tends to focus on the moment, and on the task to be accomplished. This way of thinking may have worked for a street kid in Mexicali, but it helped ruin his first romance. The breakup was messy and painful. Distressed and ultimately heartbroken, Esteban had trouble focusing on his play. He canceled plans to compete at a couple of midyear tournaments so he could take time off, go back to the house on the hill in Milpiltas, and recover his emotional balance. He eventually did go back on tour. But the damage was done. He would lose his card.

Even as he struggled to accept this setback, and a return to minor league golf, Esteban met the woman who would eventually become his wife. Colleen worked as a waitress in the clubhouse restaurant at a golf course in southern California. A petite blond with brown eyes, she met customers with a cheerfulness that hid the strain in her private life. She had just divorced her husband. She was adjusting to the demands of work, being a single parent to a little boy, and attending college classes. She could not have been less interested in dating.

Colleen declined when Esteban first asked her to go out to a party. He persisted. She finally relented the fifth time he asked. She didn't realize that he was a professional player—not a caddie—until well into their date. Even then she was not overly impressed. Though she worked at a golf course, she didn't know the difference between a wedge that'll get you out of the rough and a wedge you put on your foot.

"He was a perfect gentleman," she recalls, "and when he took me home he asked me if I would like to go running and have breakfast the next morning." She went running and shared breakfast and didn't even mind that he forgot his wallet and she had to pay. The following week she went to see him play in a tournament. Esteban decided right then that he wanted to marry her. It wasn't too long before she felt the same way. They were married in Las Vegas on New Year's eve, 1996. She would spend much of the next two years traveling the Nike circuit with him.

Despite their different backgrounds, Esteban and Colleen have much in common. Like her husband, Colleen is willing to sacrifice now for the chance that long-term security can be earned in professional golf. So far, this has required cutting expenses to the bare minimum in order to finance Esteban's life on the road. Until he made it back to the PGA Tour, the Toledos had just one credit card, and used it only for emergencies. Home was a modest apartment. They drove inexpensive cars and lived with the knowledge that their future depended on pay-checks that might never come.

Esteban's latest Q. School success, and the endorsement money that followed, relieved much of the financial
pressure. The Toledos began to think about buying their
first home. "Every year, on the Nike Tour, I would play at
these courses where there were houses along the fairway. I
started looking at these houses and thinking I'd like one
for myself," recalls Esteban. "I almost can't believe we are
going to have one."

Among the country club set, this moment would have
required at the very least a freestanding house in a pricey
neighborhood. But for the journeyman golf pro who
comes from poverty, a comfortable townhouse would be
enough. The Toledos found a three-bedroom model in a
part of Irvine with good schools. Even though it was a
modest amount, Colleen and Esteban were nervous about
paying the mortgage.

"Our dream is that Esteban will make enough money
this year to pay it off," says Colleen. "We're hoping and
praying."

•

In Mexicali, the hopes and dreams that Esteban shares
with Colleen swirl in his mind along with the memories of
struggle that are stirred by the sights and sounds and
even the smells of his past. During the charity tournament at the country club, he can't help but recall that at
least two of his brothers once showed more promise than
he did on the course. He wonders what would have happened if they had dedicated themselves to bigger dreams
than quiet lives in Mexicali. And he cannot explain, to his
own satisfaction, why he was the one who made it. In his
heart, pride mixes with a kind of survivor's guilt. He was

the one who climbed highest on the mountain, but he wants his family and old friends to accept him as they always did.

After the round, in the bar at the club, Esteban sees a picture of himself—enlarged to poster size—that's been placed in a spot of honor next to one of Tiger Woods. Do they ever think about the times they made him feel like less than zero? Do they ever reflect on how they treated the boy who waited in the dark to pick up the trash left behind after their parties? Do they know that he and the man in the picture on their wall are the same?

In the evening, Esteban attends a private little party at his sister's house, which is in one of the overcrowded barrios near the club. It's a tidy little place, one of the best-built homes in the area. Esteban eagerly paid for its construction when he first started making money on the Nike Tour, back when a Sunday check for a few thousand dollars seemed like all the money in the world.

Mexican music plays on the radio. Meat sizzles on a little grill that blazes in the corner of the dirt yard. Nicholas plays with the kittens that scamper around the house. Colleen struggles through chitchat in broken English and simple Spanish.

Esteban is surrounded by the faces of his past and of his future. He loves this place and these people. But he knows they are unaware of the sweat and tears he spent to reach his goal. As much as he yearns to be accepted as "still the same," he is not the same. He has outgrown Mexicali, outgrown his past, and everyone can see it.

None of Esteban's friends in the states, not even Jon Minnis, can fully grasp the pain he experienced in his old world. And no one here in Mexicali can appreciate the effort that was required for him to get as far as he has in his new world. In the middle of the celebrating in Mexicali, Esteban can feel that he and Colleen are truly on their own now. And whether the future holds pride or pain depends on him and his talent for getting a little white ball into a tin cup.

3

The Caddie

When Esteban returns to California from Mexico, he
begins to prepare for the Tour season. He practices and
makes travel arrangements for the months of January and
February. (The schedule will take him from northern California to San Diego and then Hawaii.) His main concern,
though, is settling on a caddie. Jon Minnis urges him to
find a veteran who knows the courses that the Big Tour
visits and can offer the wisdom of experience. Jon wonders if a better caddie could have made the difference the
last time Esteban played the Tour. The right one might
have even talked him through his romantic crisis.

But Esteban has other ideas. He doesn't want a personal counselor or a wise old-timer who remembers how
Charlie Coody won the Masters back in '71. Esteban values
dedication and hard work over experience. He doesn't

care about reputation. He respects character. This time he goes against Minnis's advice and calls a forty-seven-year-old rookie who first carried a bag a few months ago and has never worked a day on the PGA Tour.

Robert Szczesny (pronounced Sez-nee) had seen Esteban through the second half of the 1997 Nike season, learning to caddy as he went along. Esteban had promised to call on him if he made it through Q. School. He keeps his promise. "You come with me and we're both going to make some cash," he tells Robert.

Esteban is surprised when Robert doesn't seize the opportunity right away. He asks for time to make the decision. Esteban agrees to wait, but not for long.

•

Caddies don't hit the driver or the wedges, or use the putter. But a bad one can get you disqualified and a good one can help you win. Just ask John Daly. He gives much of the credit for his PGA Championship win in 1991 to Jeff "Squeeky" Medlen, the caddie who coached him along a course that he had never before played. When Rocco Mediate won the Phoenix Open, microphones caught him Sunday on the eighteenth fairway telling his caddie, "I don't win without you." When a rookie Tiger Woods hired his caddie for the PGA Tour—a white-haired, mustached walrus of a man from Maine named Mike Cowan—he considered him important enough to merit a six-figure salary.

On the golf course, the best caddies know the terrain and offer solid counsel on club selection and putting. He (99.9 percent of them are men) also serves as a governor on a player's emotions. He offers the calm perspective, or the wit, that can save a player from both the mania and depression the game evokes. In the loneliest sport, the caddie is a player's only friend. He is also, more than likely, an eccentric.

The image of the wise but strange caddie has become such a familiar cliché that even the TV show *Seinfeld* once featured a squirrelly little bag-toter, complete with cap, as a trusted adviser to the character Kramer. In his short story, "Farrell's Caddie," John Updike creates a caddie who not only elevates his player's game but offers uncanny advice on matters of love and business, which he could only provide through some paranormal means. In the movies, caddies are either idiots, savants, or wise-but-weary sages.

Intelligence and a certain oddness—the life of the professional caddie is close to the old-time hobo's—are as common in caddies as nicknames. But the cliché of the eccentric caddie is also based partly on the wishful fantasies of golfers. The ultimate caddie of a player's imagination is part genius, part magician, part psychologist. His insight covers all of life's mysteries, especially golf, and he gladly shares them.

The typical PGA Tour caddie is something slightly less than the myth. He knows yardages and course layouts. He can keep the equipment in order and stay out of a player's way. Most can read a green pretty well. Many fancy themselves to be experts on human nature. Some claim to know so much about golf that it's a wonder they haven't won the Masters themselves. As a group, caddies do seem to drink more than other people and they gamble more too. Everyone on Tour knows that you never lend a caddie money during the last month of the season. And when you give him a ticket to the tournament, or a free parking pass, you can bet he's going to scalp it for twice its face value.

●

Looking back, it is easy to see how Robert Szczesny's life had prepared him to join the fraternity of professional caddies. But this is only clear in hindsight. Little in Robert's early life suggested he would come to travel the world in service to pro golfers.

A leathery-skinned man with twinkling blue eyes, a taut body, and short brown hair, Robert J. Szczesny was born in 1950 in the gritty factory town of Erie, Pennsylvania. He was raised in a devout Catholic family. His Polish immigrant parents demanded that he serve as the family standard-bearer, and he complied, excelling at almost everything. He studied hard enough to be admitted and then graduate from a Catholic high school for gifted students. He was a good enough athlete to play on a championship basketball team and to be drafted by the Philadelphia Phillies for the minor leagues of baseball. At age 17 he was ranked in the top twenty amateur youth bowlers in the United States.

But Robert's achievements came at a price. He took his parent's urgings and frequent expressions of disappointment so seriously that even the smallest failures made him feel guilty and then angry. Defeats led to arguments and fights. More than once, he hurled his bowling ball off a bridge and into one of Erie's many little rivers. Eventually he became recognized around Erie for two things; his competitiveness and his terrible temper.

Like many a child of overly demanding parents, Robert gradually became his own harshest critic. A merciless judge of his own talent, he concluded early on—at about the same age that Esteban had committed himself to his dream of being a pro boxer—that he would never make it as either a ballplayer or bowler. He turned down the Phillies, choosing instead to pursue a business degree at Gannon University in downtown Erie. His athletic life was pared back to the school golf team and occasional amateur tournaments.

After college Robert fulfilled his Vietnam-era military obligation by going to flight school in Texas, but his temperament convinced the United States Air Force that he wasn't quite pilot material. Returned to Erie, he went to work at the sprawling General Electric locomotive plant, the same plant that had employed his father for decades.

Robert became restless and confused; he considered a lifetime spent at GE and in Erie and quickly realized that he wanted more. He found it two hours away at Thistledown race track in Cleveland, Ohio. From the very first time he saw it, he fell in love with thoroughbred racing. It wasn't the thrill of gambling that snared him—it was the entire racing scene. He loved the track, the people, the excitement at post time. And most of all he loved the horses. Strong, and well-trained, the best ran without fear, or hesitation, or self-doubt. They ran with what he believed was pure joy.

For about a year Robert spent most of his free time at the track. He met trainers and jockeys. He worked part-time for a betting sheet, reporting race results and track conditions. Then, two days after Christmas in 1975,

Robert quit his job at GE and drove to Tampa, Florida. He had heard there was a job there for someone willing to walk horses and clean stalls for a trainer named Bill Miller. He was determined to get into the horse business.

In Bill Miller's stables, Robert found work that paid him less than minimum wage, and demanded total devotion. He happily threw himself into the task of learning everything he could about horses and racing. He slept in barns, and when horses were sick, he curled up in the hay right next to them. Then, as now, Robert did not believe in making halfhearted efforts. If he was going to be a horseman, he was going to get so good at it that he could practically think, and feel, like a horse himself.

There was both social and physical risk in this work. On the social side, Robert found himself almost entirely isolated in the horse world, and within that world, he was often too busy to forge many real relationships with actual humans. The job was also physically demanding and dangerous. Once, while he was cleaning a stall, a horse spooked by a bird kicked him squarely in the chest. The blow cracked Robert's sternum almost all the way through. He lay there gasping for ten minutes before he started breathing normally. He spent several months sleeping upright before the fracture healed and the pain subsided. Through it all, he continued to work—with his entire rib cage bandaged and compressed—because the horses needed him.

Bill Miller gave Robert the training and education he needed to become an expert horseman. The most important fact he taught Robert was the one thing that the majority of trainers didn't understand: Most horses are over-trained.

"You can't become fitter than fit," explains Robert. "Once a horse is in top shape you have to back off. You have to make him happy. You give him treats, take him out to graze, change his water five times a day. Give him attention. Then he'll run for you."

In the twenty years Robert spent in the horse business, he grew into a more patient man. With the help of some psychotherapy he got control of his temper, and he adopted a philosophical outlook on his life. He eventually found time to date, but once again made a rather brutal decision based on a scathing assessment of his own chances for success. He chose to abandon the idea of ever marrying, because he couldn't offer a spouse financial security. He would value friends, work that was personally rewarding, and accept his own strengths and weaknesses. "I'll never be a ladies' man or famous or rich," he says. "But I know I can be happy."

Robert's fondest memories from his racing days involve failing horses that he nursed, rather than whipped, into winners. But as the business grew, and stables became larger, he saw the romance leave the sport. He saw some of the chicanery practiced by dishonest owners and trainers. One favorite trick involved holding horses back when they ran, to hide their true strength, and then, when the odds against them rose, betting they would win when they were finally allowed to run.

"This kind of deception was terrible, but what bothered me the most was that the horses were like pieces of machinery to the people who owned them," recalls Robert. "They didn't care about them. And you had so many horses that you couldn't give them the right attention."

•

In 1995, Robert's disillusionment with racing was becoming almost unbearable. At the same time, his father was sliding toward death from Alzheimer's disease. In the spring Robert left his job and home in Florida to go back to Erie. He wanted to spend time with his father. They had the better part of a year together, and Robert never regretted going home. In 1996 he returned to Florida, but not to the horse business. Eager to find a low-stress position that would give him time outdoors. He found just such a job in the cart barn at a golf resort that was the home course of Nike Tour player Guy Hnatiuk (pronounced Nat-chick). It was Hnatiuk who eventually suggested that Robert try to become a professional caddie by serving a self-made apprenticeship on the Nike Tour.

Robert already loved golf, and competition. And he seemed suited to the rather lonely, vagabond lifestyle that caddies adopt. You can see it in the shy way he has when around people. Robert is like the most uncomfortable boy at an eighth-grade dance. He tends to look down at the ground, and speaks only when he's addressed. His personal life, or lack thereof, also fits the caddie mold. He was a spore on the wind, so unattached that he hadn't had a permanent address for twenty-two years.

Few professional caddies—especially those who are middle-aged men—are willing to travel the Nike circuit for the three or four hundred dollars they typically earn make in a week of hard labor. But Robert was willing to try, because he knew it could be a training ground and a stepping stone to the big time. He saved some money, plunked down a big chunk of it to get his old Pontiac in top shape, and took to the road. He caught up with the Tour in Louisiana and put his name on a list of men willing to work. He got his first job, a practice round, from a player named Bob Friend, who paid him $30. At the end of the day Friend told Hnatiuk that the new guy would make a good professional caddie if he just stuck with it. Robert did, following the Nike Tour across the country and working for a different player each week.

He made some mistakes. One week he stood on the tee and reminded his player, Tom Kroll, of the out of bounds that lay on the left side of the fairway. Kroll immediately chewed him out. Players always know where hazards lie. When a caddie points them out, it can plant a thought in the mind that seems to draw the ball right into the trouble. "Don't tell me those things," said Kroll. "I don't need to be reminded of the trouble." At another tournament, Robert left a player's sand wedge in a bunker and had to run back to find it before play could continue.

Through such trial and error, and intense observation, Robert gradually learned the trade. Most of the practical demands were simple. He had to keep the clubs clean and dry, and speak up if his man were about to break the rules. Most of all, he must avoid interfering. With one misstep, a caddie can do terrible damage. One of the most vivid examples of this happened at the U.S. Open in 1946. Byron Nelson was leading the tournament when his caddie accidentally kicked his ball. The one-stroke penalty forced Nelson into a final-day playoff with Lloyd Mangrum, which Nelson ultimately lost.)

Robert also had to learn the keys to surviving on and off the course. On the course, caddies conserve their strength by walking in a measured way. They lift the bag only when necessary. On hot days, they find shade wherever possible, and drink quarts of water. Off the course, Robert did everything he could to avoid going broke. This involved sleeping in his car as often as not, and eating only at the least expensive places.

Beyond practical matters, Robert had to learn how to relate to players. His experience training horses had been good preparation, teaching him how to read any animal— including man—without a word being spoken. He could feel a player's tension, sense his fatigue. Horses had also taught him much about patience, commitment, and self-sacrifice. A good trainer never failed to feed and water his horses, and was so attuned to their moods that he could feel the smallest shift. A good caddie showed up on time, knew when to speak and when not to, and considered his player's needs first. Robert could do all these things well.

Nike players cannot promise high pay for a caddie. Many rely on friends, family, wives, or girlfriends to carry their clubs. Others are willing to hire a different local caddie every week, accepting that they are likely to get a teenager who can do nothing other than haul the bag around. Robert was one of very few unattached, adult professional caddies who stayed with the Nike Tour, moving from state to state, offering himself for work every Monday morning. He was waiting for the moment when a player who kept a regular caddie was ready for a new man.

With the season half over and the Nike Tour pulling into Hershey, Pennsylvania, Robert heard that Esteban Toledo was looking for someone to take his bag full-time. Esteban had fired two caddies in less than a month. One was a old-timer who had argued with him right in the middle of play, dropped the bag in the fairway, and walked away. The other had shown up at the wrong tee, delayed Esteban's starting time and cost him two penalty strokes. Though the caddies had obviously messed up, there were two sides to each of these stories. Many caddies thought Esteban was too demanding, too temperamental. But Esteban was also one of the more talented players on the Nike Tour, and he was willing to pay $350 a week. Robert took the job.

What began as a lucky break for a rookie caddie quickly became a remarkably productive partnership. Until Robert's arrival, Esteban had struggled just to make cuts. With Robert on the bag, he went on a tcar, making the cut in ten of the next eleven tournaments. More importantly, he began finishing tournaments higher than before, and cashing bigger paychecks. By September he was in twentieth place on the Nike Tour money list. He was within striking distance of the top fifteen, who would get to bypass Q. School and go directly to the PGA Tour for the next year.

"Esteban had not come even close to winning before then, but we did so well in those tournaments that he could have won any one of them," recalls Robert. "He may not see it this way, but I think I had a little something to do with it. I didn't know as much about golf as a lot of the guys, but I know people, and I figured out that he played his best when he was having fun. When he joked with kids and the people in the gallery he just played better."

Robert saw this most clearly during a tournament round played in Springfield, Missouri. Esteban was being trailed by a gallery of kids who had attended a clinic he had taught the day before. After a neat birdie on a par three, a ten-year-old said that it wasn't good enough. On the next hole, a par five, he challenged Esteban to make an eagle.

"Esteban looked the kid in the eye and said, 'Okay, let's do it,' " recalls the caddie. "He gets up and kills the drive. He hits a second shot to just off the green, and then he chips in. On the way to the next tee he gives the kid the ball. It was wonderful."

Unfortunately, it's difficult for anyone to maintain such good humor. The tour doesn't issue each player an adoring ten-year-old at the start of every round, and as the pressure of a long season grows, enthusiasm can fade. In late summer and early fall, Esteban had half a dozen opportunities to win a tournament, jump into the top fifteen, bypass Q. School, and graduate directly to the Big Tour. But as he tried harder and harder, he grew mentally and physically drained. He still practiced as hard as he could, willing himself to succeed. But he was like a racehorse driven past the point of fitness.

"The more serious Esteban got on the course, the worse he played," says Robert. "I tried to talk to him about this, but he wouldn't really listen. He's a lot like Bill Miller was.

Smart, but almost too proud. And I think he just saw me as a servant, a guy who should carry the bag and mostly shut up."

Out on the course, Esteban was not at all diplomatic about rejecting Robert's advice and reminding him who actually hits the ball. "It was not easy to take," recalls Robert. "I'm a forty-seven-year-old man. And I'm not stupid."

In the last three weeks of their Nike season together, Esteban succumbed to the stress and fatigue and missed every cut. He did not make the top fifteen. Robert was disappointed and convinced that Esteban considered him a poor caddie. But when they parted, Esteban gave him a $400 bonus and made his unexpected promise. "If I make it to the PGA Tour, I'll call you."

•

At Q. School, where Esteban ultimately earned his card with Jon Minnis by his side, Robert had caddied for a much younger player from Great Britain named Iain Steel, who also made the top thirty-five and got his card. This was a delightful surprise for Steel and he made sure to tell Robert that his help had been an important part of his success.

At twenty-seven years of age, Steel could hardly have been more different from Esteban. A college All-American, he had been a prominent amateur and even played in the last British Open. During his first Nike season he had won the Boise Open and finished twenty-seventh on the money list. The 1997 PGA Tour qualifying tournament was the first he had ever played. When it was over,

Steel said that he too would like Robert to join him on the Big Tour. It was an appealing offer. Generally relaxed and eager to take Robert's advice, he seemed to want a partner more than a servant. Robert knew that with Steel he would be more involved in devising strategy than he would be with Esteban.

For a while, it seemed that Robert would have to decide between two offers from markedly different pros. But then Steel's mother died in England. He flew overseas, and Robert never heard from him again. When Esteban called one last time, Robert accepted his offer.

The outlines of the deal were simple. Robert would be paid a minimum of $500 a week, and $550 when Esteban makes the cut and plays all four days of a tournament. From this he will have to pay all of his own travel expenses, and try to cover things like insurance and health care. The salary Esteban offers is less than average for PGA Tour caddies, who earn closer to $700 per week. Fortunately for him, Robert will also be eligible for a cut from Esteban's winnings. He will get 10 percent for a win, 7 percent of a top-ten finish, and 5 percent out of any other paycheck. Since first place can net a player as much as $630,000, it will be possible for Robert to earn a one-week bonus big enough to buy a small house in Erie.

Altogether, the bargain seems fair. Robert is not the average caddie on Tour. Indeed, he is still more of an apprentice, who will have to learn as he goes. Esteban is taking a risk with him. On the other hand, Robert is committing himself to work much harder than other caddies will work. Besides carrying the heavy bag for four or five miles per day, Robert will walk the course (or courses) prior to the start of each tournament, checking the grains on greens and using a laser device to get measurements from various points in the fairways to the greens. He will attend Esteban during practice sessions—fetching balls, water, and anything else he needs—before each round and afterwards. And he will no doubt be required to work Monday pro-ams, Tuesday practice rounds, and Wednesday pro-ams. At times it will be a seven-days-a-week, sixteen-hours-per-day job. Unless Esteban does very well, this means Robert will work for something less than minimum wage. Still, he relishes the prospect.

•

In late January, Robert gets into his car at his brother's house in Florida to drive cross country to Pebble Beach, California—site of Esteban's first competition. It's the same 1988 Pontiac Grand Prix, white with black interior, that he took on the Nike Tour. Though it has clocked well over 100,000 miles, it is so clean and meticulously maintained that it would merit a sign reading "Mint" on a used car lot. The trunk is organized and divided as neatly as a *bento* box. Special golf course yardage books—fluorescent green pamphlets that chart each hole at each tournament site—are stacked in one space. Travel documents are in another. Clean clothes and dirty clothes are kept in their own separate places.

Robert arrives on the Monterey Peninsula on Tuesday, two days before the tournament is to begin. He checks into a Howard Johnson motel, but when Thursday comes, and the room rates rise for the weekend, he will move into his car, where he will fall asleep to the sound of rain on the metal roof.

Tour caddies seem to fall into two categories. On one side are party animals who always seem hungover and broke. Before a match, they can be seen laughing about what happened the night before and attempting to borrow lunch money. In the other group are the more serious caddies who work hard and go to sleep early. They can see in Fluff Cowan an example of how far a caddie can go, and they want to join him at the top. Robert is in this second group.

On his first day at Pebble, Robert walks the three courses that will host the tournament, using his laser sight to measure exact yardages from various landmarks and making notes about the rough and other hazards on each hole. When the tournament begins, he will be poised to offer a precise answer to almost any question that Esteban might ask about the playing conditions.

•

Though he dreams of a Tour victory and a big paycheck, Robert is realistic about how much he can affect the outcome of Esteban's season-long campaign for his Tour Card. He cannot analyze Esteban's swing and suggest changes. The man is self-taught and will not accept this kind of advice. He decides that when Esteban's game strays off course, he should offer only encouragement. Having read sport psychologist Bob Rotella's books on golf, he insists that success is a state of mind shaped by Rotella's three "C's"—confidence, composure, and consistency. These he can help Esteban achieve.

Deep down, Robert feels respect and affection for Esteban. He also recognizes the dread that he will avoid discussing: that this team of caddie and player might not make it on the PGA Tour. At this moment, when his first competitive shot is still to come, Esteban may talk boldly of grinding his way to the top 125, and even winning a tournament. Robert doesn't buy it.

"If he's human," says Robert, "then he's at least a little bit afraid."

Show Time

All of professional sport is show biz. The competition is both a display of skill and a story for the audience. Football games are war stories. Baseball games—nuanced and subtle—are tales of intrigue. On the PGA Tour the story always follows the ancient model of the hero's quest. The golf course is both the backdrop for the journey and the obstacle that provides a test of character and physical strength that must be overcome to end the drama. A little wind, or rain, or perhaps some searing heat, will help the plot.

Like the small town carnivals that travel from one church parking lot to another all summer long, the PGA Tour delivers its stories in a caravan of tractor-trailers. The difference is that this show stops in many of the nation's richest zip codes, and the midway attractions involve high-tech driver demonstrations instead of bearded ladies.

Of all the tournaments on the Tour, the AT&T Pebble Beach National Pro-Am is the most vaudevillian. Founded in 1937 by Bing Crosby, the tournament was originally a golfing holiday for Hollywood stars, a week of drink and debauchery. Typical of the celebrity participants was the actor Phil Harris, who carried a bottle of bourbon with him on the course and declared himself the pro from "the Jack Daniels Country Club." In the TV age, the exploits of entertainers have become important draws for viewers who hope to see Bill Murray drag a woman into a bunker or Jack Lemmon bean a spectator.

Of course, in recent times the charm of Pebble Beach has been somewhat sanitized by the manners that come with corporate sponsorship. Besides AT&T, which puts its name on every program, ID badge, and caddie's blue vest, the tournament is gaudily decorated with the logos of Coca-Cola, IBM, Oldsmobile, and a dozen more corporations. Along with the money they pay to be associated with the tournament, these companies bring a more buttoned-down attitude. Big business will pay only for good *clean* fun.

Though sponsors have been a significant part of the pro golf scene since the 1950s, they came to dominate the landscape at tournaments in the 1980s. Many events have lost their original identities entirely. The Los Angeles Open is now the Nissan Open. The Tournament of Champions is the Mercedes Championship. The Magnolia State Classic is the Deposit Guaranty Classic. The tournaments sell their names so they can pay larger purses. The PGA

Tour will not visit any site for less than $2 million these days, and tickets sales don't raise nearly enough to pay players this kind of money. Corporations make up the difference.

What do they get in exchange? In most cases, major sponsors each get a white canvas tent in the 'corporate village' along a fairway, and tickets for executives and customers. They also get some spots in a warm-up tournament—they are usually held on Mondays or Wednesdays—that puts amateurs on the course with the pros. A single playing spot in one of these pro-ams goes for between $2,000 and $7,500 or even more.

At Pebble Beach and a few other tournaments, the amateurs continue to play with the professionals once the regular competition begins. In no other sport is a fan invited to play with the pros when it counts. Nervous amateurs clamor to participate because they get close to their sports heroes. The pros do it because it is tradition, because it brings them in contact with powerful and interesting people, and because it pays the bills.

•

It is raining on the morning of the Pebble Beach tournament's first round. This is typical for the Monterey Peninsula in winter. In 1996 it rained so much that the whole event was canceled. This time play is merely delayed for a few hours. When the downpour stops, grounds crews rush onto the course with squeegees to push water off the greens, leaf blowers to dry fairways, and pumps to drain bunkers. The players, celebrities, and gallery look for ways to pass the time.

Over at the corporate village, executives and their

spouses drink Bloody Marys and Irish coffee. A mile away, at a polo-field-turned-driving-range, Kevin Costner, Bill Murray, Alice Cooper, and a dozen other entertainers hit practice shots with the pros. In the nearby woods a couple of unwashed and bleary-eyed caddies grab a free breakfast at the outdoor kitchen run by the local YMCA. Everywhere in between, thousands of fans wander, their hands clutching cameras and cans of beer, their eyes agape like children visiting the midway at a circus. The smell of cigar smoke fills the air.

Enter Esteban Toledo, riding in the front passenger seat of his old Honda. Esteban's wife Colleen—brown hair, brown eyes and a serious expression on her face—is driving. Their seven-year-old son Nicholas is belted into the back seat. No one in the crowd that walks the narrow roadways and presses up against the car recognizes Esteban. Everyone is too busy looking for Tiger Woods and Bill Murray.

This may be entertainment for the masses, but Esteban is serious about his performance. He has planned a way to make this year different from 1994, his previous PGA Tour year. He will be patient, make a lot of cuts, and pile up his earnings, as modest as they may be. He can reach his goal—The Card—even if he never comes close to winning. He has Colleen's support, and the wisdom that comes with having been on Tour once before. All he has to do is play steady golf.

Naturally this sensible plan does battle in Esteban's heart with anxiety and excitement. This is the first day of his PGA Tour season, when all that he has dreamed of achieving is laid out before him, waiting to be taken. What does he stand to lose if he fails? It's not money. No matter what happens this year, sponsor dollars are going to keep him from going broke. Nor is it love. Colleen is with him for the duration. But what he could lose is that precious faith—in himself, in the game, in the very nature of life—that has sustained him all these years. These beliefs are the foundation of his character and personality. His entire sense of self depends on them. That is what is at stake this season.

In the car, Colleen steers between buses and pedestrians to find a parking spot in the mud next to the polo field. They all get out and Esteban raises the trunk lid to remove his bag. Suddenly a golf ball comes sailing over a six-foot fence. It hits a nearby car with the sound of a rifle shot.

"Look out!" shouts Esteban. He pulls Nicholas behind the trunk lid. Colleen ducks between cars as the ball ricochets from fender to fender like a cartoon bullet.

When the Toledos finally raise their heads, a passing fan says that the errant shot was hit by Jack Lemmon. Every year millions of people watching on TV pull for Lemmon to survive the cut in the professional/amateur team play at this tournament. In more than twenty tries, he has failed every time, but each attempt increases his popularity.

Now, in the parking lot, more than a dozen fans stand in the mud and wait for Esteban's reaction to the beloved Lemmon's mistake. Esteban, whose face flushed dark with anger when the ball first landed, forces a smile. Reassured, the fans resume walking. Esteban turns his back to close the trunk. "Unbelievable," he mutters.

•

The path from the lot to the practice tee and adjacent players' tent is a strip of mud the consistency and color of chocolate cake frosting. When the Toledos finally slog their way to the security checkpoint, the elderly volunteers on duty refuse to let Nicholas enter. "No children allowed," they say.

From where they are standing the Toledos can peer inside the tent and see the children of other competitors playing hide-and-seek behind folding chairs. Struggling to keep his temper, Esteban shows them his PGA Tour identification. Colleen flashes the one that wives are issued. These status symbols are not enough. The volunteers—wealthy retirees—hold their ground with their chins out and their hands on their hips until Esteban catches the eye of a Tour official who rushes over to make things right.

Esteban has been caught in this kind of mix-up before, and it's hard for him to avoid thinking that it has something to do with the color of his skin and his accented English. A few years ago, at a tournament in Palm Springs, he was directed to the service entrance by a volunteer who refused to believe he was a player and not a gardener. In Texas he almost missed his tee time when a tournament official decided he was acting a bit too uppity at the player's entrance and refused to let him in.

At Pebble Beach, a Tour official pulls apologies out of the volunteers, which smoothes things over. With Nicholas and Colleen safe with the other players' families, Esteban goes looking for his caddie. He finds Robert standing with a small group of caddies outside the players'

tent. Though Robert and Esteban might prefer to make
their plans inside the tent, over a cup of coffee, they cannot. On the PGA Tour, caddies are forbidden to enter any
area reserved for players and their families, and the players are discouraged from inviting them inside. Esteban is a
little uncomfortable with this rule. It reminds him of waiting outside the Mexicali clubhouse while the members
had their parties. But he's not going to risk breaking it.

Standing in the mud outside, Esteban checks to see if
Robert is prepared. Does he have enough dry towels for
cleaning clubs in the wet conditions? How about extra
gloves? Are the balls marked with Esteban's trademark circle of red dots? Is the yardage book in order?

With his starting time still hours away, Esteban wanders
off to help Nicholas get an autograph from Tiger Woods.
Tiger obliges, but he never once looks Esteban in the eye,
and turns away as soon as he signs.

Tiger's reaction could be a not-so-subtle reminder that
he and Esteban occupy opposite ends of the Tour pecking
order. One group flies the world in Gulfstream jets, and
stays in five-star hotels. The other travels coach, and looks
for discounts at motels. Esteban is staying at the
Econolodge this week. But there's a more benign possibility. Tiger may be acting coolly out of self-defense. No
golfer in history has been mobbed by fans the way he is at
every tour stop. Even when he's with other players and
their families, signing a single autograph could start a
stampede. It's no wonder he is reticent, in almost every
setting.

Esteban is uncomfortable enough about what happened with Tiger to mention it more than once. Robert

uses the occasion to explain that he hates the one-ups-manship on the Tour.

"A lot of those guys got on the Tour with sponsor exemptions and never had to play Q. School," he says, half under his breath. "A lot of them couldn't handle Q. School it if they were forced to. The one thing I don't like about the Tour is that so much has to do with the players being like celebrities. There's a lot of politics involved in who gets sponsor exemptions to play in tournaments. A lot of it depends on what you look like, how you smile, whose ass you kiss. And a lot of people out here will do anything for money. Esteban isn't one of those guys. He knows there's more to life than money."

Still, a little money never hurts. Top prize at the Pebble Beach tournament is $360,000 and an automatic exemption for the next year on Tour. Second prize is $216,000, which would go a long way toward guaranteeing that a player's card will be renewed at the end of the season. Though this kind of finish would be wonderful, Esteban knows it is unlikely. This is just the beginning of a long season of opportunities. He'll play about thirty tournaments between now and November. At any one stop along the way he could find The Zone and finish high on the leader board. Esteban reached The Zone at Q. School. He prays it will happen again.

Most of his fellow grinders—those thirty-something veterans who came here through Q. School—are following the same strategy: Play well enough on Thursday and Friday to make the cut and earn something on Saturday and Sunday. Add up enough Saturdays and Sundays and it equals a card for next year. Many players earn a good living for years on end without ever winning. Between 1975 and 1996, Bobby Wadkins made more than $2.5 million without ever finishing first. Another non-winner, Kirk Triplett, earned nearly as much in half the time. He has never enjoyed the fame and popularity of a frequent tournament winner. But he makes a very good living playing golf.

•

Of course, no one will make a penny at Pebble Beach if the field doesn't play at least three out of the planned four rounds. Unfortunately, the weather is not cooperating at all. Before a single shot is hit, officials decide to pare back the tournament from four rounds to three. They will limit play this day to nine holes. The same number will be played on Friday. None of the players is happy about this. Most haven't played a nine-hole competitive round since they were twelve years old.

Although it is explained that this format is intended to make the tournament fair for all—because each man will play each of the three courses the tournament uses one time—the players know better. The main reason the PGA Tour has cut the tournament short is that it wants the final round to be played on Sunday, no matter what, so the TV audience at home can see it all, including Tiger's shot-making and Bill Murray's antics.

When Esteban's tee time finally draws near, he climbs into one of the brand-new vans that are reserved for shuttling players. Colleen, Nicholas, and Robert join him for the ride to the tenth tee. Unlike the designs at most courses, where the tenth tee is next to the clubhouse, number 10 at Pebble Beach is as far away as it could be without being located in downtown Carmel.

On their little journey to the tee, Esteban and company pass some of the most intimidating golf holes in the world. The 107-yard, par-three seventh is probably the most famous. The green is set on the very end of a peninsula where the surf is so rough that golfers are frequently soaked by the salt spray. It is reached from a tee that is at least forty feet higher in elevation. The wind can blow off the sea and into a player's face at sixty miles per hour or more. Making a tee shot on this hole can be the equivalent of standing on the roof of a Manhattan brownstone in a gale, and attempting to hit the ball into a parking space across the street. Depending on the force of the wind, players have used everything here from a wedge to a driver.

On hole number 10, where Esteban will hit his first shot of the season, the ocean forms the right-hand boundary of a fairway that curves to the right. A thirty-mile-per-hour breeze blows in off the Pacific. Six-foot swells churn the pewter-colored water. On the tee Esteban performs a few bouncy squats, the same kind that boxers do as they hold onto the ropes in their corners before a fight. He smiles at his amateur playing partner, a stockbroker from New Jersey named Joseph Willet. He shakes hands with the other pro in his group—a visiting Japanese player named Kaz Hosakawa. Hosakawa, who speaks no English, is a rising star on the Japanese tour, with six wins in four years. The name of his main sponsor—a car wax called Mr. Magic—is branded on his golf bag, and on his trousers. By the end of the week fans who have never heard of the wax will be calling him Mr. Magic. Kaz's amateur partner is Sam Bronfman III, an heir to the fortune of the family that owns the Seagram Company and Universal Studios.

With a drive that lands safely on the left side of the fairway and an easy iron to the green, Esteban plays the first hole of his long season on tour in a regulation four shots. He manages a birdie three on the next hole, and misses making birdies on the next three by a sum total of two inches. He came here believing that he could succeed, and nothing happens during the first five holes to change his mind.

As many of the players expected, the rain-soaked course yields low scores. Tom Lehman will shoot four under par on the front nine at Pebble Beach. The wet course helps in two ways. First, shots hit onto the greens tend to dig themselves little craters—it's called plugging—and stop right where they land. Players can take advantage of this by landing their balls as close to the hole as possible without worrying about them rolling past it. Second, when water puddles in the fairways, the PGA Tour allows players to "lift, clean, and place" their balls before each shot. The result is a perfect lie, every time, even in the rough.

But there is also a downside to these conditions. The grass in the fairways is so heavy with water that it grabs the club when it passes through, slowing it and causing it to twist. Esteban discovers this when he hits a heavy shot that costs him a bogey on the fifteenth hole, a par-four where players must drive the ball over a gulch where a sign for walking tours reads, "Let's Learn About Bats." After six holes, he is at even par.

As they slog around, Esteban, Mr. Magic, and their amateurs play for an audience of fewer than a dozen. Each member of the tiny gallery has a personal connection to one of the players. Kaz Hosakawa's young Japanese wife is in attendance, gently tapping her gloved hands together in silent applause after every shot. Sam Bronfman's wife Kelly, an athletic, perfectly manicured woman with long blonde hair, tags along with her husband. She chats almost continually, and considers it her personal responsibility to stop and pick up every bit of litter she sees marring the perfection of the course. She does this rather elegantly, and every once in a while the movement of her hand produces a glint as the diamonds and emeralds on her ring finger catch the sunlight. Esteban's fans include Jon Minnis, Colleen, and Nicholas, who spends much of his time digging for worms in the turf and kicking pinecones.

Following a group of no-name players on a soggy Thursday is far different from watching a tournament on television or accompanying the champion as he plays the final holes on Sunday. Though the golfers hit some impressive shots, and score their share of birdies, on days like this a spectator's mind tends to wander on the journey from tee to green to tee.

Colleen Toledo can only say so much about golf. She's still learning, after all. In the long pauses between shots she tells me about the home she and her husband have bought and the mortgage she's lining up (7 percent, and two points). She ruminates about the arrangements for an upcoming trip to the Hawaiian Open. Colleen is also concerned about Nicholas, an active little boy who would rather run and throw rocks in puddles than stand still while his stepfather putts. The Tour has a traveling day care staff that sets up a center at every stop. Colleen is considering using it.

A devoted wife, Colleen has willingly accepted the roles of accountant, travel agent, and child care specialist. Although these chores are demanding, they are not the most difficult part of life on the Tour. She is more compelled by the challenge of managing relationships—with her husband, other Tour wives, and even Nicholas—within a vagabond lifestyle. Though Esteban is adamant about preferring that Colleen travel with him, many players are ambivalent about their wives attending tournaments. Many don't want to be bothered with the demands of family while they are in a tournament. This may explain the not-so-cute terms some players use to refer to the folding spectator seats most wives carry and the ID pins they must wear.

"I've had people tell me this is the bitch seat," explains Colleen. "And this," she adds, pointing to the gold PGA Tour pin on her sweater, "is what some people call the bitch pin."

Though she assures me her husband doesn't use these terms, or share the attitude that they reflect, Colleen is aware of the stress the Big Tour puts on marriages. Nick Faldo is the most glaring recent example of this problem. In 1995, he left his wife of eleven years, for a twenty-year-old college student. He was thirty-eight at the time. Three years later, not long after Faldo's divorce was finalized, he broke up with the girlfriend and she made headlines by beating his Porsche sports car with a golf club.

"Guys have women throwing themselves at them all the time," says Colleen. "And it's not much better for wives who stay home. They have all kinds of temptations when their husbands are away. One guy on the Nike Tour had to quit because he went home to find out his wife had blown $30,000 on cocaine."

Given the stresses and strains on personalities, Esteban and Colleen don't expect to make many friends among the players. Tour golfers are, in general, obsessed and self-centered. Few people reach the top without these qualities, and it is the rare person who can keep the money, adulation, and attention in perspective well enough to be a real friend.

In some ways, the ego problems among the lower-ranked pros may be even greater than they are at the top. Their status is precarious, and their shortcomings are very publicly announced in the Tour's weekly money list. This insecurity may explain why a disproportionate number seem to marry younger women who are especially suited to looking pretty and keeping quiet. These women are the ultimate supporting cast members, subsuming their own desires and impulses.

Colleen isn't one of these wallflowers, so she has had to work at the role of pro golfer's wife. She does it out of love, but it is not easy. "I had to learn that when we're out here, it's his job and his schedule. If he needs to practice after he plays, I just have to wait. It took a while for me to adjust to it, but I have." She insists that the trade-off is worth it. She likes to travel. She enjoys watching her husband play golf, hoping that he'll reach the final day of play high enough on the leader board to compete for a big paycheck.

At this early point in the competition, it's impossible to say where Colleen's husband will rank on the last day of the tournament. But he does finish nine holes at even par, like more than a dozen other players. Forecasts are calling for a series of storms–all generated by the El Niño currents–to sweep in from the Pacific at a rate of one per day. Considering the forecast, many of the players doubt that even the truncated tournament will be completed.

•

El Niño is not the only storm the Tour faces. While the Pebble Beach Pro-Am limps along in the rain, Casey Martin and his lawyer are challenging the golf establishment in a federal court in Oregon. Martin's lawsuit, which allowed him to use a golf cart for Q. School, is finally going to trial. He is suing for the right to use a cart at every tournament, and the PGA Tour is resisting him with all its might.

No matter what the merits of the case may be, Martin—whose leg is withered by a congenital defect—is clearly winning the public relations war. Media commentators and members of Congress are rallying to his cause. The Nike company has even filmed and begun broadcasting a commercial featuring Martin as a sports hero. His story fits perfectly with the company's current advertising theme, which stresses the infinite variety of players in all sports. In contrast, the PGA Tour is presenting a lineup of old rich men, including Jack Nicklaus and Arnold Palmer, whose opposition to Martin's request seems rigid and cold.

But while members of Congress and editorial writers across the country line up behind Martin, almost every player at Pebble Beach seems opposed to him. Jack Nicklaus tells reporters that though the public wants to see Casey prevail, "I just don't think the game of golf can have that happen." This sentiment is reflected in Esteban's response when I ask him about it. He says he admires Martin's determination and his skill on the course. "But in professional golf, you walk the course," he says. "They should not force us to change the rules."

Critics say that the golfers are being greedy and heartless. This may have been true of some, but if you heard the casual conversation among players at Pebble Beach you would reach a different conclusion. They are not greedy. They are insecure. Golfers have long been defensive about their game, which can easily be caricatured as the softest sport around. In what other athletic competition can a middle-aged man with twenty pounds of belly hanging over his belt still win a championship?

To counter this image, pro golfers point to the strength, skill, and training required to propel the ball. They also talk about the physical stress of walking up and down miles of terrain in summer heat or gale force winds. The ultimate example of this is Ken Venturi's 1964 victory in the U.S. Open, played in suburban Washington, D.C., during a summer heatwave. Venturi completed thirty-six holes at Congressional Country Club on the last day. With the temperature hovering around the 100-degree mark, he collapsed at the end of the first round, barely remaining conscious. Revived by salt and fluids, he was accompanied by a doctor for the entire second round. On the final hole he was in such poor shape it seemed he wouldn't make it down the fairway. But he did, and he made a ten-foot par putt to win. It was one of the greatest golf stories ever lived.

The fact that PGA Tour golf can demand such a performance allows players to claim to be real athletes. The spectacle of someone riding around in a cart and stopping to hit shots would put golf in the same category as billiards or bowling. Besides, the players say, walking is as much a part of the game as running is in other sports. No one would argue that a great slugger who is disabled be allowed to ride a go-cart to first base after swinging the bat.

These are all good arguments, but what Jack Nicklaus, Esteban, and the PGA Tour don't seem to understand—but Nike does—is that Casey Martin has priceless public appeal. Among the vast majority of casual observers, who don't know the difference between golf as it's played on the PGA Tour and golf at the local country club, carts are synonymous with the game. Indeed, everyone who has ever passed by a golf course is likely to have seen players in carts racing all over the place. Given the popular perception, the Tour was in a no-win situation. No matter what is argued on a legal basis, denying a cart to a gifted young man with a disability seems cruel. For a sport that depends on corporate sponsorship, this insensitivity to public opinion could be a financial disaster. People don't buy products from coldhearted pitchmen.

But public relations is not the only flaw in the PGA Tour's stance. To make matters even more complicated, the Tour has already opened the doors of cart barns all over the country to accommodate members of the Senior Tour, who ride whenever they choose. Senior events were created for the sole purpose of generating income for older players and the Tour organization. The carts make it possible for the public to see their aging heroes in action. Other rules have been changed to lessen the strain on players. As far back as 1964, after Venturi's valiant struggle through the heat, the tradition of playing thirty-six holes on Sundays was banished for good. The golf writer for *The New York Times* bemoaned this decision noting that "the stamina has been removed" from professional golf. The change was made to increase TV revenues.

Taken all together, the Tour's track record on the matter of stamina and golf carts is inconsistent with the argument that the rules and tradition must be upheld. When money is at stake, pro golf seems more than willing to bend. Ironically, bending for Casey Martin would improve the Tour's image and reinforce the idea that golf is a game for everyone. The marketing bonanza would be worth the inconvenience. Instead, the Tour faces the inescapable embarrassment of the villain's role in an emotional trial.

•

On Friday, as the parties return to the courtroom in Oregon, the players go back to work at Pebble Beach. The California sun shines all day long, but much to the frustration of the competitors, play will be restricted to the completion of the first round. A large crowd gathers at the first tee. They applaud politely when Esteban is introduced as part of the 11:30 group. But after he drives the ball into the right-hand rough, the gallery that follows him down the fairway is small. It's the same contingent that tagged along on Thursday. Colleen has her hair in a French braid. Nicholas wears a white visor just like Esteban's, except it is flecked with dried mud.

Esteban's drives are not as straight as they were yesterday. After going right on the first hole, he goes left into the rough on the second. Colleen starts to worry. But as the day wears on, it becomes clear that Esteban is doing this on purpose. Usually PGA Tour–style rough—six inches high or higher—is wicked enough to make a normal swing impossible. Players who miss the fairways are often doomed to bogeys. But under the lift-clean-and-place rules, which are still in effect, there's no danger in the rough. In fact, under this rule, Esteban can strain to make his drives fly a little further, and even use the rough to improve the angle of his second shot. It's all fairway out there, today.

Despite this advantage, Esteban suffers through bogeys on the first and third holes. Just as disappointing is a par of five on number 2. On this hole he smashes his second shot—a three wood—230 yards to reach the fringe of the green in two shots. A chip-in would yield an eagle. At the very least, he expects an easy up-and-down for birdie. Instead, he needs three shots to get it in the hole and squanders an important opportunity. Tour players are supposed to make birdies and eagles on par-five holes.

Discouraging though it may be, Esteban has played enough golf to know that at any moment a round can go from sour to sweet. He's hitting the ball well. He's beginning to sense the speed of the waterlogged greens. On the sixth hole, he sinks a twelve-footer for birdie. On the very next hole, he stands on the elevated tee and looks down at the famous seventh green, 107 yards away. Waves crash into the rocky point on three sides, sending salt spray high in the air. A brisk wind carries the sound of barking seals from nearby rocks.

For a moment, Esteban stands still and absorbs the sights, the sounds, the feeling of the warm sun. It is a privilege to be here on one of the most scenic golf holes in the world. When his turn comes, he makes a tricky little knockdown shot that leaves the ball on the green, eighteen feet from the hole. Minutes later, with the sound of the crashing waves in his ears, he makes the putt for another birdie. He turns to face the hillside where friends and family watch. He smiles broadly and thrusts his fist into the air.

Esteban goes on to finish at one-under, seventy-one. Kaz Hosakawa scores a seventy-three. Seven strokes ahead of Esteban, at the course record of sixty-four, is Tom Lehman.

•

It is Saturday, and we are somewhere on the Poppy Hills course at Pebble Beach, watching Colleen Toledo's husband play the second full round of the tournament, when she discovers that the huge diamonds and emeralds on Kelly Bronfman's hand are real. She also learns that the Bronfman family's wealth dwarfs the riches of Tiger Woods and any other of the world's great golfers. "And here I've been talking to her like she was just like me," says Colleen. "It's amazing who you meet and what you see at these golf tournaments."

The surprises had been much less pleasant on the Nike Tour. Back then, Esteban had often ventured into dangerous neighborhoods in search of cheap motels, and he played on many courses that were isolated and devoid of spectators. At the Dakota Dunes Open, a caddie stumbled onto a marijuana crop cultivated just out of bounds. It was harvested for later use. At Pebble Beach, the surprising discoveries fall into the Kelly-Bronfman's-jewels-are-real category. Here, the men wearing knickers and badges that identify them as volunteer marshals are likely to be retired CEOs. Many of the elderly women volunteers who direct the shuttle buses walk to the course from million-dollar cottages.

Though Colleen is free to take in all of the atmosphere, Esteban ignores it. So far he has scored four pars and a bogey. On a day when everyone is teeing it up in the rough and firing right at the flags, he is losing ground to the leaders. He must start making birdies soon, or miss the cut.

He stands on the sixth tee with a three iron in his hand and looks at the flag that waves 190 yards away. He sets up over the ball, shuffles his feet, and then is still for a split second. He draws the club back and sends a low shot that lands on the squishy green and rolls twelve feet past the hole. He wrestles a tricky downhill putt into the cup for a birdie.

Unfortunately, this success does not begin a streak. The only remarkable event that occurs on the next few holes is a drive that John Daly, who is playing one group behind, smashes over Esteban's head while he is waiting to hit on the par-five ninth. It's the kind of intrusion that could enrage a country club player on a Sunday afternoon, but here everyone is simply amazed at how far Daly can hit the ball. Esteban smiles, removes his visor for a moment, and then puts it back on.

As the day wears on, the sun and the wind dry out the course and conditions improve. Esteban scores clutch birdies on two par-fives. He likes the Poppy Hills course, but not for any of the reasons you might expect. He likes it because it was here, in 1991, that Jon Minnis finally said, "Esteban, I love you like a son." Jon was serving as caddie at the time. Esteban had gotten into the tournament during a Monday qualifier. He doesn't remember much about the round, but he'll never forget what Jon said.

In the present, Esteban scrambles to three under par, with six holes to go. But instead of going on a hot run of birdies, which is his intention, he continues to struggle. On a fairly straightforward par-four, he overpowers a greenside chip and leaves himself a long putt for par. He misses and loses a stroke he had gained just moments before.

In the tiny, mobile gallery, friends and family try to offer encouragement without calling attention to the mounting pressure. Nearly five hours have passed by the time Esteban, Kaz Hosakawa, and the two amateurs reach the tee for the last hole of the day. With the sun setting in the Pacific, brown deer with flicking tails have started to wander out of the woods to graze on the lush fairway grass. They seem to find the grass on the eighteenth fairway especially delicious.

The eighteenth at Poppy Hills is a twisting, 500-yard hole that bends first left and then right before ending at a steeply sloped green. Under drier, faster conditions, a ball hit to the middle of the green would tend to roll back down toward the fairway.

The odd angles of the fairway and a stand of pines on the right side about a hundred yards from the green make it almost impossible to reach in two shots. But somehow,

Kaz does it. With his longest drive of the day and a three wood that he hits so it drifts from the left to the right, he scores an artful four and finishes with a one-under-par seventy-one round. Esteban needs three shots to get to the green, but he is close enough—at ten feet—to hope for a birdie.

And then he seems to lose his concentration. He misses and then misses again from just three feet. The three-putt bogey reduces him to even par for the day and one-under for the tournament. He's in danger of missing the cut and starting the year with a big fat zero in earnings.

Esteban seems dumbfounded. He looks down at the hole, as if to make sure that there really is one cut there. He comes off the green saying that the three-footer was perfect. He cannot understand why it didn't go in. His little band of followers agrees that it's a mystery. It's as if some evil god of golf denied him on a whim.

But of course this isn't the case. PGA Tour pros make three- or four-foot putts as a matter of routine. When they miss, it's because they didn't read the green right, failed to compensate for footprints around the hole, or just didn't stroke it cleanly. Robert Szczesny knows the miss is Esteban's fault, but he doesn't say what he is thinking. It's only the first tournament of the year. Now is not the time to show how much he knows. Maybe over time, he hopes, Esteban will consult him more, and let him help.

•

The leader board shows that Tom Watson has passed Lehman to seize first place at nine under par for the two days. At age 48, Watson is one of the most successful players in history. He has more than thirty tournament wins, including a U.S. Open victory at Pebble Beach in 1982. In all, twenty-one players are within four strokes of first place, which suggests an exciting finish. At a press conference, a smiling Watson says that the weather, and how a player reacts to it, may determine the ultimate winner of this tournament. He estimates that he has played Pebble Beach about 150 times over the years, so he has a bit of experience with the conditions here.

While Tom Watson is charming the press, Esteban is back in his car and fuming. Gone is the grin he flashed yesterday after he scored a birdie on the famous oceanfront par-three and thrust his fist in the air. Now he can't believe he missed such an easy birdie putt. Fortunately he made the cut, tying for seventy-sixth place. But with the tournament shortened by the weather, he cannot count on two days of play to catch up to the leaders. He'll be lucky to play one more round, move up a few spots, and earn a few thousand dollars.

"It was right there, going in the hole," he says. "I don't believe it."

Esteban's ill temper persists as we drive away from the course. He had insisted on giving me a lift to the distant parking lot where I had left my car. But none of the Boy Scouts enlisted to direct traffic at Pebble Beach seems to know how we can get to this lot. Neither do I. When we circle past the same point for the third time, Esteban demands to know why I don't know my way around. I remind him that I've never been here before. The normal traffic patterns had been changed to accommodate the tournament. Two-way roads had become one-way. Others had been closed altogether.

He listens, but I'm not sure my explanation makes sense to him. Thankfully, we finally find a twisting road that takes us where we have to go. As I say good night, he's telling Colleen why he doesn't want to drive thirty minutes to Monterey for dinner at Bubba Gump's. He may not admit it himself, but he is acting like a very worried man.

•

Dawn on the tournament's last day comes with patches of blue sky amid the clouds. Esteban arrives at the Spyglass Hill Golf Course smiling again and eager to start play. If not forgotten entirely, yesterday's blown putt is no longer torturing him. Any pressure he might have felt to finish the tournament high on the leader board is gone, too. Now his sights are set on another goal: simply playing better golf.

As he waits for his tee time, Esteban watches the clouds thicken. When he moves to the practice green, raindrops start to fall. Robert holds an umbrella over his boss as he practices putting. The rain comes harder as they walk to the tenth tee, where they will start today's round. Undaunted, Esteban lets the rain soak him as he hits two solid shots and scores an easy birdie on the par four hole. It rains harder.

Another straight drive lands in the fairway and leaves Esteban in good position to attack the par-five number 11 hole. But as he reaches the ball and prepares to hit, airhorns begin to sound all over the course. This is the signal that play is suspended. As of this moment, he is nine strokes behind the leaders.

From the fairway, Esteban looks in my direction. I'm standing on a cart path in a grove of pines that deflect some of the rain. He takes the umbrella from Robert and walks over to me. He holds it over my head. I interpret this as a proud man's gesture of reconciliation, an unspoken apology for the grumbling in the car a day before.

As we walk back to the clubhouse, Esteban tells me the rain and the suspended rounds make it difficult to get into a playing rhythm. "But everyone has the same problem," he adds. "It's frustrating to everyone." Rain is so common at Pebble Beach in the winter that many players, including Lehman, are suggesting that the tournament be permanently rescheduled to autumn. "They complain," says Esteban, "but I bet none of them would give up their place. We all want to be here. Rain, wind, hurricane, we all would be here. There are times when I've even felt like sleeping on the golf course. I love it that much."

It takes about two hours for officials to recognize that El Niño has defeated the PGA Tour. The tournament will not be resumed. Bill Murray and Jack Lemmon are sent home. There will be no final act in this drama, at least not right away.

The players are invited to return to Pebble Beach in August for one round that will determine a winner and final rankings. All the scores posted on this day—including Esteban's birdie—are wiped out. Of course, he is not the only soaked and discouraged player. Among the other Q. School grinders, Tom Pernice, J. P. Hayes, and Jeff Gallagher are within four shots of the lead and rightly anticipated earning enough money to settle their nerves for a few months. Instead, they leave with nothing but the hope that they will play as well in the next tournament.

With the rain washing down in sheets, most of the

players scurry to the cars and vans that will take them to area airports. Esteban rides over to Jon Minnis's house in Carmel to visit with some nephews. He, Colleen, and Nicholas then load up the Honda for a six-hour drive home. It is February 2. Esteban's winnings still total zero. Anyone would feel discouraged. But the Buick Open will start on Thursday in La Jolla, outside San Diego. Colleen has found a discount room at the Embassy Suites hotel. And Sea World is just down the road, in case Nicholas gets bored.

•

In the weeks that follow Pebble Beach, Esteban and his band of supporters will march through tournaments in La Jolla and Hawaii. In those two events, he survives both Friday cuts, and plays on the weekend. His performance in Hawaii is especially encouraging. In the Monday pro-am, he shoots a sixty-five, the lowest score of the day. In the regular tournament he scores 69-68-67-70. He takes pleasure in beating his Sunday playing partner, a longtime Tour regular named Billy Mayfair. Mayfair's wife Tammy, who has been watching pro golf for a decade, tells Robert that she thinks Esteban has what it takes to win.

On almost any other week, Esteban's score would be enough put him in the top ten, but in Hawaii the perfect playing conditions and a comparatively easy course make it possible for many of the players to do far better. John Huston wins by shooting twenty-eight under par and breaking Ben Hogan's record for lowest-ever score in a PGA Tour event. The $324,000 prize moves Huston's lifetime earnings total over the $4.5 million mark. A college star who needed just four years to become a Tour regular,

Huston is anything but a grinder. With a fourteen-under-par total, Esteban has to settle for twenty-seventh place and $11,981.23.

•

Esteban feels a surge of confidence as he heads for Valencia, California, just north of Los Angeles, and the Nissan Open. The Open is the final event of the Tour's annual "West Coast swing" of eight tournaments. "I feel really good," he tells me. "I think I can give these guys a run for the money."

But Valencia turns out to be nothing but trouble. It begins when an off-duty cop hired for security insists that Esteban go to the caddie entrance. A little arguing persuades the cop, but unsettles Esteban.

Things get worse in the pro-am outing. Esteban is paired with a red-faced Nissan dealer who is either deeply disappointed that he isn't playing with Tiger Woods or just plain mean. For sixteen holes, he badgers Esteban about his sponsor—Toyota—and his game. "Hit the goddamned ball, kid, hit the goddamned ball," he keeps saying. On the sixteenth hole, the amateur hits a terrible shot into the rough and turns to scowl at Esteban, who just can't resist the opening.

"Just hit the damn ball," he says.

From this point on, the car dealer complains about everything. He threatens to contact his pals at Toyota's U.S. headquarters and demand they drop Esteban's sponsorship. Esteban is so upset that when the round is over, he calls Toyota himself and volunteers to cancel his contract. They won't hear of it.

When play begins for real in Valencia, Esteban misses

the cut by one stroke. His West Coast swing is over, and it is not at all clear whether his dream or his dread is going to come true this year. Meanwhile Billy Mayfair, the same Billy Mayfair who trailed Esteban in Hawaii, wins the Nissan Open in Los Angeles by defeating Tiger Woods in a playoff.

Though he tries to maintain a facade of confidence, it's obvious that crashing in Valencia has affected Esteban. He is, by turns, brooding, fearful, or blustery in denying that he's afraid he will fail to grasp the dream he has chased for more than a decade. But in one unguarded moment, he confesses to me that he's not certain he belongs on the Tour. "I know I earned it," he says. "I think I can play with these guys. But I haven't proven it to anybody." Most of all, he hasn't proven it to himself.

•

If Esteban is feeling a little shaken, then Robert is truly upset. He's already wondering if things might have worked out better if he had gone with another player, say, Iain Steel. Robert is frustrated because he thinks he sees things—how the pressure makes Esteban play too quickly, how he does his best when his mood is light—and he is sure he could help. But so far, all Esteban seems interested in is whether he gets the yardage right and the equipment in order.

As caddie and player prepare to leave the West Coast, Robert hopes that disconnecting from family and friends will help Esteban focus. "He can't say no to them," he complains to me. "One night in San Diego they took him out to Sea World at seven-thirty. He didn't get much sleep that night. In Hawaii, they gave him Valentine's Day presents and made a big deal out of it. He didn't have the time to get anything for them. It made him feel bad. I know it.

"They obviously don't understand how hard this is. He needs to practice and relax and stay focused. Most of all he needs to practice. He's self-taught. Everything is feel with him. That's why he has to hit balls every day."

While Robert frets, he might be comforted to know that most of the other grinders are doing no better than Esteban. The exceptions are Jeff Gallagher and Steve Jurgenson. Gallagher, whose brother and sister are both pro Tour players, has the advantage of some recent Tour experience. He made $114,000 after getting his card in 1996. It was not enough to retain his playing privileges, but enough to suggest he was ready for the top level of competition. At Valencia he tied for sixth and earned more than $67,000. Jurgenson also played on the Big Tour in 1996, besting Gallagher by $4,000. At thirty-seven, he is one of the oldest of the grinders and overdue for success. At the Buick Invitational in San Diego, he made $61,350 by capturing sixth.

Despite their progress, Gallagher and Jurgenson cannot relax any more than Esteban. Each week brings a new challenge, and no player can be sure he will survive another cut or win another dollar. But when I ask Esteban if he is nervous, he responds coolly. "I am going to succeed," he says. "I am going to keep my card. You watch."

THE SCORECARD

Remaining tournaments	27
Esteban's earnings	$15,866
Money still needed to keep card	$214,134
Rank	200th plus

5

El Caballo

Esteban and Robert are spending almost as much time together as conjoined twins. Their work days are eight, nine, even ten hours long. (This is three or four hours longer than the average Tour golfer's work day, but Esteban is living up to his legendary reputation as a practice hog.) The schedule is made even more difficult for Robert by the fact that he refuses to spend his money on airplane tickets.

In a typical week on the Tour, Robert literally dashes to his '88 Grand Prix moments after the final round of a tournament and begins driving to the next site even before the winner's finish. Some PGA Tour events are more than 500 miles apart, so Robert drives on, stopping only for fast food, bathrooms, and half-hour naps at highway rest areas.

When he reaches his destination, Robert goes to the clubhouse to pick up the yardage book that charts the hazards and distances between landmarks on every hole. He then walks the course to make his own measurements, a dozen or more per fairway. He also inspects the greens, and checks the height of the rough. Each bit of data goes in the book. During play, the book will be consulted on almost every shot. It's a wonderful tool, but it adds to a caddie's responsibilities. There were no books in the days of Palmer and Trevino. Back then, the caddies offered eyeball estimates and advice based on experience. *All* of the players operated on feel.

On most Mondays, after he's charted the course, Robert will carry Esteban's bag for a pro-am tournament. The Monday pro-ams are typically junior events at these tournaments, attracting corporate vice presidents instead of presidents, chiropractors rather than MDs. Few top players participate. However, they are all required to appear for Wednesday pro-ams, and that's enough contact with the public for most.

Those who play on Mondays do it because they can make between $500 and $2,500 for each appearance. Added together, pro-am checks can double a low-ranked player's annual income. But it comes at a price. Often, a player must travel through the night, or sacrifice practice time, in order to appear on the pro-am tee Monday morning. Meanwhile, the upper-level players are resting, spending time with family, or attending to business at home. Most don't even arrive at a tournament until Tuesday or Wednesday.

Caddies follow the schedule set by their bosses. So while

many of his peers are resting, Robert carries Esteban's bag for Monday pro-ams and attends to him during practice afterwards. He pulls the clubs, fetches baskets of balls, and generally keeps things moving.

Robert has surrendered entirely to his job. When he's not at the course, he's sleeping in his car or at a cheap motel. He never seems to have anything but work on his mind, or any place to go. On the practice range, he waits in a Zen-like silence, watching ball after ball fly. He knows that because Esteban hates to stop hitting while there is still light, the sun controls the schedule. With summer coming, Robert's days are getting longer and longer. His skin is already brown. The lines that radiate from the corners of his eyes are getting deeper and longer.

The more I get to know Robert, the more I understand that he is desperate to do more than the routine tasks of the caddie. Though he can't offer much direct help with his swing, Robert spends hours analyzing Esteban's ability and character, and tries to imagine ways to help him do better. The trouble is that Esteban doesn't offer his trust easily, and he isn't one for self-analysis. He doesn't seem at all interested in reviewing poor rounds to see what might be learned, and he does not listen to advice with much interest.

"You can't just tell him something, because he has to experience it himself," says Robert. "That's just the way it is. But I try to just say little things to get him thinking about how he plays, his swing, how he manages the course. I think about these things because I want him to do well, mostly for his sake, but also for mine."

In his own way, Robert is as obsessive as Esteban. This

kind of devotion cannot be bought for the $500 per week he is paid as a salary and his thin slice of Esteban's potential weekly winnings. He does it because he is becoming attached to Esteban. He is beginning to think of him as a brother, and he says as much during moments of candor.

Like many brothers, this caddie and player are very different. Esteban cares about golf and little else. He is task-oriented, always preferring to do something rather than talk about it. And he is self-absorbed. When he is at a tournament, he expects family and friends to bend to his needs, whether they are choosing a restaurant or deciding when to leave the golf course. And if the topic of conversation wanders very far from golf, Esteban can grow restless.

Of all Esteban's personal qualities, perhaps his most valuable is his ability to forgive himself for anything that goes wrong on the course. He'll blame uneven greens, a gust of wind, almost anything or anyone but himself. This ability to externalize problems is actually essential to his success and commonplace among Tour pros. Though they say they hate to make excuses, most do it compulsively. But it is a useful compulsion. It allows a player to keep going after a bad shot, a bad hole, a bad round, or a bad year. A less egocentric man who takes the blame upon himself would likely quit before he succeeds.

"He's a very intelligent, very strong, very proud guy. I mean, he made it so far on his own," says Robert. "But he has trouble looking at himself objectively. I mean, no matter how much he practices, Esteban can't see his own swing or check out his own attitude. We all need someone we trust to give us the truth about ourselves."

Robert worries that without objective help from an

outsider, Esteban will be vulnerable to the kind of head-banging meltdown that defeated Woody Austin at Q. School. This is why Scott Verplank consults with a sports psychologist. It is why Tiger Woods depends on a teacher, a veteran caddie, and his ever-present father.

"Esteban doesn't have someone he can turn to for perspective," says the caddie. "I know I could do that for him. Help him. But he can't accept it yet. I think it's a problem that a lot of people who pull themselves up by the bootstraps have. No one can go it all the way alone. But they don't see that."

In a lonely sport, Esteban may be the ultimate loner. In the past, he has told Colleen that he is "El Caballo," a horse wearing blinders and plodding toward his goal. Though El Caballo has come a long way, the glory in life more often belongs to those who know when and how to run free like a thoroughbred. No one knows this better than a former trainer of racehorses like Robert Szczesny. He believes that Esteban does his best when he lets himself play joyous golf. This is not easy for Esteban to do. His passion for success is matched by his frustration with failure. But frustration does not help Esteban's performance, says Robert.

What does?

Playfulness. He saw it when Esteban was challenged by the kids in Missouri and responded with a birdie and an eagle. He's seen it this year too, when fans call out and Esteban replies with a joke or offers drinks from the player's water jug to spectators lining a tee box. Esteban always seems to hit better shots when he's having fun with the gallery.

Esteban is a natural entertainer, an extrovert. Somehow, Robert must help him overcome his anxiety and dread so that he can be himself. He hopes it will happen once they leave the West Coast, and the distractions of family and friends, and play the series of tournaments slated for the South in the month of March. In the South, there will be fewer distractions. Esteban will concentrate on golf and golf alone. "Everything will be better in the South," he says.

•

But it is not better. At the Doral-Ryder Open, a vicious golf course nicknamed the Blue Monster tortures every player with more than 100 bunkers, a beguiling layout, and water on all but two holes. More than once, Esteban is deceived by the gently undulating terrain, which makes it almost impossible to judge distances. At several key moments, he can't reconcile what his eyes tell him and the yardage figures Robert reports from his book. Esteban goes with his eyes and shoots a seventy-nine on the first day. Tomorrow he'll need to break par by four or five strokes—a fourteen-shot swing in his performance—to make the cut.

On Friday, Esteban is paired with Rocco Mediate, who is in his thirteenth straight year on Tour and last saw the Q. School in 1986. Mediate is a friendly but quiet man with a huge, gap-toothed grin and a playful streak—off the course. When he's at work, he says very little. Having slain the Blue Monster to win this tournament 1991, Mediate is comfortable in his surroundings. The calm rubs off on his playing partner. With five birdies and no bogeys on the first eleven holes, Esteban begins to believe he'll make it to Saturday. Then he and Robert suffer a communication breakdown.

It happens on the 591-yard, par-five number 12. Esteban is standing on the fairway, facing a green that is protected by bunkers on all sides. The caddie recommends a three iron, with which Esteban can easily hit the ball 200 yards. Esteban looks at the hole and thinks it is closer to 180 yards away. He asks for the distance, and Robert tells him not to worry.

"I'm out here to help you," says Robert. "Trust me."

Esteban doesn't trust him. He picks his six iron out of the bag and settles over the ball. He hits the ball into the bunker. A birdie opportunity becomes a bogey. For the second time in a row, Esteban misses the cut.

Later on, both men will say they learned something from this. Esteban will say that he will trust his caddie more. Robert promises to give his player all the data in his book, instead of just handing him a club. But in the moment, both of them are annoyed and confused. It's another week without a paycheck. That's three zeros in five weeks. This is not the way you keep your card.

No matter what they say about learning their lessons, the tension, and fear, are growing inside both men. Robert decides he's going to stay away from Esteban when they are not working. The distance may help both of them relax. Resentment is starting to creep into what he says about his boss.

"He's great to be around if he's the center of attention. But I don't know if he really knows how to have an equal relationship with somebody. I mean, he likes to be the king. He's a benevolent king. But when things aren't going well he gets testy and can blame everyone and everything but himself. That's why I'm not going to stay with him, or go out with him for dinner. I'm there for him on the course and at practice, but it's not good to be together twenty-four hours a day."

Esteban seems, to me, to be more nervous than despotic. If he is self-absorbed, it is because he cannot stop worrying about failure. Anyone who is paid to perform knows how it feels to fight for an opportunity and then stumble when it arrives. First films flop. First books get panned. Rookie pitchers are sent back to the minors. Failure is never more painful than when it arrives on the heels of a long-sought opportunity. Esteban experienced this kind of loss in 1994, when he failed to keep his card. He has waited three years for another chance. Now that it is here, he cannot escape that awful memory.

The pressure is evident on his face, which rarely shines with the little-boy grin I saw at Q. School. When we are together, even off the course, every conversation winds back to the topic of his obsession, keeping his card. "It's a hundred dogs going for one bone," says Esteban. "I feel like I'm fighting against them all.

Though he would never admit it, I think he is depressed. After missing the cut in Los Angeles, he let his usual routine slip. He lost his enthusiasm for his daily run—a holdover from boxing—and complains more often about the lonesome lifestyle of the Tour. Friends and family do prefer to be with him when he's playing well. "They never call when you are playing bad," he says.

It is now mid-March. The Tour season is about a quarter gone already. So far, every week has brought a new winner. No one is dominating like Tiger Woods did in 1997, when he won four PGA Tour events and the Masters, all before May 1. The prize money is being spread more evenly. But Esteban is still stuck at $15,866, around 150th on the money list.

●

Few of the Q. School grinders of '98 are doing much better than Esteban. In fact, most rank behind him on the money list. Two—Tom Loustelot and Lan Gooch—have yet to make it through a single cut and actually play for a paycheck. Only Tom Pernice ($35,000) and Robert Friend ($81,000) are ahead of him. Friend, who is ninety-eighth on the money list, is the envy of them all.

Two years younger than Esteban, thirty-three-year-old Friend is one of the most open, talkative men on the Tour. He's built like a small linebacker, and has a linebacker's determination. Though he didn't grow up poor—his father was a Pittsburgh Pirates pitcher—Friend has much in common with Esteban. He, too, started as a caddie. He played many years on the Nike Tour and had one previous shot at the Big Tour. It was 1992, and he also failed to hold onto his card. Unlike Esteban, who went right back to tournament golf after losing his card, Friend decided to abandon his dream and took a job as a club pro.

"But I was never really happy. My friends on the Tour would call me and tell me what they were doing. I'd be standing there selling some guy a pair of socks and they'd be telling me how they played that day. I had to go back."

So far, Bob Friend is making more cuts, and more money, than Esteban. The main difference between them may be Friend's willingness to let go of some of his grinder ways. "Last time I tried *waaaay* to hard," says Friend. "I was always gritting my teeth and making everything a struggle." After failing in his first PGA Tour year, Friend turned to several sport psychologists—including the famous Rotella—and framed a new approach. "I've decided not to think about keeping my card or winning a tournament. I'm just going to have fun and try to hit a good shot every time.

"Don't get me wrong. I still practice all the time, and I'm very competitive. But the idea is to get away from the one problem that grinders have. We've all worked so hard, all our lives, to get to the point where we will win golf tournaments. But that's putting the cart before the horse. You can't think about winning. You just think about each shot. Then, between shots, I relax. We are getting paid, we get free equipment and clothes and we're flying all over the world playing at the best golf courses. If you can't have fun doing that, something's wrong with you."

While Bob Friend is having fun all the way to the bank, self-doubt is running rampant among the other grinders. When I bump into Lan Gooch in an airport, he looks far more harried than any of the other frequent fliers dragging Samsonite through the terminal.

Short, with short hair, a round face and a compact body, Gooch looks a little like Charlie Brown and a lot like a nervous wreck. He has given up almost everything, including true love, to play on the PGA Tour. (His fiancée dumped him because he insisted on continuing the quest when she thought he should have surrendered.) Now that he's finally reached his goal, things are going terribly. Gooch has only broken par twice so far, and he hasn't come close to making any cuts.

"I'm losing so often that I'm afraid I'm getting used to it," he says, shifting uncomfortably from foot to foot. "I got a choice. Either I tuck my tail and go home or I improve. I'm not going home."

Each player has his own set of beliefs—sort of like a religion of one—when it comes to dealing with slumps. Lan Gooch tries to get away from golf. He plays tourist in whatever city he is visiting, or goes to a movie, anything to give his mind, body, and soul a rest. Bob Friend reaches out to Bob Rotella, who reminds him to stick to his original plan. Esteban Toledo grabs for the one antidote that has always worked for him: practice.

Practice is a time-honored remedy. Even in their old age, Arnold Palmer and Lee Trevino both say that they wake up every morning eager to go to the golf course and work on their games. They feel most comfortable and relaxed surrounded by shades of green. Esteban feels the same way, and it's hard to avoid thinking that it all goes back to the days when he was a scrawny kid in bare feet carrying a seven iron around the Mexicali Country Club in twilight. The deserted golf course was an oasis for the boy from across the river. Everything was quiet, calm, and green. Whether he played alone, or with his brothers, he didn't have to feel self-conscious about his clothes or his class. He could succeed there, like anyone else.

Our experiences early in life leave a deep and lasting imprint. The sights, sounds, and even the smells that soothed us as children have the same effect decades later, sometimes without us realizing it. This is the way it is with Esteban Toledo and golf. For him, the scent of freshly mowed grass and the sight of the flag fluttering on a distant green evoke a sense of calm. As much as golf tortures him, it is also a refuge.

So after missing his second cut in a row at Doral, Esteban goes immediately to the practice range and begins hitting balls. He does this alone, studying the flight patterns of hundreds of shots. "The ball is the teacher," he says. "It tells you what to do."

If Esteban represents one extreme, on the other is Bruce Lietzke, a tall, slim, forty-seven-year-old Texan who practices less than many weekend amateurs. Lietzke has won thirteen PGA Tour titles and more than $6 million without ever practicing between tournaments. Lietzke is as serious about *not* practicing as Esteban is about his routine. But he does share Esteban's aversion to teachers and tinkerers. He admits to accepting one lesson—from his brother—in his twenty-three years on the PGA Tour.

Neither Lietzke nor Esteban represents the norm on Tour. Most players depend on teachers. Some report extraordinary results. Skip Kendall more than doubled his earnings after he began working with Gary Smith, a pro from England. Pro golfers also rely on video replay machines and anything else they can find to help them fix flaws or improve their skills. Equipment is a source of constant conversation on the Tour. New drivers, wedges, irons, and putters are always coming along with promises of straighter, longer, or higher shots.

This is another area where Esteban is different. He knows less about equipment than many amateurs, and practically refuses to learn. When asked if he uses a putter with an "flat lie" shaft he says, "I don't know what that means." The Taylor Made driver he uses was selected by default, because the manufacturer gave it to him, and he declined the offer to fit it to his body and swing. His irons—all Mizuno blades except for a Ping 2 iron—have never been checked for lie. Some have been used so much that the grooves on their faces are wearing out. Manufacturer representatives, who attend every tournament in order to cater to the pros, have given up asking if they can help him with his equipment. Golf clubs are golf clubs, he says. A player's performance is all that matters.

This doesn't mean that Esteban ignores all of the finer aspects of the game. During years of practice in Mexicali and around the world, Esteban taught himself to bend the flight of the ball, to hit it low or high, to stop it, or back it up on the green, or let it roll with a touch of a hook. He has spent enough time practicing in bunkers to be one of the best sand players anywhere.

"All these guys talk about the balls, the shafts this and the titanium that. It means nothing if you don't get it into the hole," he says. "That's what I think about. 'How can I get the ball from where it is, into the hole?' "

He's not absolutely alone in this way of thinking. And in fact, there's some psychological wisdom in his instinctive approach. Seve Ballesteros, also a self-taught former caddie, became an instant success when he joined the American Tour with his free-flowing, idiosyncratic game. Then he listened to people who advised him to adopt the mechanical style he saw in younger American phenoms. He sought out teachers, tinkered with every part of his motion, and played worse and worse.

On the Doral range, Esteban hits enough balls to turn his corner of the practice tee into a grassless desert. Other pros, who can see him as they finish the front nine and start the back, can't help but marvel at Esteban's work ethic. When he finishes his round, Jim McGovern comes over to exclaim, "You're still here? I saw you when I made the turn, and that was three hours ago!" Rocco Mediate offers Esteban both encouragement and advice. "You hit the ball well," he says. "But out here it's all putting."

When the weekend comes, Esteban leaves the Blue Monster behind and drives to the next tournament, the Honda Classic, in Coral Gables, Florida. Over the next few days, he plays the course, fires 1,000 range balls, and puts hours and hours into putting. He also returns to his daily running routine, which he had neglected. On the night before the first day of play, he dreams of finishing fifth in the Honda Classic.

The dream is a poignant reminder of how the grinder's experience on the PGA Tour bears only a faint resemblance to the lives of those at the top. On the Sunday that Esteban spent practicing in Coral Gables, young millionaire Michael Bradley won the Doral tournament and $360,000. John Huston, having already earned nearly half a million dollars and set a Tour record low score, added a second-place finish and $176,000 to his pot. Off the course, General Mills announced that Tiger Woods will become only the eighth athlete in forty years to become a permanent endorser for Wheaties and a fixture on the outside of box. General Mills and IMG refused to say how much the cereal would add to his $100 million–plus endorsement total.

In contrast, Esteban is on the phone most nights with Colleen, discussing the perils of buying their first home when they can't be certain that he will earn another dollar this year. Both of them are lonely, so they try to discuss everything that happens in each day. Convinced that it is vital to his mental well-being as well as his physical condition, Colleen never forgets to ask if he has squeezed in a run during his day.

They also talk about his working relationship with Robert. Esteban remembers that a caddie's mistake—picking up a ball marker on the green at the wrong moment—cost him a victory in a playoff for the Nike Tour Reno Open championship in 1991. Since then, he has never come so close to winning on American soil.

●

While Esteban runs up his hotel phone bill talking to Colleen, Robert curls into the backseat of the Grand Prix to sleep. Before he closes his eyes, he thinks about what has gone right, and what has gone wrong so far this season. Esteban's lack of earnings is an obvious problem. He's got to start making higher finishes. As for his own performance, Robert thinks that he has learned to take care of the small things, tees, balls, the clubs, yardages, etc., so Esteban can focus exclusively on making shots.

Robert has developed a very detailed view of Esteban as a person and as a player. When we meet, a few weeks after Doral, he tries to explain it. "The biggest plus is that he's very creative, especially around the greens," he says. "He knows how the ball will behave in the rough and the short grass and how to use the slope and grain of a green to his advantage." During one stretch, Esteban made a dozen "sand saves" in a row, meaning he got the ball out of a bunker and into the cup in just two shots.

"He's got a very individual swing," says his caddie. "I mean, very individual, like, he swings differently every time. He moves his feet ten times before he hits it. Sometime his feet are still moving when he starts his backswing. You have to think his aim is off. But it isn't." Indeed, Esteban is one of the most accurate hitters around, especially with his long irons shots, which tend to fly straighter than those of other pros. This helps make up for the fact that his drives do not go especially far.

When the two men work together, it is easy to see how Robert is trying to help. Frustrated by too many three-putts in Valencia and at Doral, Esteban is worried that he's moving his head as he putts. Robert won't say whether Esteban's head is moving. He doesn't think it matters. All he will say is, "You're not trusting your swing. Trust it and follow through." When Esteban finishes a bad round and wants some feedback, the caddie just says, "Let's go to the range, hit a lot of balls, and get the feel back."

Of course, the contemplative caddie is not always calm and collected. He is a 'feel' player, too, groping his way through his first year on the Tour. Handicapped by what he suspects is an undiagnosed case of attention deficit disorder, he is easily distracted, and has trouble juggling more than one task at a time. He compensates by constantly making notes, and he is compulsive about keeping Esteban's equipment in order. The clubs are always arranged, by number, in the same way. Balls, tees, towels, and other sundries are always in the same pockets of the bag. But notes and compulsions are not foolproof remedies. An hour before tee time on the first day of the Honda Classic, he discovers that a sand wedge is missing.

"What do you mean it's missing?" says Esteban, his face darkening. "It was there yesterday."

Robert recalls that the last time the club left the bag was during the Monday pro-am round, on the sixteenth hole. Esteban used it to get out of the rough. The ball landed on the green, Esteban handed the club back and took his putter. Though he recalls wiping the wedge off and sliding it back in its proper place, Robert starts to doubt himself. What if he dropped the club right there? Could it be lying in the tall grass?

The caddie runs to the sixteenth green, but finds no club. With his heart pounding, he then races to the driving range, the pro shop, and the shed where the greenkeepers equipment is stored. No one has found a club. Finally he goes to the doorway of the players' locker room—a place he's barred from entering—and asks an attendant to look around. There, tucked behind a locker, is the wedge. Since caddies aren't allowed in the locker room, it's likely that Esteban left it there himself, and forgot.

As in Valencia, where the run-in with the cranky amateur foreshadowed misery, the debacle of the lost wedge begins a day that will go badly. Esteban misses the fairway with almost every drive—some veer left, some right—and scores a seventy-five. He comes off the eighteenth green with the specter of another missed cut clouding his mind. He wants to go to his hotel, but Robert knows that Esteban will be restless and sleep fitfully if he leaves the course without fixing what is wrong. It doesn't take much coaxing to get him to the practice tee where he hits 100 drives, ninety-six of them perfectly straight.

The practice pays off. Friday yields a sixty-eight—aided by a chip-in on the seventeenth hole—which gets Esteban into the weekend competition for prize money. He matches this score on Saturday, and then manages a seventy-one on Sunday. He ties for thirtieth place and earns $10,240. Coming after the defeat on the Blue Monster and the rough start on Thursday, these three rounds show that Esteban has the mental resilience to handle setbacks. His earnings are now just over $26,000. He's 140th on the money list. And he finally makes it into the golfing news, but not in the way he might like. The Associated Press uses him to illustrate just how poorly the ailing Greg Norman is doing. Norman is "in 141st place . . . right behind Esteban Toledo . . ." the wire reports.

•

In an ideal world, Esteban's momentum from Coral Springs would be carried directly to the next tournament. Unfortunately, for the next two weeks he and most of the other Q. School grinders will be forced to step aside while the premier players attend the Bay Hill Invitational and the Players Championship, both in Florida. These opportunities are more examples of the advantages that flow to the established stars. The Players Championship offers the biggest purse in golf—$4 million—and it's all reserved for the elite. Even eleventh place wins $100,000.

The grinders must each decide how to use the two weeks off. Robert Szczesny thinks his man should take some time away from the stress of tournament play. But Esteban considers his new house and mortgage and ignores the warnings about just how much his thirty-five-year-old body and mind can take. "I know my body very well," he says. "It will tell me when I need time off. Besides I need the money."

During his two-week break, Esteban decides to earn some money by using his status as a PGA Tour regular to claim spots in the field for Nike Tournaments in Monterrey, Mexico, and in Louisiana. Esteban recalls that he resented it when Tour players "dipped down" into a Nike contest. But now that he has the privilege, he will use it.

Though he says he is returning to the Nike Tour for the money, I think he is also seeking the comfort of old friends and competitors. He's hoping to get his bearings. Unlike the Big Tour, which is often a lonely grind, the Nike is like a family-run carnival. Players, wives, and children all socialize. He will be among friends.

In Monterrey, Esteban fails to make the cut, but at the Louisiana Open he shoots the lowest round of the tournament—sixty-four—to seize fourth place and the biggest single paycheck of his life, $18,750. Even though the winnings cannot be applied to his PGA Tour total, the money eases some of Esteban's financial concerns, at least temporarily. And when we discuss the tournament on the phone, Robert tells me that Esteban got something more important, and more valuable, out of his little dip into the Nike Tour; a reminder that golf is fun.

The conditions in Louisiana were terrible. Cold winds and rain combined to make every player miserable. "But it didn't matter," the caddie tells me. "Esteban was joking with the guys and not feeling any pressure. They were mostly guys he knew from before and they were pretty happy to see him. On the last day, you could see that he had remembered to have fun. That's how he shot the sixty-four, by letting go and enjoying golf.

"This is what makes all the difference with Esteban. If he learns how to enjoy himself out here, how to really feel good playing this game he's going to be good. He's got the game. I'm telling you, if he just gets his mind in the right place he's going to beat a lot of people."

THE SCORECARD

Remaining tournaments	23
Esteban's earnings	$44,593
Money still needed to keep card	$185,407
Rank	140th

6

Turnabout

There is no rest for the grinder, even when he is sick with a heavy chest cold. During Master's week, while the golf elite is celebrated among the azaleas, Toyota summons Esteban to a outing at a country club outside Los Angeles. He has yet to receive the car he was promised in lieu of a sponsorship payment, but this doesn't matter. He now wears Toyota's name stitched onto his shirt and over his heart. He is as loyal as a twenty-year-worker on an assembly line in Japan. So while he's still fighting the germ he picked up in Louisiana, he gets in his old Honda car and drives to the exhibition.

Most of the car dealers, executives, and customers at the outing have only a vague idea that Esteban Toledo is a real pro. Their attention is focused on Toyota's aging star, Chi Chi Rodriguez, a sun-dried wraith of a man whose routine would play as well at a comedy club as it does on the practice tee. Chi Chi's presence gives Esteban a chance to relax, for which his weary body and mind are grateful. He had recently picked up some pills at a drugstore in Mexicali, but they didn't seem to be helping his cold very much. He feels exhausted.

After a trick shot display and a few holes with amateur partners, Esteban and Chi Chi are liberated. In the locker room, the elder statesman of Hispanic-American golfers asks Esteban about life on the Tour. He confesses that he's worried about keeping his card. Esteban recalls Chi Chi's reply:

"Oh, you shouldn't worry about that," said Chi Chi. "Don't even think about keeping your card. You go out there and you try to win. That's all that matters. Win. Then the card will take care of itself."

Esteban files away Chi Chi's advice with all the other words of wisdom he's been offered by well-meaning fellow pros. Much of it is contradictory. Some have told him to focus on making the cut each week, because then he would be assured some sort of paycheck. Other pros have said he should just relax when he doesn't make the cut, because next week he might win everything. All these points of view are staples of pro golf philosophy. Players use whatever suits them at the moment.

One article of faith among the journeymen and the grinders is the belief that the fields are weaker at certain tournaments, especially those that take place after majors. The Greater Greensboro Open, which is held two weeks after the Masters, is one such event. Many of the top players pass on Greensboro, which means the field could be easier to beat. Of course technically, PGA Tour pros do not set out to beat each other. No one plays defense in golf, and winning involves doing your best without regard for the other fellow. But every tournament is won by the man with the lowest score, and when there are fewer players with a habit of shooting low in the field, a top-ten finish seems a little less elusive to the weekly also-rans.

This is what Esteban is thinking as he boards a Delta Airlines flight and hacks and coughs his way from California to North Carolina. While he is away, Colleen will manage the packing, the move, and the unpacking at their new home all by herself. Esteban will try to follow Chi Chi's advice. It's time to try for a win. But on Tuesday morning's practice round, the cold he's had for two weeks settles in his chest with the weight of a medicine ball. The pills he got in Mexicali are gone.

On the back nine of a morning practice round, he begins to feel weak. At lunchtime, he lies down on the bench in the locker room. The attendants start to worry. He looks pale, and he's sweating. They call paramedics, who take him to the Tour's doctor. The cold has become bronchitis bordering on pneumonia. Esteban is loaded up with antibiotics and sent to the house of the local family hosting him for the week. He'll spend the next two days watching trash TV—Jerry Springer features feuding transvestites—and rise on Thursday to tee it up, no matter how he feels.

•

Though it may be a low-prestige event in the eyes of some top pros, the tournament in Greensboro caps a week that is sheer frenzy in the local community. The twice-yearly furniture convention—North Carolina is home to hundreds of manufacturers—coincides with the tournament, so along with the golf fans, thousands of buyers from stores across the country fill the city. They swell the galleries and turn the tournament into a bigger event.

I fly into Greensboro on Friday and manage to catch Esteban as he's coming up the seventeenth fairway with Barry Cheesman, a journeyman who moved up from the Nike Tour this year, and John Riegger, another Q. School qualifier. The bark of Esteban's cough carries more than 100 yards. The little scoreboard held by a teenage volunteer shows he's two over par. His face, ashen with fatigue, shows he's in no condition to finish well, even if he does make the cut. Pars on numbers 17 and 18 bring him in with a chance to play for pay on Saturday.

Esteban tends to wear his feelings for all to see. At the entrance to the clubhouse we meet Robert Gamez, who won the very first tournament he played when he joined in 1990 and has been on the Tour ever since. The American-born son of Mexican parents, Gamez owns a luxurious home in Vegas and is known as a party animal. He is an infrequent and reluctant visitor to the practice range, and he seems to grin even when he misses the cut. "Hey Esteban cheer up. The cut's probably going to be two over," he says. "You'll make it."

"No, I won't," mutters Esteban.

Inside, he finds the oak locker where the brass plate reads "Esteban Toledo" and plops down on the bench. He is exhausted, frustrated with his illness, and angry with one of his playing partners, Barry Cheesman. Golf was once a gentleman's game built on trust, he says. Now it seems like arguments are a regular occurrence and he's not so sure anymore that his opponents are willing to play fair.

Twice today, Cheesman challenged Esteban when he attempted to move his ball out of so-called casual water, as the rules allow. (Steady rain had left hundreds of puddles—casual water—on the Greensboro course.) In both instances, Esteban found his ball sitting in fairway grass that was flooded with half an inch of water. Cheesman marched to Esteban's ball and insisted he place it in the rough. Both times he was overruled by the third man in the group, John Riegger, who approved Esteban's placements on dry fairway. These were not just annoying events to Esteban. They were insults.

It's likely that Esteban is taking these incidents more seriously because he is sick and he has played poorly. He is in a negative mood. However, spats and mishaps do occur more often at professional tournaments than any casual television-watching fan could know. Take, for example, the argument Tim Simpson once raised during a Nike tournament when Esteban hit his ball into the water. Under these circumstances, a player is supposed to place a new ball on the shore at the point where the lost one last saw dry ground. This isn't easy to do when the ball hits the water a hundred or two hundred yards away from where it is struck. Players understand that placement is often a guessing game and routinely extend the benefit of the doubt. This time, Simpson insisted Esteban was wrong and told him to place his ball twenty yards further from the hole. Again the third man in the group—this time it was

Lan Gooch—ruled in Esteban's favor, but not after a heated debate. An annoyed Esteban hit his next shot into the lake, too. He scored a triple bogey.

More stories of mix-ups and mayhem spill out of Esteban as we share a high school cafeteria–quality lunch in the players' lounge. All around us, other pros, their wives and children, chatter and laugh. Gradually Esteban starts to lighten up. He even smiles a bit as he describes the adventure he was forced to endure the night before because the Tour transportation team forgot to pick him up.

Though tired and battling a slight fever, Esteban had hit balls until dusk. At the clubhouse, he telephoned a volunteer office to summon a ride. "We'll be right over," they said. Esteban waited, and waited, and waited. At 8:30, he called again. The transportation office was closed. Taxis don't run out to the country club, and all the other pros were gone. He set out on foot, knowing his hosts lived near the sixth fairway, but not remembering their names. About all he could recall about the house was a decorative flag that hung on the porch. He wandered around the unlit neighborhood for more than an hour, discovering that about a quarter of the homes had a flag displayed. Finally he bumped into someone who helped him find the right house.

By the time lunch is over, Robert Gamez is walking around the locker room with a beer in each hand and a grin on his face. The cut is going to be one over par. He made it. Esteban did not. But he doesn't seem at all upset. He uses the telephone reserved for pros to call Colleen. She's in the middle of packing. The moving vans will arrive in a few days. She says it's a blessing that he missed the cut. He could use the rest. When he hangs up, he says that instead of heading to the range with six buckets of balls he's going to the green to practice putting.

In the first three months on the Tour, Esteban has learned the value of good putting. Though he is ranked in the top twenty for reaching greens in regulation, he uses too many strokes to get the ball in the hole. It's one big reason why he hasn't made more money. Players at the top of the money list average fewer than 1.75 putts per hole. Esteban's average is 1.82. The difference seems statistically minuscule, but it matters when you look at what's called "birdie conversion." Right now Esteban is 'converting'—turning his fine iron play into birdies—about one quarter of the time. The top ten players are all closer to one third.

Of course, Esteban doesn't need the statistics to understand all this. As with everything else, he bases his assessments on practical experience. He recalls one round he played at the Freeport McDermott Classic near New Orleans with Ian Woosnam. Woosnam, who has won more than forty tournaments, hit his driver and irons all over the place, but scored under par because he putted so well. Esteban saw the same thing in a round he played with Rocco Mediate at Doral. Mediate missed almost every fairway but broke par for the round because he chipped and putted superbly.

The lesson is obvious. Low scores and paychecks are earned on the green. If Esteban can improve in that area, and trust the rest of his game, he will succeed. "I'm not worried about my swing. It's solid," he tells me after Greensboro. "If I get my putter going, then you watch out."

Having missed the cut at Greensboro, Esteban wasn't around on Sunday to see Trevor Dodds, a fresh Nike graduate, win his first PGA Tour event. At thirty-eight, Dodds is even older than Esteban, and he had earned and lost his card four different times before. He began the last round at Greensboro three shots behind the leaders, Bob Estes, Skip Kendall, and Scott Verplank. In a vivid illustration of how quickly things can go wrong on the golf course, Kendall shot a seventy-eight and gave away his chance to win. Estes stumbled with two bogeys, which left Dodds and Verplank tied for first at the end of regulation play. On the very first playoff hole, Verplank hit his drive into the high rough and doomed himself to a bogey. Dodds made a safe par to win $396,000. He became the fifteenth different player to win this year.

●

PGATour.com/scoring/ is the Internet address for the scoreboard that reports the results of every tournament on the Big Tour. Operated in real time, the board provides each player's score, hole by hole, as it is punched into the little laptop computers that volunteers operate beside each green on the course. There is no better way to follow a player, unless you walk stride-for-stride with him down the fairways.

On a Thursday night in May, I log on to check the scores at the BellSouth Classic, which is being played outside Atlanta. So far this year, every time I have turned to the Internet to check Esteban's score I have been forced to search through several pages of small print before finding his name near the bottom. This time I take a short cut, scrolling quickly to the bottom. His name is not there. I scroll up. Still he's not there.

Though it's unlikely, given his stubborn streak, I begin to wonder if Esteban has withdrawn from the competition. Maybe he's sick again. He's already told me that he dislikes the course where the tournament is being played. Designed by Greg Norman, it is long—7,259 yards—hilly, and mischievously dotted with hazards. As if to prove his displeasure, Esteban shot a seventy-eight in the Monday pro-am and seventy-nine in a Tuesday practice round with Peter Jacobsen. It's possible that he stumbled so badly on the first day of competition that he just gave up and withdrew.

After scanning the list of names a second time, I close down the Web site. As I do, the top of the scoreboard flashes onto my computer screen for a fraction of a second. There it is. The name in second place. Esteban Toledo.

Racing back to the PGA Tour site I find his name again. How could he be in second place? A few more clicks of the keyboard brings his scorecard up on the computer screen. It shows he posted a first-round sixty-six by making just one bogey and six birdies. One of these he scored on the treacherous eighteenth hole, a 576-yard par-five that twists right and left and threatens those who can't resist going for an eagle with a pitched green that tends to send the ball sliding back down into a waiting pond.

Esteban is one stroke behind Mark Calcavecchia. Definitely not a grinder, Calcavecchia has been a fixture on the Tour since 1983, winning eight times and amassing more than $7.6 million in prize money. Lurking behind, but not too far behind, are seventeen players with scores of 67, 68, or 69. Among them are two long-hitters who should feel more comfortable than most in the scramble for first on a long golf course: Tiger Woods and John Huston.

•

"It was really exciting. After my round they pulled me into the press room to answers questions. I told them that I stopped worrying about making the cut and just started trying to make birdies. I told them I'm hungry. Tiger Woods and David Duval have millions in the bank. I'm hungry."

Esteban didn't have to say he was excited. When he called on the phone he spoke so loud, and so fast, that anyone could tell he was revved up. He had played his best—hitting sixteen of eighteen greens and needing just 28 putts—and the golf world had noticed.

In the transcript of his pressroom appearance, the reporters ask Esteban for a detailed review of his performance. Instead, he tries to explain why he played so well. True to his personality, he speaks from the heart. "When I missed the cut in Greensboro a couple of weeks ago I told my wife that I was going to practice two and a half, three hours every single day," he explains. This week those hours were put into putting. The reporters want to know if his back ever gets tired from so much work. "I can stay there for a long time," he tells them.

When another writer asks him how many fairways and greens he hit, Esteban brushes him off. "I don't really care about this fairways and greens stuff," he says. "I want to care about scoring. That's number one in my mind. I've got to score."

•

Since this is only Round One, it is natural to wonder if Esteban will choke. It happens all the time. A newcomer on the Tour gets near the top, notices that he has a chance to win, and falls apart in the very next round. Esteban is aware of this possibility when he goes to sleep on Thursday. On Friday morning he gets the chance to worry about it some more, as black clouds roll in, lightning begins to flash, and the rain starts to fall.

On a normal tournament day, Esteban gets to the course an hour or two before his tee time. He works on the putting green, hits some balls on the range, putts a bit more, and then reports to the tee. On this day, he waits in the clubhouse as the rain falls and the hours pass. Noon comes and goes. Sometime around 2 p.m. the rain lets up. His tee time is fixed at 6:09 p.m. But even this doesn't hold. His group doesn't start play until after seven o'clock. Tight and tired from so much waiting, Esteban makes a double bogey on the very first hole. He follows with a par, a bogey and a par. Four holes. Three shots lost. Then suddenly, somewhere, an airhorn is sounded. Play is suspended for the day on account of darkness. Lucky for him.

When Esteban calls California, Colleen tries to be reassuring on the telephone. She says most of the right things. "Hang in there. Don't give up. Play your own game. Try to enjoy it." He feels better, but he still sleeps fitfully.

•

What a difference one day and four awful holes can make. Esteban has fallen off the leader board. On Saturday, he must complete the second round and then play a full eighteen holes. All together it's thirty-two holes of golf on a course that he never liked in the first place.

On the trip south, I know only that Esteban is facing the biggest opportunity in his golfing career. Qualifying School was probably a bigger challenge. But it only offered admission to the PGA Tour. This time he has a chance to prove, at long last, that he belongs.

After flying into Atlanta, driving to the course, and checking in at the press center, I find Esteban on the fifteenth tee. He's finishing Round Two. The little scoreboard that a teenage boy carries down the fairway has a big red number 3—meaning three under par—next to his name. The putts aren't falling and he's missing too many greens.

Esteban is determined to steady himself. The leaders, Jay Don Blake and Craig Parry, are six shots ahead, but that is not an insurmountable gap. No one is running away with the tournament. Not yet, anyway.

On the tenth tee, where he will start Round Three with Jay Haas and Kenny Perry, the crowd is bigger than any that has watched Esteban all year. A few of the fans mention that they saw him featured on a TV sports show. The piece focused on his past as a boxer and his transformation into a golfer. After Esteban hits his drive a young boy shouts, "*Vamos Esteban!*"

Vamos he does. Birdies on 12 and 16 are followed by another one on the long eighteenth hole. This last score is especially satisfying because he does it by laying up and then hitting a soft, low-flying, left-to-right wedge shot that flirts with the pond and then rolls up near the hole. He taught himself to do this on the range in Mexicali and has practiced it thousands of times. Now he has his reward.

As he makes the turn at seven under for the tournament, it's clear that Esteban is having fun, probably more fun than anyone on the course. The smile that graced his face at the beginning of the round has become a grin he can't contain. It is the smile of a man who has found some magic in his putter.

On the par-three, number 2 hole—Esteban's eleventh of the round—his first shot lands seven feet above the flagstick and he putts it in for a 2. As he makes his way to the next tee, he slaps the hands of half a dozen kids who line the ropes and reach out for him. Haas and Perry follow, staring straight ahead and letting the outstretched little hands flap against their legs.

Exceptional golf begins with a relaxed, confident state of mind. On the fourth hole, Esteban shows he's reached this nirvana when his drive stops behind a large tree that stands alone in the center of the fairway about 250 yards from the hole. It's a bit of bad luck, but he's unaffected. An iron hit to within 100 yards leaves him a wedge to the green. On his fourth shot, the ball bounces past the hole by a yard or two until the backspin takes over. Like a yo-yo that has reached the end of its string, the ball scoots backwards and directly into the hole. Esteban is eight under par and on his way to another 66.

Somewhere on the course, Tiger Woods is making birdies too. The blimp that carries the TV cameras has been hovering over Tiger all day, like a giant honeybee. The roars that follow almost everything he does echo around the golf course. When Esteban reaches his fifteenth hole, one of the electronic leader boards shows that Woods and Jay Don Blake are now 11 under. And there, in a group clustered in fourth place, is the name "E.

Toledo." By the end of the day, Tiger will set a course record of 63. The Sunday paper will be filled with accounts of his greatness. Esteban will get his name in the paper too, but only because the *Atlanta Constitution's* golf writer wants to illustrate that Woods faces few credible challengers. He is referred to as "Esteban 'Holy' Toledo, a Mexican just back from another Q. school, 140th on the money list." At least they spelled his name right.

•

Robert is having fun, but he's also a natural-born worrier. On Sunday morning we meet at a Shoney's Restaurant where truckers and families headed for church fill up at the breakfast bar. He's obsessing over how to do more for his boss. One problem would be easy to fix, he says. Esteban needs new irons. The grooves on his two iron are wearing out. His other irons have been hit so much that the angles of the clubheads are off. Robert estimates that some of them have lost five or ten yards in distance. Others are bent so they are permanently hooded, and send the ball further than they should. He keeps suggesting the clubs be recalibrated, but Esteban refuses to have them checked. He will not tinker.

In the middle of fretting about all the simple things that Esteban just refuses to do, the caddie suddenly stops and smiles. He remembers that it's only May. He's about to carry the bag for a player who has a chance to win a PGA Tour event. Less than a year ago he was a rookie caddie on the Nike Tour. "I really got nothing to complain about," he finally confesses. "It's just that I can't stop thinking about these things."

•

Sunday is Mother's Day and Esteban calls Rita Minnis to tell her he loves her. Esteban is a sentimental man, and when all the world around him seems to be talking about mothers, he can't help but feel sadness about his own mother in Mexico. She's more than 1,000 miles away, and even further away when he considers the huge gulf that separates her world from his. Esteban knows he's supposed to accept that she'll never understand him, never truly know him. But with Mother's Day on the front page of the Sunday paper and on the radio, it hurts.

In the hour before his tee time, Esteban goes to the practice tee to shake out the kinks in his body and put himself into his pre-round trance. He's wearing his usual Sunday uniform: a white shirt, black pants, black shoes, and a white visor. He cannot contain his smile. As usual, he works through his bag, grabbing first a wedge and hitting a few shots, then moving on to the nine iron, eight and so on. As he watches the balls fly true, a smile forces itself across his face. He has waited his entire life to be here, in this place, playing for high stakes. He is nervous, but he loves it.

"I called my mom in Erie this morning," says Bob. He pours a bucket of balls on the ground. "She wants you to know, she's praying for you."

When they are through with the driver, Esteban and his caddie move on to the practice green. As he putts, Esteban sings a few lines from the Joe Cocker song that played on the car radio as he drove to the tournament this morning: "You Are So Beautiful."

"Something good is going to happen today," says Esteban. "I can't tell you why, but I can feel it, like you feel the wind."

Trevor Dodds, fellow Nike alumnus and the winner in Greensboro, wanders by to wish him good luck. This week in Atlanta, several Nike graduates are in the top ten on the leaderboard including Steve Flesch, Stewart Cink, and Guy Hnatiuk. For years, Nike players have said that the level of play on their tour is not much different from the big league. This group is proving the argument.

On the other side of the practice green, Tiger Woods makes a few strokes and then walks to the hole to collect his golf balls. Wood positively glows in his customary final-day red shirt, black pants, and a pair of black and red Nike golf shoes.

Tiger is a complex phenomenon. Everywhere he goes, he is followed by hundreds of fans, young and old. People are constantly begging for an autograph, a golf ball, or a smile. They call out to him, even scream. In Atlanta, I stood on the practice tee while Tiger took the very last space at the far end of the range. When I turned to look at the spectators who filled the little grandstand I could see that every face was aimed in Tiger's direction. This was despite the presence of a dozen other truly gifted players who were hitting impressive shots of all shapes.

It is like this whenever Tiger comes to a tournament. All the other players seem to fade in his light. On the practice tee, where Tiger warmed up, the fans were so intently focused on him that Esteban could have landed a right hook on Robert's jaw and the police would have had trouble finding one reliable witness among the hundreds in the gallery.

Though almost everyone on the PGA tour would refuse to say it on the record, Tigermania has produced so much jealousy that young Woods is shunned by almost all the other pros. On Sunday morning in Atlanta he goes alone to the putting green. In the awkward silence, he seems like an isolated, socially awkward young man. When he passes me and asks the time, he doesn't quite catch my answer and must ask again.

"Thanks, I'm a little nervous," he says, revealing something that would suprise most of his fans. "I just want to get to the tee on time."

He returns to his routine, talking to no one; and the rest of the players leave a minimum of twenty feet between themselves and the phenom.

•

Esteban is paired with John Huston and Craig Parry, a steady player from Australia who has earned more than $2 million in the United States since 1992. Thirty-one years old, Parry is a cheerful man with massive forearms that have earned him the nickname "Popeye." He has four second-place finishes in American tournaments and fourteen international victorics to his crcdit, including three Australian masters wins. At age 37, Huston has held his Tour card for ten straight years. Ranked in the top fifty career money-winners, he has had nearly 100 top-twenty-five finishes. Lately he has been beset by the aches and pains of tendinitis. He recently began sleeping on a magnetic mattress cover that is supposed to ease his pain. The science behind the magnets is still unproven, but Huston is a believer. Pain-free, he is in the midst of his best year ever on the Tour.

At 12:10 p.m., Parry, Huston, and Toledo are announced on the first tee. Each identifies the ball he'll play—

Esteban's is a Titleist 1. At 12:12, a few raindrops fall, warning of showers that may come. At 12:14, Parry steps up to hit the first shot.

The tone of the match is set with the very first shots. Parry and Huston both out-drive Esteban by more than twenty-five yards. But as the group moves down the fairway, it becomes plain that Esteban's ball is in a better position, dead center. The crowd lining the hole is huge. Most have come to see Tiger, whose tee time is roughly thirty minutes away. They cheer loudly as three routine pars are scored.

Huston, a small man with a narrow waist, is as cheerful and engaging as the beige shirt and pants he has chosen for the day. He ignores the crowds, and his playing partners, and his face doesn't change even as he scores his first birdie, a two on the par-three second hole. Parry is a bit more outgoing, at least with his playing partners. He's famous for having won a cow at a tournament in Japan, and enjoys telling the story.

By the fourth tee, with three pars in his pocket, Esteban has obviously decided that he is going to enjoy himself. As his group waits for slow players ahead, a young woman spectator complains about being thirsty. Esteban serves her a paper cupful of the sports drink that's available on each tee for the players. He takes a drink himself. While Parry and Huston stand with their hands on their hips looking down the fairway, Esteban discusses the weather with the crowd. Dark clouds have hung over Atlanta all day, and rain from the night before has made the course soggy and humid.

Again Esteban's drive is the shortest, which means he'll

need three shots to get onto the green of this 541-yard hole. Hoping to get in position for an eagle, Huston lashes a three wood from the fairway that fades into light rough on the right. Then he shocks the crowd by knocking in a seventy-yard wedge. Despite making this dramatic eagle, he barely smiles. Esteban and Parry settle for fives.

On the next hole, the sun finally comes out and it is bright and hot. The radiant energy hits the turf and turns the water squishing beneath the grass into a warm vapor that drifts up like heated fog. All three players make the green in regulation. Huston three-putts his way to a bogey 5. Esteban gets his first birdie on 6, and then Huston suffers another bogey on 7. On the tenth hole, Esteban benefits from a two-shot swing as he scores a birdie and Huston a bogey six. Parry keeps pace, and they all reach the fifteenth hole at eleven under for the tournament. Here, Parry scores a bogey as the others make threes. Parry falls further behind with a par on the next hole as Huston and Esteban birdie.

On the way to the seventeenth tee, Esteban looks at a leader board and sees that he is thirteen under for the tournament, tied with Huston for fourth place. He won't be the winner, but he could earn a nice big check and make a huge stride toward keeping his card.

As he walks, Esteban slaps the hands of a few kids who line the ropes. He is grinning so broadly that I expect him to burst out laughing any minute. Overhead the blimp is floating into position, its motor humming. After hitting his drive, Esteban follows it down the fairway, splashing in the standing water like a kid. On the green, he sinks a par putt while Huston misses a four-footer and takes a bogey.

Now Esteban is ahead of him for the first time today—at thirteen under—and alone in third place.

The leader board shows that Tiger's closest pursuer, Jay Don Blake, is not scoring enough birdies to catch him. This will be Tiger's first win this year. The gallery seems to be growing bigger by the second as spectators stream toward the eighteenth green in hopes of seeing the winner crowned.

As Esteban stands on the tee for the last hole of the tournament, he is four shots off the leader. I can't help thinking about the bogey/double-bogey debacle he suffered in the gloom of Friday evening. If he had managed simple pars on those two holes—holes he played successfully every other time—he would be standing on the tee with a chance to tie Tiger Woods and force a play-off. Of course, he isn't thinking about his lost opportunity. He's thinking only of the next shot.

At this moment Esteban's immediate challenge is a 576-yard, par-five finishing hole that tempts a player to imagine an eagle and is more likely to deliver disaster. The length of the hole and the pond in front of the green are intimidating enough, but number 18 offers one more bit of psychological torture. Most players land their drives on the crest of a hill that is roughly 250 yards from the green. The drop-off from this hill to the putting surface is severe, perhaps thirty feet. From this height, the green looks tantalizingly close. But it's a sucker's setup. Few players can land the ball on the green from this distance and keep it there.

To make matters more interesting today, the hole is lined by several thousand fans waiting to see Tiger Woods finish and win. Esteban, Huston, and Parry hit their drives and walk to where they've landed. When they reach the spot, fans in the gallery start screaming for them to risk the water and go for the green. They want the thrill of watching an extraordinary shot, or disaster. Either one will do.

"Be a man!" shouts one onlooker.

Two shots down to Esteban, Huston can't resist going for it. He's one of the biggest hitters on Tour and if he catches the ball just right, he can put himself in position for an eagle and a share of third place. Adrenaline pumping, he draws a three wood out of his bag and swings hard. The ball explodes off the club face and flies directly into the sun.

"I can't see it," says Huston to his caddie.

"Neither can I."

A tense moment passes and then a cheer erupts in the grandstand behind the green.

"I guess it was good," says Huston, finally showing a little smile.

Esteban refuses to be greedy. He won't fall for the eighteenth hole's tricks. He will play it his way, the way that has allowed him to make birdie two times before. He lofts an iron to the right side of the fairway, just about 100 yards from the green. As he walks toward it, Huston's ball finally becomes visible. It is on the putting surface, but a good twenty-five feet past the hole. For eagle he'll face a long, tricky, downhill putt. It will be nearly impossible to make. When it is his turn, Esteban hits a wedge to a spot less than fifteen feet below the hole. He's played from this spot before. The putt will be long, but comfortably uphill, with no break. If he lines up right and hits it hard, it will go in.

At a little after 5 p.m., Esteban walks onto the green and smiles at the huge Sunday gallery, which applauds his arrival. The fans know he's an underdog, a former boxer turned golfer, and that he is finishing the most important round of his life. This moment, and the crowd's attention and approval are the reward Esteban has sought ever since he decided to make golf his profession. Even more importantly, it confirms the faith he has invested in himself, his dreams, and the value of hard work. This is the proof that he was right all along.

Real golf fans pull for every player, especially on the eighteenth green. They want to see long putts drop. Huston comes close, and the groan that follows his ball as it passes the cup can be heard several fairways away. The second try drops the ball in the hole and for the moment Huston has again tied Esteban, this time at thirteen under.

As he lines up his birdie try, Esteban is thinking about making the shot, about Colleen watching him on TV, and about beating John Huston. He doesn't think about the fact that he will make roughly $40,000 more if the putt goes in. He seems perfectly calm—El Caballo with his blinders on—as he settles into his stance. The TV network cameras swivel to capture his stroke. And just as he did when I first saw him on the practice green at Q. School, he makes a smooth, steady swing that sends the ball rolling right into the center of the cup.

The gallery's applause turns to cheers when Esteban throws a right-handed uppercut into the air. It's a spontaneous and gleeful moment of celebration and the energy is infectious. The cheer becomes a roar. Esteban Toledo hasn't won the tournament, but he has achieved almost as much. He has earned enough money to get halfway to his goal of keeping his card. He has established, for all to see, that he's got the ability to compete at the top of the PGA Tour. And he has proven to himself that he can handle the pressure. He has the heart to succeed on Sunday. With the privilege of a "behind-the-ropes" pass, I've had the pleasure of walking every step of the round. As he comes off the green and heads to the scorer's tent, Esteban puts his arm on my back and whispers in my ear.

"D'Antonio, I was shaking like a little chicken."

•

The roped-off runway that players walk to leave the eighteenth green is lined with kids who beg for autographs. In his brief moment of glory, Esteban stands and signs everything. Some of the kids beg Robert for his autograph too. He shyly steps back. He doesn't have the ego, or the time to sign autographs or celebrate the success. Next week's tournament is in Texas, and he's going to drive there. Desperate to get on the road while there's still sunlight, he hands me Esteban's golf bag and disappears.

In the locker room, Steve Flesch, the other third-place finisher, slaps Esteban on the back. "Nice playing, Esteban. Nice putt, you turkey." The attendants take Esteban's shoes for polishing and hand him a pink telephone slip. It's from Colleen. It says, "I'm going shopping."

When Esteban finally gets her on the telephone, he can't contain himself. "Honey, did you see me?" he shouts. "It's $104,000. We got the house paid for already!"

Colleen did see him. In fact, she had spent the day with her parents, watching the tournament on TV and simultaneously following Esteban's score on PGAtour.com. She was cheering when the TV cameras showed Esteban's putt on number 18 fall.

Even as they laugh about their plans for the money, Esteban reminds Colleen that his success will come at a price. Two weeks have passed since they were last together. Esteban had planned to go home for a couple weeks soon. He had expected the time off because two upcoming tournaments—the Colonial in Forth Worth and the Memorial in Ohio—are invitationals, the exclusive kind of event that won't admit the 140th player on the money list. But his third-place finish here has vaulted him to sixty-fifth place. Now many of the rules and restrictions that benefit the top performers, and that made it so hard for a newcomer to succeed, work in his favor. The people who run the Colonial and the Memorial will want Esteban Toledo in their fields. After that, there are two more regular tournaments leading up to the U.S. Open. If he continues to play well, and continues to make all the Friday cuts, Esteban will be on the road for another month.

From a delayed-gratification point of view, this is all good news. Esteban's absence is a sure reflection of his success. But alone in California, Colleen must handle all the hard work of creating and maintaining a home without her husband. She's delighted with the house. It's a brand-new, two-story corner unit in a townhouse development south of Los Angeles. It's got a Spanish tile roof, an extra bedroom, and a two-car garage. Unfortunately, the garage is not quite filled. Toyota has still not delivered their new car. This means that Colleen is driving the old Honda sixty miles per day so that Nicholas can finish the term in his school.

The stress of the move and Esteban's absence is affecting Nicholas. The school principal has called several times recently to discuss his behavior. Colleen wouldn't mind having a husband home to help with him. But this is not the time to say any of this, so she simply tells Esteban she loves him. He says he loves her too.

•

Esteban has stayed this week in Atlanta with a family who live alongside the golf course. At the end of the day, his hosts give him a little party—take-out barbecue, soft drinks, chips, beer—to celebrate his success. Friends and neighbors are invited. They are delighted to be close to one of the top golfers of the week and warm themselves in the reflection of his success. But it's hard to avoid noticing the obvious—that they don't really know Esteban. They would be saying and doing all the same things if another golfer had come into their midst after finishing in third place.

For his part, Esteban is gracious and, by all appearances, perfectly happy marking the biggest moment in his career with a crowd of people who are mere acquaintances. He has spent his entire adult life traveling the world in the lonesome pursuit of golf glory, sacrificing many of the comforts of familiar surroundings and relationships. He has explained this quest to me in three ways. First, he says he loves the game of golf. Second he wants to prove to himself that he is the best at something. Third, he wants to prove to the golf world that he is worthy of respect.

These are reasonable explanations, but it's hard to ignore all the signs that a deeper emotional need drives him. As an orphan boy, the constant hard work that Esteban accepted as a matter of survival kept him too busy to feel much of the grief, loss, and anger that would follow losing a brother, a father, and the support of everyone else in his family. It makes sense that he would continue this almost desperate striving, and constant activity, as an adult. His obsession with golf and its promise of both riches and social acceptance provide the same kind of relief from his anxieties. Practice, struggling, and dreaming help him to forget the past.

•

The isolation of Esteban's pursuit—and perhaps the isolation experienced by most Tour golfers—is even more obvious and poignant on Monday. I have agreed to give Esteban a ride to the airport for his flight to Dallas. At 4:30 a.m., he stands in the dark on his host's doorstep, dressed in a Toyota shirt and golf pants. He's so tired, he barely speaks as he gets in the car. A little coffee warms him up enough for him to say he's still high from the previous day, but he misses Colleen.

Traffic is light and we get to the airport more than an hour early. We have time for breakfast at a Waffle House just beside the highway off-ramp. I buy *USA Today* so Esteban can see his name on the front of the sports section.

"I knew this would happen one day," he says, shifting in the plastic booth as the waitress pours more coffee. "If you keep trying, you can go pretty far." When the waitress takes our order, he points out his name in the paper.

"Oh, you're one of the golfers," she says. "Great. How do ya want your eggs?"

THE SCORECARD

Remaining tournaments	21
Esteban's earnings	$157,806
Money still needed to keep card	$72,194
Rank	65th

7

The Grinder King ○

It's all about the shrimp. At least that's what people in the banquet business say. If the shrimp are large, fresh, peeled, and plentiful, the party will be a smash. At The Memorial, the tournament Jack Nicklaus hosts in Dublin, Ohio, the shrimp are piled up into a glistening pink promontory at the head of the buffet table in the VIP dining room. This Mt. Shrimp is so impressive that the TV commentators tell the folks back home about it, citing it as proof that this is, indeed, a top-rate event.

The Memorial is played on a course that Nicklaus designed and placed in the midst of a huge real estate development called Muirfield Village. Hardly a village, Muirfield includes thousands of luxury homes along with restaurants, retail shops, schools, and parks. Players flying into Columbus reach Muirfield by traveling on a highway named for Nicklaus. Along the way they pass billboards plastered with his face. At the tournament, everything down to the spectators' programs bears his signature.

The fact that this corner of Ohio has been turned into a virtual Jackland demonstrates the wealth and power that can accrue to the world's greatest golfers. (No doubt Tiger will have his own land one day.) But though the Memorial is an annual reminder of his own stature, Nicklaus actually created the tournament to honor his golfing comrades. Each year, a historic figure in the sport is inducted into a Muirfield Hall of Fame in a ceremony that includes the unveiling of a plaque in a special garden. The first in this pantheon was Bobby Jones, who died less than a year prior to the inaugural Muirfield tournament.

Though they don't get garden plaques, all of the tournament competitors are treated like the princes many consider themselves to be. And it's not just the shrimp. Consider, for instance, the practice area the pros use at Muirfield Village. A shimmering expanse of perfect grass, fenced to keep spectators at bay, the tournament practice area is groomed and maintained all year long to be used only by the pros at this one tournament. The range has a 270-degree circumference, allowing players to test the prevailing winds at almost any angle they'll encounter on the course. On the putting green, players are protected from the distraction of fans by extra security guards. Reporters, who are free-range animals at other tournaments, are admitted to the Muirfield putting green only by invitation. The locker room, which is fitted in brass and filled with overstuffed furniture, is also off-limits.

Even the caddies are treated well at The Memorial.

Instead of a charity tent in the woods like they get at Pebble Beach, the caddies at Memorial are treated to their own buffet table right in the clubhouse. They also get a $50-per-day stipend for wearing a cap with the tournament symbol.

The Memorial is almost as exclusive as one of the Majors. The field is limited to 105—almost one-third fewer than most tournaments. Seventeen criteria govern the invitations to play, and most of them require that a player already be a winner at some other recent tournament. Exceptions include Ryder Cup team members and ten sponsor exemptions. The last doorway to enter the tournament, criterion number 17, lets the tournament directors fill out the field with players in the top seventy on the current PGA Tour money list.

At the moment Esteban, who has earned more than $170,000, is ranked sixty-fifth on the PGA Tour money list. He is King of the Q. School Grinders. The nearest of his peers is Jeff Gallagher, who is eightieth with about $125,000. Next is Bob Friend with less than $90,000. Following a very good start to the year, Friend has dropped to 115th place.

Esteban feels more suited to the Tour than he did back in 1994. He actually prefers the PGA Tour's course conditions—high rough, narrow fairways, fast greens—to the long, wide-open courses favored by the Nike Tour. These layouts "set up well" for his creative, accurate game. "You have to stay out of trouble," he says, "and know all of the shots."

A close look at Esteban's playing statistics from April and May provide a precise explanation for his success. He has improved in almost every important measure of his play: driving accuracy, putting, greens in regulation. In fact, according to the PGA Tour record-keepers, he's now forty-fourth in all-around play, a measure of his performance in every area of the game.

Mathematically speaking, the difference between the Esteban of April and the Esteban of May can seem infinitesimal. For example, his putts-per-round figure is only about half a stroke better than it was a month ago. But this alone equals two shots per tournament. For Esteban, those two strokes made a $40,000 difference in Atlanta and guaranteed him a moment in the media spotlight and a trip to Jackland.

•

All new things, even life's rewards, require a bit of adjustment. This is true for Esteban at The Memorial. When he arrives at Muirfield Village, he is a little uncomfortable, still feeling like an outsider. In the private players' dining room another contestant—he refuses to tell me who—makes a wisecrack: "Who let you in here?" Still a bit uncertain of his place in the hierarchy of golf, Esteban isn't sure whether it's good-natured teasing or a slam. In his wary mood, he thinks it's the latter.

Then comes his reunion with Colleen and seven-year-old Nicholas, who have flown to Ohio to join him. Esteban is happy to see them, but a little unsettled. In the testosterone-soaked world of the PGA Tour, the very top players traveling alone tend to do what they want, when they want, without a thought for anyone else. Week in and week out they are lavished with free gifts, banquets, and the adoration of fans. They are coddled by caddies and Tour officials. Attendants shine their shoes and awestruck volunteers chauffeur them from place to place. A private travel agent, provided free of charge, serves them right in the locker room. With all this, it is easy to become self-centered off the course as well as on. Families notice this immediately.

Determined to be "the same" man he always was, Esteban makes a conscious effort to avoid becoming one of these "jerky guys." But it is nevertheless a struggle to leave his self-absorption on the golf course. It's especially difficult now that he has had some success and fans everywhere are starting to recognize him. Immediately after he plays a round, when Colleen and Nicholas wait for him outside the scorer's tent, people start to gather to ask for autographs. Esteban's mind is filled with the performance he just finished, and he is assaulted by the adults and children pushing programs and hats for him to sign. He may be physically present, but his mind is still on the game. He scrawls his name on everything that's offered, but doesn't seem focused on the task. A question from Colleen or Nicholas is met by a blank stare. Finally Colleen shouts "Esteban!" and he is jolted into focus.

Few people can move effortlessly from center stage to domestic life. It must be especially difficult for someone who has been more-or-less alone from the age of 5. As a child wandering the hills and fields near his home, Esteban learned to live without much conversation or interaction with others. Relationships were a comparative luxury. Until Colleen and Nicholas, Esteban had never had a stable family life. Little wonder that he must work at it.

One example of this struggle is the hotel Esteban has

chosen this week for his family. Despite his recent step up the financial scale, his survival instincts continue to rule the way he thinks about his travel expenses. ("I am not a Sheraton Hotel type of guy," he says.) For The Memorial he has booked one room at the Red Roof Inn for himself, Colleen, and Nicholas. When eight suitcases are thrown into this space, it shrinks to the size of a walk-in closet. It is hardly what one might expect from a man suddenly flush with money, who hasn't seen his wife in a month, and is eager for a new baby.

Other problems arise. Meals are delayed while Esteban practices and seems to forget all about his family. Disagreements arise over little things, like arranging for Nicholas to get to day care. These aren't serious problems, just a matter of their lives being out of synch. But Esteban and Colleen had high hopes for this week. They are both a little disappointed and upset. Esteban never feels comfortable when he's on the outs with Colleen. He won't feel right until he smoothes things over. It's not easy being a PGA Tour husband and father.

On the first tee on the opening round, Esteban shakes off his worries and tries to focus on the course. Lush and exquisitely groomed, Muirfield is a beautiful torture chamber of golf that is both long—7,163 yards—and complex. Water comes into play on eleven holes. On most of the doglegs, tall trees are found right where the fairway bends, making it hard to cut the corner.

During his round, Esteban is recognized by hundreds of the people in the gallery. Every few minutes somebody says, "There's that boxer!" or "Holy Toledo!" Esteban manages a one over par seventy-three, which will put him in the middle of the leaderboard.

He's never received so much gallery attention. Later on he'll find out that most of the fans who call out his name have seen a TV report about him on the Cable News Network. CNN has begun to broadcast it worldwide every few hours. In this piece, the obvious angle of the boxer-turned-fighter is played to the hilt. Photos from Esteban's fighting days and a visit to his old gym in Mexicali are contrasted with tape from the BellSouth tournament.

●

By Friday morning it seems that everyone at The Memorial has seen the CNN report, except Esteban. He takes a ribbing about it in the locker room, and on the course a buzz goes through the gallery whenever he passes. If the fans fail to identify Esteban by the name tag on his caddie's back, they can pick him out by the unusual new headcovers on his driver and three wood. They are bright blue boxing gloves. On one, is written "Esteban," on the other, "Toledo."

The gloves are the gift of a sportswriter from the newspaper *Reforma* in Mexico City, who has come to interview Mexico's new golfing sensation. José Luis Tapia speaks with Esteban in Spanish, and asks the kind of questions that only a reporter from Mexico might ask. "Why didn't you marry a Mexican woman? Why don't you live in Mexicali?" (Esteban explains that pursuit of the PGA Tour has controlled the course of his life—including where he lived and the women he met—but he also says that Mexico still has a hold on his heart.)

The blue boxing gloves, which were used as props for

photographs, don't work very well as headcovers. They are too heavy and tend to pop off, forcing Robert to stop and reinstall them time and time again. Robert will complain about them the entire tournament. But in the becalmed ocean of blandness that is the PGA Tour, a little flourish like these headcovers attracts a great deal of attention.

On this day, pars pile up on Esteban's scorecard, one after another, for ten holes. His iron play is strong. But though he's is landing the ball close enough to make a birdie on every hole, his putting won't let it happen. His smile disappears as he comes off of the tenth green, until a nine-year-old girl named Ashley Cahall, who had gotten his autograph before the round started, calls out to him. She wants to introduce her mother. Esteban stops, says hello, and accepts a scrap of paper on which Ashley has written a note declaring that Esteban is her favorite golfer of them all. The whole exchange takes about fifteen seconds, but it lifts Esteban's spirits as he proceeds to the next hole.

A 539-yard par-five, hole number 11 at Muirfield is one of the least difficult on the course, but it is still full of tricks. From the tee area, a little creek wanders down the left side for about 250 yards. It then veers right and heads straight down the center of the fairway. Before the stream reaches the green it makes another turn, back to the left, where it disappears in the trees. True to the Nicklaus design style, the hole can be reached in two by a big-hitter, but these must be nearly perfect shots.

With an average drive of less than 265 yards, Esteban doesn't even think about reaching the green in two. He skirts the creek with his drive and lays up for a wedge shot to the green. This third stroke lands the ball within twelve feet of the hole. He finally makes a birdie putt. In the distance, Ashley Cahall yells, "Yeay!" and forces a laugh out in the otherwise silent gallery of several hundred.

With a birdie, Esteban is finally even for the tournament. He gets another birdie on number fifteen—a straight, 486-yard par-five that's the easiest hole on the course—and then makes pars to finish just before thunderstorms move in and play is suspended. He walks off the last hole one under for the tournament. His second-round 70 means he will make the cut, by three strokes, and play for money on the weekend.

After scrambling to the middle of the field, Esteban should be more at ease. But he seems unhappy. He and Colleen climb the stairs to the VIP dining room, pass the guards posted at the door, and head for the players' lounge, which overlooks the eighteenth green. Once he's seated at a table, Esteban glances around the room and bounces his knee as Colleen chats with some of the other Tour player's wives. A lineup of wives waits at the little table where a computer terminal provides instant updates on scores. Kris Dodds, whose husband is near the top of the scoring, is obsessed with the little laptop and what it reports about her husband, Trevor. Her hands shake as she works the keys and stares at the screen. She departs, and then returns moments later for another look, and then another.

Outside, a rainshower sweeps over the course, stranding Trevor and a quarter of the field on the back nine. Though he could leave, Esteban decides to wait out the storm in hopes of getting just a little more practice before the sun sets at around 9 p.m. The thunder and rain stop at about 7:15. Esteban goes looking for his caddie. Robert had abandoned his post at 7 p.m., when it seemed that the storm would linger past sunset. When Esteban discovers that Robert is gone, he makes enough of a fuss—complaining loudly about his wayward employee—that the other caddies will still be talking about it in the morning.

•

On Saturday morning at the Red Roof Inn, Colleen lays out a pair of khaki pants and a colorful patterned golf shirt. Esteban, who is superstitious about these things, instead puts on his traditional weekend outfit: a white shirt and black pants. The family piles into the free car supplied for their use this week by a local auto dealer, and heads for the golf course. They will be there for ten hours.

At Muirfield, the caddiemaster—this is one of the few clubs that still has one—has already warned Robert that Esteban was complaining about him. When Esteban arrives, he's still upset about Robert's absence the night before. The two men argue over what should have happened and what did happen. Robert says that Esteban had told him it was alright to leave after seven o'clock. Esteban says it was 7:30. They finally agree to disagree.

They walk silently to the practice tee, Esteban a few steps ahead. When they get there, Robert fetches some balls from the boys in charge of the range. He spills a pile of balls onto the turf. Esteban asks Robert how he slept the night before. "What club do you want, boss?" asks Robert. Esteban smiles. All may not be forgotten, but it is forgiven.

The Saturday gallery at The Memorial is so big that Esteban and Robert have trouble just walking from the practice tee to the putting green. The crowds have come because twenty of the world's twenty-one top money-winners are at the tournament. The only one missing is Mark O'Meara, who was reportedly paid a $350,000 "appearance fee" to play in Germany this week.

At this particular moment, the game's marquee draw, Tiger Woods, is practicing his putting. So many people are gathered around the green that Esteban cannot reach it. He makes one try and then another, but still can't penetrate the wall of people around the green. Finally a security guard the size of an NFL lineman makes an opening big enough for the golfer and caddie to squeeze through.

Once on the green, Esteban and Robert find themselves performers in a theater-in-the-round, only the stage is velvety grass. But they needn't feel self-conscious. As usual, all eyes are on Tiger.

Esteban will play today with Vijay Singh, who won The Memorial last year and has already made $380,000 this year. Born in Fiji and the same age as Esteban, Singh was PGA Tour Rookie of the Year in 1993 and has won five tournaments. At six feet, two inches, he is one of the taller and more powerful players on the Tour. He practices almost as obsessively as Esteban, remaining on the range long after others have departed. He is also one of the longest hitters on the PGA Tour. He drives the ball, on average, fifteen yards further than Esteban. He's accompanied by David Renwick, a small, Scottish caddie who calls him "Veej" and has helped both Steve Elkington and Jose Maria Olazabal win Majors.

As they start play today, Vijay Singh is in no better position than Esteban Toledo. Both are at number thirty-nine
on the leaderboard. Eight strokes ahead of them, in first
place, are Fred Couples and Len Mattiace. Almost all the
big names in golf—David Duval, Justin Leonard, Davis
Love III, Tom Lehman—are in contention. Esteban and
Vijay Singh would have to set course records to win the
tournament. Still, they have an opportunity to move up
several places and claim a bigger check. With a purse of
$2.2 million, The Memorial pays less than $10,000 for
thirty-ninth place, but three times as much for nineteenth.

●

As it is at every tournament, the real opponent at The
Memorial is the course. Though they play in groups of two
and three, each man faces only the challenge of the layout. The triumphs and travails of a playing partner should
have no effect. But it always seems that when one player
gets hot, so do those around him. If he sticks his ball five
feet from the cup, the next man's shot may well land
closer. Unfortunately, the process works the other way,
too. Spend a few holes with a struggling player, and you'll
start hacking too.

So it is with Vijay and Esteban. On hole number three,
Vijay lands his drive in a fairway bunker. Disgusted, he
fires a second shot that skips across the green into another
bunker. Bogey. Two holes later, Esteban needs three putts
to get the ball in the hole and score a bogey six. Vijay loses
another shot on the eighth hole. Esteban drops one on
the ninth.

As they walk to the tenth tee, the sun is shining and the
clouded sky begins to show patches of blue. Airplanes tow-

ing banners buzz overhead. One of the ads offers roof repairs. The other sells power washing for decks and fences. Down on the ground Esteban stops to tickle the chin of a crying baby girl—like the baby girl he wants to have with Colleen—and the child is startled into silence. "Works every time," he says.

Pleasant as the atmosphere may be—what with sunshine and a pretty baby—the golf is about to get worse. On number 11, where yesterday Ashley Cahall cheered Esteban's birdie, Vijay's drive lands in the creek on the left side of the fairway. After he plucks the ball out of the water he still has well over 200 yards to the front of the green.

"Alright now Veej, here we go," says Renwick.

Veej hits the ball thinly and finds the creek again, this time in the spot where it curves to the center of the fairway. He's fortunate to escape with a seven.

Esteban has his own problems as he and Vijay head for the clubhouse. He three-putts for a bogey on the sixteenth hole and fails to get up-and-down from a bunker on the seventeenth. On the par-five final hole, he three-putts again for a six. He loses all the progress of the day, and then some. Vijay Singh finishes with yet another humbling double-bogey on the last hole. He must write seventy-six on his scorecard. Esteban settles for seventy-three.

On the other end of the scoreboard, Fred Couples, who held a share of the lead with Len Mattiace at the start of play, now claims first place all for himself. The nearest competitor, David Duval, is three behind. Esteban has dropped to number fifty on the scoreboard. Veej is even further back.

•

A player who starts Sunday fifty places away from the leader doesn't think about winning. He thinks about improving the numbers on his paycheck, and about sharpening his game. When he is in this position, Esteban likes to play well enough to leave town in the right frame of mind: confident and optimistic about the next Tour stop. Robert tells me that to accomplish this, his boss must do something to break the funk that shrouded him on the final three holes yesterday. "I'm worried about him falling apart," he says. He intends to slow Esteban's pace by taking more time to give him yardage reports and clubs. He's going to do everything at half speed. "It might help him focus," he explains.

Esteban and his playing partner, Brent Geiberger— adopted son of former PGA Tour player Al Geiberger— are fortunate to have a morning tee time. Thunderstorms are expected by late afternoon, and play could be suspended for hours.

Young Geiberger—one under par for the tournament— is six feet, four inches tall and has the perpetually relaxed air of a young man who has always known where he is going and how to get there. He was born in Santa Barbara, California, and raised in a prominent golf family, and played golf at Pepperdine University in Malibu. Geiberger worked for just two years on the Nike Tour before succeeding at Q. School in 1996. In that, his first year, he earned nearly $400,000 and kept his card. This year he's already made well over $300,000. Why shouldn't he be relaxed?

Esteban is the opposite of relaxed. On the first hole, he hits his second shot into the rough on the left side of the green. As he and Robert walk down the fairway, one of the boxing gloves slips off its clubhead and falls to the ground. Robert mutters something and stops to pick it up. He struggles to jam it onto the driver and make it stay put.

They find Esteban's Titleist buried in eight inches of rough. Unable to get the club on it cleanly, Esteban sends it into a greenside bunker. He is fortunate to get up and down in two shots to save bogey. He goes on to three-putt the next green for another bogey. As Robert passes, he reminds me in a whisper that counting yesterday's finish, "That's *five* bogeys in a row."

As discouraging as it may be for Robert, Esteban's performance won't be the worst at Muirfield today. That distinction will go to Payne Stewart. He had a reasonable chance at a top-ten finish on Sunday, before he reached hole number 12. A par three of just 160 yards, 12 is one of the easiest holes of the course, despite the pond that fills nearly all the space between the tee and green. Ironically, Stewart's drive did not land in the water, but in the left-hand rough near the green. His chip, alas, skipped past the hole and into the drink. His next two shots landed in the water too. The penalties and a single putt led to a score of ten. All of this was shown, blow by blow, on national television.

While Stewart is splashing his way to a humiliating score of 83, Esteban and Brent Geiberger play ordinary, uninspired golf. They drift from one side of par to the other. On the last hole, the sky darkens and clouds blow in from the West. On the green, Esteban bends down to mark his ball, but before he can touch it a sudden gust of wind blows it ten feet further from the hole. A rules official must be summoned to determine that he can put the ball back where it was. At the end, Geiberger is right where he started—one under—and Esteban loses a stroke to finish plus-one. Rain starts to fall as they enter the scorer's tent just off the eighteenth green. For Esteban, who will earn $4,884, it is an appropriately glum end to a week of ambivalent golf.

As Esteban empties his locker, Fred Couples races against thunderstorms to victory. He will beat Andrew Magee by four strokes and David Duval by five. In a year when it seems like a different player wins every week, Couples, who won the Bob Hope Chrysler Classic in January, will become only the second pro to claim two victories. His prize, almost $400,000, will raise his year's total to $1.4 million and put his name at the top of the money list, for now.

•

After The Memorial, the golfing circus travels to the Kemper Open in the super-wealthy suburb of Potomac, Maryland. Esteban, Colleen, and Nicholas are part of the caravan that wheels down the two-lane roads that pass mansions and horse farms on the way to the Tournament Players' Club at Avenel, one of more than twenty golf courses that are either owned or managed by the PGA Tour. The Toledos are fortunate to be staying with a family who live near the course, instead of in a hotel. The area's roads are so inadequate to handle spectators that traffic will be gridlocked for the week. Any player staying more than a mile or two away constantly risks missing his tee time.

Esteban and Colleen are adjusting to being together again. They begin to re-create the cooperative, relaxed attitude that saw them through the previous summer on the Nike Tour. He played better on those weeks last year when she was watching. She enjoys seeing the country and being a part of his success.

In Maryland, life gets better for Esteban on the golf course, too. Scores of 69, 69, and 71 put him in position to win a substantial check, perhaps even enough to guarantee his card. Robert checks the math and figures that a final round of 69 might be good enough for third place, $90,000, and a clinch of the card. He and Esteban both wonder: Could this be the weekend?

On Sunday morning, a forty-mile-per-hour wind is scraping the fairways, blowing paper cups and candy wrappers in every direction. Showers dart through the area. The weather will keep the gallery small and unnerve some players. But Esteban feels confident. He naturally hits the ball lower than most, which is an advantage in this gale. He picks up a stroke on the front nine and makes the clubhouse turn brimming with confidence. The gusts are growing more powerful, though, strong enough to blow putts off line.

As they come to the tee on hole number 10, Robert is hoping for the second birdie of the day. He's still certain that two-under for the day would mean a top-five finish. The hole is a birdie opportunity. It's a short—374 yards— par-four with just a small turn to the left at the end of the fairway. The only significant hazard is a wiggly little creek that runs down the left side of the fairway and then veers toward the green. The stream is only a few feet across, and under normal conditions should pose no real threat to a PGA Tour–level player.

Esteban's drive is perfect, down the right side about 265 yards. But here the wind complicates matters. It's blowing toward the hole, which means the ball will fly further no matter which club he hits. With the wind, a little shot hit with a fifty-six-degree wedge would go 115 yards. Since the greens are hard and fast, it could even go further, ending up in a bunker or worse, the devilish rough behind the green. If hit perfectly, the more lofted sixty-degree wedge would fly 100 yards, land softly, and roll just a few feet.

"Long is better," says Robert, who fears the creek and trusts Esteban's skill in the bunkers and rough. "I like the fifty-six."

Esteban pulls the sixty-degree wedge from the bag. He wants to get it close and putt for birdie.

Later, Robert would say that it was the wrong time to try for a perfect shot. He would say that Esteban could have saved par from the back rough or the bunker. "We didn't have a perfect lie to hit from. The wind was unpredictable. But he thinks he can hit it as far as all the other guys and he can't. It's a macho thing."

Robert is never the one who must make the ultimate decision. He does not swing the club, or cash the prize checks. It is all on Esteban. He stands alone over the ball. In his mind's eye he sees a perfectly struck ball in wind-assisted flight, landing short of the hole and rolling toward the cup.

Now a golf ball is designed to ride the wind. As it spins, the dimples actually turn it into something like an airplane's wing, with the air pressure underneath somewhat higher than the pressure above it. This is why some Tour pros can hit shots that seem to take off on a stable angle and then suddenly leap higher into the air. As it spins, the ball develops lift.

Unfortunately, the same aerodynamic properties that make a golf ball soar also make it vulnerable to gusts. At the Kemper Open, a sudden crosswind catches Esteban's wedge shot just as it reaches its apogee. Buffeted by the gale, the ball descends too quickly, falling on the crest of the far bank of the creek. Another inch or two and it would have skidded forward, perhaps onto the green. But instead, all of the ball's energy is rammed into the bank. Its forward momentum dies and then it tumbles backward, pulled by gravity, into the rock-strewn water. Esteban is penalized a stroke. He needs three more shots to finish the hole.

The double bogey six is just the beginning of a miserable back nine. Esteban scores three more bogeys, and one birdie, to finish with a 75. Instead of picking up a couple of shots and a pot of money, he slides back down the leader board to a tie for twenty-fifth place. It's $13,713.18 instead of $90,000-plus.

Anyone would be vexed by watching so much money and progress on the golf course slip away in a final disastrous round. But the troubles that two pros experience off the golf course in Maryland put Esteban's problems in a reasonable perspective. Robert Gamez, who is known for a rollicking lifestyle, gets into a one-car crash that ruptures his spleen and sends him home to Las Vegas for a long term of recuperation. And the downtrodden Lan Gooch, having missed the cut again, gets into an argument with a traffic cop that ends with his arrest. This is how Lan explains it:

"I was leaving the golf course and this cop said I couldn't make a turn to go to where I was staying. I had made that turn all week, but now he's going to stop me. I tried to explain, but he wouldn't listen. He told me that either I move along, or pull the car over. I told him I thought it was a bunch of bullshit. Well, before I know it I'm getting charged with disobeying a lawful order and trying to elude an officer."

This kind of confrontation is not uncommon at tournaments when players accustomed to VIP treatment every week run into a local police officer who isn't willing to play along. If a conflict occurs at the tournament site, PGA Tour officials can usually smoothe things over. But this time Lan Gooch was on a public street and the traffic cop didn't care who he was.

"The whole thing was ridiculous, but it was also pretty serious," adds Gooch. "I know I shouldn't have been so difficult but I had run out of patience. Now I've had to get a lawyer. I've got to go back and appear in court. I could be fined $1,000 and even get a year of jail. I should have known better, but he also could have been less of a hard ass."

•

As Esteban leaves Washington for Westchester, just north of New York City, he is still the Grinder King. But his name is tumbling down the money list. In New York, he and Colleen and Nicholas stay in the home of a wealthy investment banker whose mansion is big enough to accommodate them in a quiet suite of rooms. The home is right next to the course, making it easier for them spend more time together, which does good things for their relationship.

Esteban will have even more time with Colleen than he expects, because on Friday a storm moves in and pounds the course with tons of rainwater and covers it in thick fog. He waits all day as officials keep saying that a break in the showers is expected. Play is finally canceled entirely at 5:30 in the afternoon. On Saturday morning, the first few groups tee off in fog so thick that their tee shots disappear like bullets fired into a mattress.

Esteban starts off at noon, paired with J. P. Hayes. Hayes, thirty-two, is one of the Q. School grinders. He has qualified for the Big Tour three previous times, but has never played well enough to keep his card. So far this year he's made just a bit over $16,000. He's been cut from the field in five of the eight tournaments he's played, and he's only completed two tournaments under par.

The rain comes again after just four holes. A five-hour delay follows. Finally, Hayes and Toledo get back onto the course long enough to play eight more before the sun sets. Hayes and Esteban are both frustrated, and so are scores of other players. It would be impossible for the tournament to run the minimum number of holes—fifty-four—and be completed on Sunday. This means Monday golf, and per-haps even a suspension for several months until players can be brought back to finish.

As bad as these circumstances are for the players, they are worse for the tournament organizers, because they are sure to have trouble just holding onto many of the com-petitors. Sure enough, on Sunday morning nearly forty players—all of them well out of contention for first place—decide not to finish their rounds. They withdraw from the competition. Some will go to their homes to rest. Others will head to San Francisco for the U.S. Open.

Esteban, who is probably not going to make the cut, feels obligated to perform anyway. If the Westchester folks were kind enough to invite him, they deserve his best effort. And who knows, maybe some day in the future the tournament officials will remember that he did the right thing this time and give him a sponsor's exemption if he needs it.

When Sunday comes, and the rain stops, Esteban shoots an 80 in the second round and knows immediately he is finished. J. P. Hayes does the opposite. He makes a string of birdies and, to the shock of almost everyone on Tour, actually wins the tournament. It is a victory with an asterisk, because of the number of rounds played. But even so, he is the low scorer—twelve under par—and he earns $324,000 and a two-year extension of his card.

The most remarkable thing about Hayes's performance is that it comes without any foreshadowing. Until this week he had earned just $16,712 and had broken 70 only twice. He had been cut from five of the eight prior tournaments. He had even been cut from the one Nike tournament he played—the Louisiana Open—where he shot 81 and 76. Despite this ragged record, in the money-is-everything system of the Tour rankings, this single performance catapults him past scores of players who have beaten him solidly week after week. Esteban is deposed as King of the Grinders. His reign lasted precisely thirty-three days.

Esteban finally gets a week off after Westchester, as those players who qualified for the U.S. Open went to San Francisco's Olympic Club to compete. He watches on television as Lee Janzen makes up a seven-stroke deficit to win on a most difficult golf course. The only one of Q. School grinders who made the cut at the Open—Lee Porter—finishes in the middle of the pack, earning $18,372. Esteban struggles with feelings of envy as he views the competition from afar. He promises himself he will play in the Open next year.

THE SCORECARD

Remaining tournaments	15
Esteban's earnings	$180,808
Money still needed to keep card	$49,192
Rank	79th

8.

A Lobster in Moline

At the start of the year, Esteban Toledo was determined to keep his card, and this goal blazed before him like a bonfire. Afraid that he wouldn't make it, he obsessed and worried and practiced hard. Now that he had almost succeeded, he could drift along for the rest of the year, make only half the cuts, and still reach the magic $230,000 mark. "There's much less pressure now," he tells me as he practices putting in the 100-degree heat at the Western Open outside Chicago. "I feel like I can enjoy this a little more."

But the terrible truth about golf, like mutual funds, is that recent results are not an indicator of future performance. If Esteban requires any reminder of this, he need only look at Charles Henry "Chip" Beck, who labors this morning on the other side of the putting green at the Cog Hill Golf and Country Club.

At age 41, Beck ranks twenty-second in all-time PGA
Tour money winners. In his career he has won four tournaments, several Ryder Cup singles matches, and come
close to snatching a major title three times. As recently as
1996, he made more than $228,000 on Tour. He lives in a
$6 million home not far from Cog Hill (monthly payment
$30,000) and is author of a popular book: A *Thinker's
Guide to Peak Performance Golf.*

At about the time his book was published, Beck fell off
his own peak. In 1997, he entered thirty-two events, made
the cut just three times, and earned less than $11,000. So
far this year, it has been fifteen tournaments and zero paychecks. His worst showing was fifteen over par at the U.S.
Open. His best was minus three at the Bob Hope Chrysler
Classic, the first tournament of the year. Going back to
1997, Chip Beck has failed to make the cut forty times in
a row.

Beck cannot escape the fleeting nature of golf's
charms. He feels the game's betrayal every time he misses
a cut, and he is a walking reminder of failure for every
other player. For months now stretching into years, Beck
has been seeking the answer to his troubles, looking both
inward and to various teachers and experts.

Other Tour pros deal with the specter of Beck's collapse through a kind of functional denial. They acknowledge the disaster, but avoid empathizing too much. They
are like the driver who passes the scene of a horrible acci-
dent. If he looks too closely and cares too much, he'll
become too terrified to continue his own trip. So while
Esteban and Beck share the putting green and together
sweat pints of fluid under the awful sun, Esteban must

believe that such a monumental slump will not happen to him. "I can't control it, so I don't think about it," he says. "You have to be careful what you think. It could come true."

•

In comparison to Beck, Esteban's slump is almost imperceptible. In his last four competitive rounds he has recorded a 71, a 75, a 72 and an 80. Experience tells Esteban that this is no crisis. He will score in the 60s again. He is bothered more by Cog Hill's heat. This week's weather has been the same every day. The temperature at dawn has been in the high eighties. By afternoon it exceeds 100. At night, explosive thunderstorms roll across the countryside, but the relief they bring lasts just a few hours. The entire Midwest is locked in this pattern. It is so hot that air conditioners are overwhelming the electric supply system. Power blackouts have hit Illinois and Indiana, and the air quality is so poor that health officials are telling even able-bodied adults to avoid exerting themselves outdoors.

Many of the other players assume that Esteban must be comfortable in the heat. After all, he grew up playing golf in a place where the summer sun turned the putting greens into mirages. "Mexican weather," they call it when they see him. The truth is, he hates the heat and suffers as much as anyone. But he sticks to his grinder routine. In the middle of the afternoon, after he's already shot a disappointing first round score of 75—continuing his mini-crisis—I find him flogging balls on the practice tee. With the humidity, the heat index is about 115 degrees. It is so uncomfortable that everyone else, including the volunteers in charge of handing out range balls, has fled for the air-conditioned clubhouse. I feel drained just watching. But he continues, sweat pouring down his face and soaking his clothes.

When Esteban stops to sip some water I realize that he's a little crazy to be out in this heat. You don't have to be Bruce Lietzke to know that at some point anyone can practice too much. In the opening offered by his little water break, I try to find out a little more about why Esteban does this. He tells me that he's trying to make sure, through repetition, that his body will make the proper swing even under pressure. It's not punishment. He actually likes it. He gets a thrill out of making the golf ball bend to his will. To demonstrate this, he hits a few exaggerated hooks and slices. Next he delicately fades the ball, left to right. Then he then draws it, right to left. He hits a few low shots, the kind that take the wind out of play, and a few high ones that land softly. After a dozen or so perfectly executed shots, he rests the club on the turf, flicks the sweat off his brow with the back of his hand, and grins. When I ask him how he does it, he offers a shockingly simple answer.

"I just think about what the shot should look like. I see it in my mind and then I swing. It just happens."

That is it. No deliberate change in his stance, like the golf magazines suggest. No forced shift in his swing plane. No adjustment in the grip. Don't misunderstand. Some of these things do occur as Esteban executes a shot. But they happen automatically. This is the way a true, self-taught, "feel" player operates. "After hitting so many of these shots, year after year, my body just does what I think in my mind," he says.

The heat has finally defeated Esteban. For the first time ever, I can see the way he must have looked at the end of a training session in his boxing days, after he pounded the heavy bag for an hour and worked the speed bag just as hard. His clothes are so soaked with perspiration that he looks like he fell into a water hazard. His hair, normally bushy and fine, is matted down. Salty beads form on his forehead and drip into his eyes. He decides to head back to his hotel—this time a suite at the Hilton—for a shower and some downtime with Colleen while Nicholas is in the day care program.

●

The entire Toledo family returns to Cog Hill around 7 p.m. The temperature has dropped to 85 degrees, but the range and the golf course are almost empty. The gallery is gone. The media and PGA Tour officials have departed. Colleen sits right down on the cool grass of the putting green and chats as Esteban rolls a few putts. She points out a young woman who is one married player's girlfriend-du-jour and laughs because Esteban is oblivious to the personal lives of his fellow players. A few yards away, Nicholas uses a wedge to whack a ball around the high grass. Like all little boys, he can get a bit manic while swinging a blunt instrument. Noticing Nicholas revving to a high pitch, endangering the precious grass of the green, Esteban suggests a move to the driving range.

The range is empty. Esteban spills out a couple of baskets of balls and lets Nicholas hit away. He does, making little explosion sounds with his voice whenever he makes contact. "Pow! Pow! Pow!"

Colleen giggles a bit as she takes her husband's copper-colored, Taylor Made three wood in hand and tees up a ball. Her swing is part field hockey and part golf, but it works well enough to send the ball 100 yards out. She hits it straight, just like her husband. And she laughs some more.

"Now, that's very good, honey," says Esteban. "Look at how you hit the ball."

Nicholas, who may be just as competitive as his stepfather, hits another ball and then challenges his mother to hit one farther, straighter, or higher. We all agree that the contest is a tie, which spares him from the agony of losing. When Colleen tires and settles down on the grass, Esteban takes his driver out of the bag and plays a little game. He points to an old wooden barn, painted green and shaded by trees, that's about 300 yards out. He then points out an open double window.

"One, maybe two bounces," he says.

The very first swing sends the ball straight at the window. It lands, bounces once, and dives through the opening like an action hero leaping to escape an exploding grenade. He hits about a dozen more. Half go into the window. He cannot help but laugh. I've never seen him so relaxed.

That night all of us, including Robert, share dinner at a Mexican restaurant near the Hilton. It is a mom-and-pop place, not a chain-style taco chip factory. We eat chicken stew and quesadilla. At one moment, Esteban teases Robert about sleeping in his car. In another he playfully scolds me for eating with a knife and fork when my hands would work better.

"Sometimes I can't believe all that's happened and how

far I've come from Mexicali," he says when the table grows quiet. "Anyone who complains about being on the PGA Tour doesn't know what a hard life is."

Esteban doesn't complain, even after a second-round 72 leaves him below the cutline at Cog Hill. He doesn't feel sorry for himself, or anyone else who happens to be leaving on Friday afternoon. Even Lan Gooch, still at zero earnings, doesn't get much sympathy from Esteban. Gooch has had the pleasure of playing some practice holes with Payne Stewart this week. He's still one of a select few who can call themselves PGA Tour players. "At least he gets a chance to compete," says Esteban. "I don't feel sorry for anyone who has that. He doesn't have a hard life. Just ask anyone who worked outside in the fields on a day like today. He'll tell you, Lan Gooch has it good. Out here, we all do."

•

A hard life for a professional golfer means running out of chances before you are ready to retire. What does a thirty-something professional do when the PGA Tour makes it clear he will never make it? Most disappear to country club jobs or get out of the golf business entirely. The fortunate few find work around the edges of the Tour, laboring for broadcasters or equipment companies.

Jeffrey Cook, whom I meet at the next Tour stop in Hartford, Connecticut, is one of these lucky ones. In 1993, Cook was a thirty-one-year-old grinder—a winner on the Nike Tour—who had finally made it to the PGA Tour. He played rounds with Tom Watson and Tom Kite and discovered there were moments when his game equaled theirs. But despite some real talent, Cook finished 164th on the money list, lost his card, and never got it back. In the summer of 1998, he stopped trying. He accepted a job from Mizuno, the Japanese manufacturer that makes the most popular irons on Tour, including Esteban's. In accepting Mizuno's offer, Cook joined the band of representatives of equipment manufacturers—Titleist, TopFlite, Callaway, Taylor Made and a dozen others—who travel from tournament to tournament ministering to the competitors with new equipment, repairs and adjustments. Some even bring mobile homes and tractor-trailers equipped with vises, grinders, and other metal-working tools to deliver service as fast as McDonald's.

"For a long time I didn't want a job like this because it seemed like that meant I was giving up," Cook tells me in Connecticut. We talk inside a white tent that we both ran to when a thunderstorm hit the Canon Greater Hartford Open. (It seems like rain is chasing the Tour to every stop, but the truth is, this season is no wetter than most.) Cook says he was forced to take a very cold look at his chances for ever succeeding on the PGA Tour.

"I had to acknowledge that the courses are much harder than any others. I could hit the ball just as good as ever and still miss the cut. I had to admit that a lot of the players knew a lot more about what they were doing than I did. Some were just more suited to it. Once I played with Tom Kite in the second to last group on a Sunday at the LA Open. He made two birdies on the last three holes and won. The difference was, he made putts when it mattered and I didn't."

Cook is a cheerful man who can appear to be happy doing anything. He's valued by Mizuno because he knows many players and can approach them comfortably. For his part, Cook says that he is delighted to be around top-flight golf every week, even if he's not in the field. But neither he nor the players who come to him looking for a new seven iron have doubts about what he would rather be doing. He may be blessed to be making a living in the golf business, but he is also cursed to be confronted every day with the dream he almost made real.

•

Most of the Q. School grinders at Hartford are desperate to avoid becoming Jeff Cook. Out of the fourteen, only one, J. P. Hayes, has his card secured and two others, Esteban and Robert Friend, are close to keeping theirs. Half of the Q. School group have earned less than $50,000. It is already July. The Grinders are counting how many chances they have left, and grumbling about tournament spots that are handed to players who haven't even earned their cards. One such player is Jay Delsing, a journeyman who has no Tour status—not even a Nike card—but has nonetheless managed to compete in more than a dozen tournaments this year and win more than $26,000. Delsing even got into the Bay Hill Invitational. Other players figure he's done it by lobbying tournament officials for exemptions. Tall, relaxed, and ever-smiling, Delsing is a charming fellow who just may be able to talk his way into tournaments. But no matter how he's managed to get into so many events, and despite the fact that his earnings are small, his presence is stirring some resentment.

The other object of complaint is Casey Martin, who has been invited to play at Hartford because of the fame generated by his petition to use a golf cart at tournaments. On Thursday of this week, Martin made a little history when he became the first player to use a cart in a PGA Tour tournament. A huge gallery followed him and his playing partners, Hugh Royer III and Iain Steel. He scored one over par for the round, seven behind the leaders.

On Thursday night, Martin and Esteban found themselves side by side on an evening cruise down the Connecticut River, a social event arranged by the tournament organizers. The boat was slow and the cruise dragged on until almost everyone aboard was exhausted and cranky. As Esteban recalls it, he bumped into Martin and told him that he opposes the use of carts and that the controversy has been bad for the game. "If I say what I feel away from him, I should say it to his face," he explains to me later. "It wasn't an argument or anything, but I wanted him to know from me how I feel."

Though the general public still sympathizes with Martin, the sentiment on the PGA Tour is hardening against him. Players on the bottom of the money list are especially irritated by the fact that the notoriety generated by the legal struggle has led tournaments around the country to offer Martin playing spots he would never have gotten otherwise. They figure that every time Martin accepts a bid, someone who has played by the rules and is qualified by his performance will be excluded.

•

Out on the golf course, Esteban makes the cut but finishes the week just one under par and makes only $4,300. His fellow grinder, John Riegger, finally plays well for an entire tournament. A seven-under-par performance wins him more than $22,000 and finally moves him past the

$40,000 mark. Riegger, who turned thirty-five in June, is a quiet man who wears wire-rimmed glasses that make him look almost professorial as he studies a putt or gazes down a fairway. He held a Tour Card once before, in 1992. He finished that year in 192nd place on the money list and lost it.

Though he hasn't been showing it on the outside, Riegger has been frustrated all year and no doubt was losing confidence. At the end of the Hartford tournament, he tells me that he got a little of it back this week from Fuzzy Zoeller, his playing partner on Sunday.

"I tried to take a lesson from Fuzzy's attitude. He walks onto every golf course like he owns it. I mean he's so relaxed and happy. He likes everybody, it seems, and he's confident. He should be, I guess. He's been out here forever. Anyway, while we were playing he actually encouraged me. He'd say, 'C'mon, kid, you can make it. Let's do it.' You don't get that from other people on the Tour. I think it helped. I think it helped quite a bit. I actually had fun out there."

He had no more fun, however, than Olin Browne, a thirty-nine-year-old, who grabbed his very first PGA Tour victory by chipping the ball into the hole from the fringe on the eighteenth green. Fifteen years of work, on and off the Big Tour, preceded Browne's success. He proves there is hope for every grinder.

●

It is now the middle of July, and about a dozen regular tournaments remain. For many, it's already too late to follow a modest strategy of accumulating cash at a rate of $10,000 or $15,000 per week and letting it add up to a card. As the weeks pass, high finishes and big paychecks become imperative for Riegger, Tom Pernice, Lee Porter, Vance Veazey, and everyone else who's closer to the bottom than the top. For these players, J. P. Hayes is becoming an object of both inspiration and envy. Inspiring as well are Mark O'Meara, Scott Simpson, Tom Watson, and John Cook, all forty-somethings who have won this year. They have proven that the game is not yet wholly owned by the young stars such as Woods, Justin Leonard, Ernie Els, and David Duval.

Of course, none of these stars—young or old—can be found at the Quad City Classic in Moline, Illinois. These are the dog days of summer. It is the time when the mighty take off to prepare for the upcoming British Open, and the grinders fight with each other at tournaments with smaller galleries, smaller purses, and little visibility. Not one of the Tour's top ten will play in Moline, or next week in Jackson, Mississippi, or the week after in Memphis, Tennessee.

PGA Tour officials insist that there is no such thing as a minor tournament. But everything in Moline, right down to the cafeteria-style food served to the players in a broiling hot tent, reminds you that it is just that. Transportation services are erratic. Few players have been provided with courtesy cars, and the options for hotels and restaurants are limited.

If any of the players in Moline didn't feel their second-class status keenly, they could be reminded by a recent newspaper report on the World Golf Championships, a series of exclusive tournaments for the elite that will commence in the coming year. Purses will be $5 million minimum, and the fields—as small as sixty-four players—will be drawn from the top ranks of the tours of America, Europe, Japan, Australia, and South Africa.

The people behind this idea, most notably PGA Tour commissioner Tim Finchem, are hoping to create more opportunities for the very best players to face each other in arenas where a valuable global TV audience won't be distracted by a pesky little no-name player who might have an unusually good week and knock Tiger Woods off the telecast.

These tournaments will also contribute to the informal division of the PGA Tour. In the bifurcated Tour of the future, the very best players will concentrate on a premier circuit, made up of the World Golf Championships, the Majors, and a handful of existing invitational events such as The Memorial. They will get even more money, and more attention, and play less often. Meanwhile, the grinders and others below the top seventy or so spots on the money list will toil at more ordinary tournaments for less money and less glory and hope that a victory moves them into the upper echelon. Tour officials insist this is not where the sport is headed, but it is inevitable that the ordinary PGA Tour will be watered down while the sponsors, fans, and elite players focus on a smaller number of high-prestige contests.

With this vision of the future, and the dog-day tournaments at hand, the normal grumblings heard among the rank and file are becoming more intense and more focused. In Moline, every player finds a questionnaire in his locker. It begins by stating that the "Tour leadership" and some players are divided on key issues. It goes on to asks for opinions about player representation on the board of the PGA Tour, and about the idea of creating an independent Tour Players Association. It also mentions a proposal for paying small stipends to players who miss a cut. Though the author of the questionnaire doesn't offer his name, the return address—locker number 78—belongs to veteran player Danny Edwards.

•

Two rounds of 70 are not good enough for Esteban to make the cut in Moline, where the Oakwood Country Club course is one of the easiest on the PGA Tour. Oakwood is so easy for the pros that the average score at the 1997 Quad Cities Classic was 69.7. As the final day of play began, twelve competitors were ten or more strokes under par, a PGA Tour record. This year Steve Jones, 1996 U.S. Open champion, will win by a score of seventeen under par. Jones had come to Moline in fifty-fifth place on the money list with more than $300,000 in winnings for the year. His card was secure, and his victory snatches yet another chance away from the Q. School grinders whose time is running out.

With his early dismissal from the tournament, Esteban is in a cranky mood when he dresses to go practice on Saturday morning. Few things bother him more than watching other people play for money while he waits on the sidelines for next week. But unlike most players, he will go to the course, even after missing the cut, to practice and face up to his failure.

As he's leaving, he grumbles at Colleen about money—the number one source of friction in all marriages. She knows that maybe for the first time, money isn't a problem. He's just upset in general. But it hurts anyway, and the pain shows on her face.

When he gets to the practice tee, Esteban has trouble concentrating. He hits a few shots, but he is unable to relax and lose himself in the happy, semi-trance state that usually comes over him when he's on the range. He keeps recalling the look on Colleen's face and the harsh words he had spoken. Unable to get this out of this mind, he puts his clubs back in the bag, pulls the leather glove off of his left hand, and heads back to the motel. He must apologize.

At the motel, Colleen starts to cry before he can even get out his apology.

"Why are you crying?" he asks.

"Because you are going to be a papa."

Colleen had suspected for days. Even though she couldn't be more than one month pregnant, she knew in her heart that it was true. The confirmation came this morning in the form of a do-it-yourself pregnancy test that sits on the table in the room with its little chemical signal indicating a positive result.

He hugs her tightly and kisses her and his eyes tear with joy. Ever since he was a boy himself, Esteban has wanted to raise a family of his own. With Colleen, Nicholas, and now a baby on the way, a dream that has always meant even more to him that golf is coming true.

Suddenly, money is not a problem. He wants to buy her everything and anything she might desire. And the sting of missing the cut in Moline, and pain caused by all the other failures in his long struggle disappear. Tonight, the Toledos will celebrate at the best restaurant they can find in Moline. Nearly 1,000 miles from the ocean, Colleen will have one of the largest lobsters she's ever seen.

THE SCORECARD

Remaining tournaments	12
Esteban's earnings	$185,108
Money still needed to keep card	$44,892
Rank	89th

9

Sleepwalking in Jackson ○

More than 800 miles separate Moline, Illinois and Jackson, Mississippi, home of the Deposit Guaranty Golf Classic. Airline service is so expensive and inconvenient that Esteban and Colleen decide to put Nicholas and all their baggage into a rented car and take a thirteen-hour drive. High on the good news from the pregnancy test, they start out in good spirits. Colleen is reminded of last summer, when she and Esteban spent weeks traveling the Nike circuit from the Midwest to Maine and back again. It was one of the happiest times of her life.

On this trip, midnight finds the Toledos pulling into Jackson and discovering that between a softball tournament and a convention, almost every motel room is taken. After bouncing from one dimly lit parking lot to another, they are almost grateful to find a place in the type of cheap, battered, and noisy dive Esteban used to frequent when he traveled alone. Even at this hour, some of the other guests are sitting on chairs outside their rooms, tilting them back against the wall, drinking beer, laughing, and talking loud.

The long trip, the gritty hotel, and loudmouths outside the room seem all that much worse because Esteban comes to Mississippi under a cloud. The glory of the BellSouth Classic is long past. He has not yet reached his goal, and like everyone else in this predicament, he is running out of time. He won't allow himself to say it out loud, but he knows this could be the week when he finally proves he belongs, or it could be another dance with fear and frustration. Despite being road-tired, he has trouble falling asleep.

•

If the heat and humidity of the Midwest were stifling, conditions in deepest Dixie in the middle of July are downright smothering. These days, the temperature in Jackson reaches 100 by 11 a.m., and moves higher from there. The humidity makes every living thing that moves miserable. Locals spend most of the summer next to their air conditioners. If they move around outside at all, they do it early in the morning and in the evening. The only ones who break this rule are laborers who are paid to do it: construction workers, gardeners, and PGA Tour pros who have not yet secured their cards.

On the first day of the tournament, Annandale Golf Course is eerily quiet. On the roadway leading up to the golf course, the guards keep waving me on until I find a parking spot in an almost empty lot right next to the club-

house. An orange tram that is supposed to shuttle spectators snakes up the driveway without a soul on board. Half
the sales booths along the little midway leading to the
entrance gate—where credit card companies and others
usually offer free golf balls—are deserted.

Of course the heat is the main reason that people are
staying away in droves, but it is not the only one. Serious
fans would probably brave the weather if they knew they
were going to see top-flight competition. But this is also
the week of the most venerated golf event in the world,
the British Open. Practically all of the planet's best players
are in Southport, England, enjoying the cool breezes at
Royal Birkdale Golf Club and soaking up the adoration of
the most knowledgeable gallery anywhere. And the whole
thing is broadcast on television right here in the States.
It's on even in the clubhouse at Annandale.

Because of the time difference, Round One at the
British is nearing completion just as the first group tees off
in Mississippi. Overseas, the American stars are in ascent.
Tiger Woods and John Huston share the lead at five
under par. Brad Faxon, Peter Jacobsen, and Davis Love III
are all in the top ten. The pictures from Southport show
sunny skies and huge throngs. Since temperatures never
rise out of the sixties, Tiger and many of the others play in
long sleeves.

In the Old South, a less stellar field includes a few especially eager refugees from the Nike Tour. One is Stiles
"Big Daddy" Mitchell, whom I last saw chipping like an ice
hockey player at Q. School. Another is Allen Doyle, a
forty-nine-year-old driving range operator who began
playing tournaments only four years ago. Doyle's home-

made swing begins with an extra-wide stance that makes him look like a cowboy with rickets. He lunges back and then forward with the club, hitting the ball long and straight.

Unlike almost everyone else, Mitchell and Doyle seem delighted to be here. But neither could be more intent on playing well this week than Lan Gooch. Jackson is a short drive from Lan's hometown of Houston, Mississippi. Family and friends have come to watch him. For the first time all season, he knows the golf course well, because he has played it many times. Before turning pro, he qualified for the U.S. Amateur Championship in a tournament played here. His experience on the course, combined with the fact the competition here is probably the weakest anywhere, means he will have no better chance than this to make a cut this year.

The local paper has noted Gooch's presence with a hometown-boy-struggles-to-make-good article on the sports page. His 1988 Southeast conference college championship is noted, along with the fact that one of the players he beat—Dudley Hart—has won $2 million on the PGA Tour. After describing all of Lan's problems, the writer quotes him as saying that the only thing he would rather do is fish for a living, "but they don't pay me much for fishing, either."

Although he is unfailingly good-natured about his terrible performance this year, Gooch would give almost anything to get out of this situation. He does not want to be known as a good loser. "The other players have been pretty supportive, but to tell you the truth, I don't need their support," he tells me over an iced tea in the clubhouse. "I don't want to be in this position. More and more guys are staying away from me because they don't want it to rub off. I play a lot of practice rounds alone."

Many of the problems that more successful players encounter are turned on their heads when you are Lan Gooch. Instead of fending off a stream of offers from caddies who want a job, Gooch has had trouble holding on to anyone for more than a tournament or two. Better offers come along and the caddie is gone before he can help much at all. Gooch doesn't need to scramble to get a airplane flight on Sunday nights because he played in a late group. Instead, he has to figure out where he will spend his extra days when he is cut once again. And while two hundred other players fret about reaching number 125 on the money list, Gooch is already resigned to another Q. School torture test. He just wants to make the cut to soothe his ego and please his family and friends.

"If I had really played well, played my best, and had the same result I've had so far then I would quit," he tells me. "But I haven't done that. This year I haven't adapted to the level of play, or the courses, and I haven't played with my usual confidence. But when I try again, and I will, I'll have had this year of experience to fall back on."

Resigned as he may be, Gooch doesn't seem at all discouraged. He makes four birdies on the front nine and a fifth on the tenth hole. For a moment, he's on the leader board. If there had been a gallery, they would have cheered. Hope lives. But then the birdies stop. He gives back two of the shots he earned on the front nine, and finishes just one over par. Esteban has the same score, as does Stiles Mitchell. All is not lost, though. If the cut were made today, they would all survive it.

•

On Friday, Lan Gooch plays better than he has all year. With his tiny gallery sweating it out beside him, he shoots 70 and actually lands above the cutline. Stiles Mitchell is not so blessed. He goes from a 70 on Thursday to 76 on Friday, which means he is out. When I pass him near the putting green, he smiles and says, "I gotta keep it out of the trees." Allen Doyle lands near the top of the leader board, four shots off the pace set by Doug Tewell and Paul Goydos, who are twelve under par.

One of the best rounds of the day, a 66, is posted by Esteban, who hasn't played this well since the BellSouth Classic, two months and twenty-four competitive rounds ago. He does it with steady, unspectacular play; six birdies and no bogey. He lands his drive in the fairway on all fourteen driving holes. He hits the greens in regulation seventeen out of eighteen times. He is never in a bunker, and he only needs thirty putts.

It is impossible to say why Esteban played so well today. But Robert and Colleen are agree that he always plays better when he is able to relax during a round. Right now, he's excited about Colleen's pregnancy, and that gives him something to think about, other than golf, as he walks from shot to shot. This tournament also provides an extremely casual environment. The galleries are so small that it's almost like an outing at a little public course. Security at the clubhouse is minimal, which means that almost anyone can walk into the players' dining room. The food set out there is classic southern country fare:

greens, fried okra, hominy. During Friday's round, Colleen and I carry a supply of cornmeal-battered catfish fillets out onto the fairway for a snack. Almost giddy with excitement about her pregnancy, Colleen teases Esteban when he lands the ball just a few feet from the cup on number 8, a par-three.

"Hey, can't you hit it any closer than that?" she shouts.

"How's my baby?" he hollers back.

"Your baby's hot."

●

As drowsy as things are in Jackson, events at the British Open are exhilarating. On Friday, two of the players least likely to succeed, American Brian Watts and British amateur Justin Rose, move into first and second place. Watts, thirty-two, had earned his way to England via the Japanese Tour. Rose played his way into the tournament during a qualifying round held at a different course directly across the street from Royal Birkdale.

All of seventeen years old, Rose has tied the record for low amateur score—66—in wind, cold, and rain that combined to create what some players considered the worst conditions ever seen in a major tournament. The weather pushed several of the world's best players into the 80s.

The drama unfolding in England captivates the competitors in Jackson. Out on the course, players ask each other what they know about Brian Watts and Justin Rose. In the clubhouse, crowds gather around the TV set in the bar. None of the players say, "I wish I were there instead of here." But they all must think it. Today there's no place in the world farther from Southport than Jackson.

•

On Friday night at the Annandale range, Esteban is con-
tent to take a break from his routine to gaze at Mac
O'Grady, who is entertaining a small gathering of pros just
a few yards away. "That guy has the best swing you will ever
see," he says. "He's also a little bit crazy."

O'Grady—the golfer previously known as Phil
McGleno—is the single most peculiar figure on the PGA
Tour. Four years before he got his card in 1982, he almost
died from pneumonia. Homeless and flat broke, he
changed his name and accepted the help of some friends
who nursed him to health. When he finally recorded his
first PGA Tour win, in 1986, he dedicated it to "people
whose spirits never fragmented along the yellow brick
road."

He holds the record for Q. School failures: sixteen.
Over the years, O'Grady has engaged in one row after
another with fellow pros and Tour officials, whom he
labeled "tin-can bureaucrats." By 1990, he was in semi-
retirement, the victim of nerves so jangled he couldn't
manage to sink a three-foot putt. He had the yips.

But even as O'Grady's PGA Tour earnings fell to almost
nothing, his reputation as a golf artist and teacher grew.
For decades, he has studied golf as intently as a rabbinical
scholar studies the Talmud. He has developed a mathematically precise model for the perfect swing, one that
takes into account almost 4,000 variables. According to
O'Grady's system, Davis Love's swing is a ninety-two out of
100. Sam Snead scores ninety-nine.

O'Grady himself possesses a swing that many pros consider the best of all time. Genuinely ambidextrous, he

once shot a 62 playing right-handed and followed it with a 69 playing from the left. Players as varied as Gene Littler and Vijay Singh have sought him out for instruction. He has helped many, but drives many away with his obsessive-compulsive personality.

On the range at Annandale, O'Grady is more charming than annoying. He demonstrates how he hits a draw, a fade, and a straight shot by making the slightest adjustment in his stance, which then causes him to swing from the inside, the outside, or along his normal path. He is making the point that the tiniest adjustment can cue the body to make a series of automatic changes. It's so subtle that when he asks the pros to look at his setup and predict where he's going to hit the ball next—left, right, or straight—they guess wrong most of the time.

"Fade."

Whack. "Wrong."

"Straight.

Whack. "Wrong."

"Draw."

Whack. "Good guess."

The chuckles turn to laughter as O'Grady imitates the slashing swing of Trevino and the pirouette finish of Arnold Palmer. It's not as funny as all the giggling suggests, but it's so hot, and the players are so drained, that just about anything could make them dissolve in laughter.

•

With all of the PGA Tour's elite young millionaires an ocean away, the rank-and-file players in Jackson feel more comfortable laughing, and they feel more comfortable grousing. Normally, Tour players say nothing more about each other than "He's a great guy." But here, half a dozen players tell me they resent the money and playing spots taken up by Jay Delsing. He has earned almost $31,000, which puts him ahead of five of the grinders who paid their dues at Q. School. Others complain about Dave Stockton Jr., saying that he gets sponsor exemptions because his father was a successful pro.

Besides these petty jealousies, some of the players have also begun to talk more openly about the issues raised by the questionnaire circulated in Moline. The fact that anyone is willing to talk openly about a union is remarkable in itself. The PGA Tour is about as conservative as the Heritage Foundation. The few who do speak out about politics are, almost to a man, free-market fanatics who see evidence of their personal superiority in their position on the money list. Many of the wealthier players, such as Davis Love and Brad Faxon, have already condemned the idea of a player organization. More than one critic says that if the dissatisfied pros want to be paid more, they should practice more. It is as if their years of work, success at Q. School, and play that draws fans and revenues to tournaments, do not merit any reward at all.

Though many of the top players immediately stand against the organizing effort, in Jackson it becomes clear that this is not a fringe movement and that something more than earnings-envy is at work here. Most players now know that three respected members of the Big Tour are behind this effort. Danny Edwards, who is almost fifty years old, has won five times and seems destined for success on the Senior Tour. He has no vested interest in changing things on the regular Tour. Larry Rinker, forty-one, has never won, but he has made a decent living on the PGA Tour and the Nike Tour for fifteen years. He's hardly poor. The youngest of the three, thirty-seven-year-old Mark Brooks, has won seven tournaments in the last ten years, including the PGA Championship in 1996, which got him a ten-year exemption. So far this year he's earned well over $100,000.

The main issue raised by these three is the percentage of PGA Tour revenues reserved to pay players. In major team sports, owners pay 50 percent or more of gross revenues to athletes. This is why major league baseball players, and there are more than 750 or them, had an average salary of $1.3 million in 1998. Golf's powers-that-be pay only about 20 percent of the Tour's gross revenues to the players who compete every week. This is why only the twenty top golfers in the country make as much as an average baseball player.

A second issue centers on the paychecks, or lack of them, given to players who miss the cut at a tournament. Many players think the time has come to give at least a couple thousand dollars to the men who play only Thursday and Friday. Those who argue for this idea say the players who are cut have nevertheless performed for the crowds. Those who are opposed say it would damage the competitive culture of the Tour. Golf would no longer be the only sport with a do-or-die pay structure.

Most of the Q. School grinders avoid the debate over the TPA. Esteban will only say that he thinks it's a good idea to ask some questions about how the Tour's revenues are handled. On the other side, Bob Friend tells me he can't understand why anyone who is lucky enough to play golf for money is complaining. But unlike most of his fellow journeymen, John Riegger is not only willing to discuss the issues raised by Edwards and company, he brings it up when we have dinner on Friday night at a Louisiana-style fish house in Jackson.

"The older guys have definitely set things up to favor themselves and to make it harder on the players who come out of Q. School. I mean, the way it is now, someone who won a tournament back in 1979 and has done nothing since gets a better shot at playing in tournaments and will even get better tee times—early in the day, before the greens are beat up—than someone who earned their way onto the Big Tour at the last qualifying tournament."

It's surprising to hear Riegger speak so openly. No one on Tour has a cooler golf course demeanor. The only way he could be quieter, or calmer, would be if he had embalming fluid in his veins. But here, he's openly resentful, even angry about what he sees as an unjustifiably skewed system. "I've had to miss the Byron Nelson, the Colonial, the Memorial, a whole lot of tournaments that other guys below me on the money have played. It's pretty damn hard to keep sharp and make money when they don't let you play. Of course, that's the way a lot of them want it."

When I ask Riegger where all this resentment originates, he recalls a players' meeting in 1992, the only previous full year he played on Tour. At the time, he was struggling his way to finishing in 192nd place on the money list.

"There was a lot of discussion about making it more fair for the new guys. I thought that at last the older players were thinking about something other than themselves. Then Lanny Wadkins gets up and says, 'I made my money already. Screw those new guys. Let them pay their dues the way I did.' "

It's more than a little ironic that this statement came from Lanny Wadkins. No one has benefited from the ranking system in quite the same way as Wadkins. With more than fifteen years on Tour and twenty wins, he is the only player who fits into a category called "lifetime member," which gives him privileges no matter how poorly he may play today or tomorrow. In the last five years, he has averaged less than $100,000 in earnings and missed the 125 mark on the money list every year, yet his privileges are continually renewed.

PGA Tour supporters would likely argue that as a whole, the Tour benefits significantly from Wadkins's presence. As winner of the 1977 PGA Championship, he still draws a number of fans to tournaments and to their television sets. Keeping him around is akin to keeping a faded ingenue on stage. John Riegger couldn't disagree more.

"This is a sport, not some kind of show," he says. "I think guys like that ought to have to go back to Q. School and prove they've still got it. A lot of them couldn't handle it."

Though Riegger has shown he can handle the pressure of the qualifying tournament, he is not frightening anyone yet on the Tour. With a little more than $46,000, he's 170th on the money list. Among the fourteen Q. School grinders, he's eighth. Riegger missed the cut nine times in the first twelve tournaments. He then called on an old friend to be his caddie. Since then, he's played for money three of four weeks. In Hartford, he picked up a $22,480 check for twentieth place. True to the grinder creed, he's certain he's about to break through, maybe even win. This hope is something more than bravado. Riegger has climbed to 123rd on the Tour's overall statistical ranking, which measures how good a player is at everything from driving to putting. His game is just good enough.

Riegger's confidence is also supplied by his sports pedigree. His father, a power plant manager, played minor league baseball, and John himself was a high school star: a pitcher in baseball and quarterback in football. He played golf at a municipal course in Paducah, Kentucky, with two older boys who grew up to be PGA Tour pros, Russ Cochran and Kenny Perry. Perry has more than $4 million in lifetime earnings. Cochran has $3.4 million. In college, Riegger was an All-American and played with Steve Elkington and Scott Verplank. He has competed with many of the Tour's best, and beaten many of them at one time or another.

A handful of unexpected, intermittent successes have kept Riegger, now thirty-four-years old, competing despite the fact that his lifetime PGA Tour earnings are just a bit over $100,000. He has sacrificed much, including two marriages. The first was crushed, in part, by his wife's insistence that he get some kind of real job. The second was a rebound relationship that might have worked if he hadn't put twice as much time into his game as he devoted to his marriage.

Twelve years after college, chain-smoking cigarettes and picking at a plate of seafood in steamy Jackson, John

Riegger can acknowledge the sacrifices he has made. But he cannot let go of his dream. If golf hasn't given him what he deserves, that's only because of a few bad breaks, a circumstance here or there. And he says that the game cannot be blamed for his loneliness, either. "I think I got to find me a nice Southern girl next," he says, in all seriousness. "They treat a man better. Stand by him, you know? With a Southern girl, it would work."

•

A not-so-grand total of twelve people represent the gallery beside the first tee when John Riegger and Esteban appear to start play on Saturday. There are only seven groups that will follow, a sign that they are playing well enough to compete for a top-ten finish. Esteban and Riegger are both seven under, five behind the leaders. But this is one tournament where the honor of teeing off late is a mixed blessing. At their appointed moment—11:14 a.m.— the sun is nearing its zenith and the air is so thick with moisture that sweat just lies on the skin, refusing to evaporate. Today, two caddies will faint from the 100-degree-plus heat and be rushed to the clubhouse to receive fluids intravenously. They will be victims of the weather and a ridiculous Tour prohibition against short pants. Over the decades, pleading, protest, and the collapse of caddies have all failed to persuade the PGA Tour to revoke the rule.

Riegger and Esteban sleep walk through the first six holes, scoring unremarkable pars. The gallery has been reduced to Colleen and me, and the occasional stray fan. We avoid heat stroke by lingering beneath shade trees and stealing water from the big barrel-sized dispensers set up for the players. It's difficult to focus on what is happening in the tournament. Instead we talk about babies, and marriage, and family—almost everything but golf—in part to keep our minds off the heat.

On the course, the doldrums are finally broken on hole number 8, a par-three, when Esteban lands his ball within six feet of the hole and makes a birdie. Riegger matches him on the next hole, and then makes a little run on the back nine, with birdies on numbers 10, 11 and 12. For a moment he is on the leader board, in fourth place. He can hope for a big finish that might cement his card. But the moment passes. He gives away a shot on the thirteenth hole and suffers a miserable double bogey on number seventeen. The round turns into a mediocre 71. Esteban finishes at par, 72. They won't be teeing off quite so late tomorrow.

•

The final day of a golf tournament is supposed to be exciting and entertaining. It will be for the new leaders—Mike Brisky and Fred Funk—and the few who have a chance to catch them. But for everyone else, Sunday at the Annandale Golf Course is so quiet that it is downright depressing. There is no blimp hovering over this tournament. The fairways are devoid of spectators. Even the grandstand around the eighteenth green is mostly empty.

This is not the case, of course, at the British Open. There, the final day of play finds Brian Watts still defending the lead that he had protected on Saturday in even stronger winds. Justin Rose begins play three shots behind Watts. Between them are this year's Masters champion Mark O'Meara, Jim Furyk, and Jesper Parnevik. The elite are at last making a run.

While Watts and O'Meara are hurtling toward a high-anxiety playoff, the most surprising performance in Jackson is turned in by Tim Loustalot, a member of the Q. School fourteen. Going into this tournament, Loustalot occupied space number 222 on the money list. A final-day 68 in Jackson will win him second place behind Funk and $89,600. This is less than one quarter of what he would have earned with a similar finish at a big-money event. But it immediately moves him up more than seventy places and puts next year's card within reach.

Today Esteban is paired with Mark Carnavale, a thirty-seven-year-old veteran who has seen better seasons. In 1992, Carnavale made $220,000 and finished in seventieth place on the money list. As recently as 1994, he was in the top 100. But he lost his card in 1995 and had to play the Nike Tour to get it back. So far this year, he's made less than $68,000 in nineteen tournaments.

No one shows the effects of the heat more blatantly than Carnavale, who claims to weigh 238 but looks much heavier. While Esteban wears his usual Sunday outfit of black pants and white shirt, which hide the perspiration pouring off his body, Carnavale is dressed in light green cotton pants that absorb every drop of sweat and turn dark with the moisture. After a few holes, the sweat stain has traveled from Carnavale's waist to his knees, making him look like someone took a garden hose to his pants. He adds to his bedraggled appearance a white towel, soaked in cold water and draped over his head.

Carnavale's personal gallery of one is a young red-haired woman named Shannon who, despite his appearance and constant moaning, follows him faithfully for the entire round. The two met in March in a New Orleans bar during the Freeport McDermott Classic. Shannon, who works at a department store in Baton Rouge, didn't immediately believe Carnavale was a Tour player. But she found him on the course the next day, and has been interested in him ever since. She doesn't seem to lose any of her enthusiasm even as Mark curses and groans his way to a 70.

Alongside Carnavale, Esteban cruises to a three-under-par 69. The most encouraging part of his round is the way he responds to three-putting for a bogey on the sixteenth. He lets this setback fade from his mind, and promptly sinks long putts on the last two holes for consecutive birdies. The putt on the eighteenth moves him from twenty-seventh place—worth $7,800—to twenty-first, which nets him $12,000.

Among other the players I have followed this week, John Riegger will make a little over $6,000, hardly enough to make a difference in his quest for the card. Lan Gooch will finally break out of the zero-earnings column by winning $3,173. Jay Delsing will pick up $27,600, and Allen Doyle will earn $36,000—enough to buy roughly 1,200 buckets of balls at his drive range back home—by finishing four shots out of first place.

Colleen and I applaud her husband's finish and begin walking toward the scorer's tent. She's happy to see Esteban back on track, but she's weary of traveling the PGA Tour. She's filled her days with spectating and shopping, but even that's becoming tedious, not to mention expensive. She is beginning to wonder if she shouldn't go home for a while.

Her ambivalence is an honest response to a tournament that many players and their families would rather not attend. Back in the clubhouse, the contrast with the British Open is made clearer by the TV highlight report. It shows Mark O'Meara besting Brian Watts in a four-hole play-off to clinch his second major championship. Besides the second-place check of $329,00, Watts will receive a PGA Tour Card. Justin Rose will take his fourth-place finish and turn professional.

Esteban has been so taken by the scenery and drama of the British Open that he has all but decided to make the trip next year and try to qualify on Monday if he isn't invited to play.

We discuss this on the front porch of the Annandale clubhouse as dusk settles on Jackson. Esteban and more than a dozen other players are waiting to board a bus that will take them to the airport and a private jet bound for Flint, Michigan. They're all going to participate in a celebrity charity outing that puts them on the golf course, and then inside race cars, with auto racing pros. It sounded like a good idea when he was invited. But as the departure is delayed, and delayed again, he starts to wonder if he should have declined the invitation.

He wonders too about his status a PGA Tour professional. After the BellSouth Classic, he dared to say that he would try to actually win tournaments. Eight weeks later, he's acutely aware of the difference between the British Open field and the pros who gathered at the Deposit Guaranty Classic. He's a Deposit Guaranty kind of player, at least for the moment. With just eleven tournaments left to play, he's still more than $30,000 shy of guaranteeing his card for next year. He knows that he could fail, that his dream could crumble, and he might never get another chance.

"I'm worried, but I'm not scared," he says, as he leans against a white column on the porch. His golf bag is propped against the wall beside the door. "I still want to prove to everyone that I belong."

In the parking lot, Jeff Gallagher calls to Esteban. He tells him it's time to load his clubs into the luggage compartment on the bus. I wish him luck as he shoulders the bag. A few days later, I will find out that Esteban, Colleen, Nicholas, and all the other players and their families had waited until almost midnight for their jet to Flint. They got to their hotels after 2 a.m., and had to rise before 7 to attend the pro-am. Such is the glamorous life of the average PGA Tour pro.

THE SCORECARD

Remaining tournaments	11
Esteban's earnings	$197,108
Money still needed to keep card	$32,892
Rank	90th

10.

Not the Only Thing ○

"I keep remembering last year on the Nike when he was close to finishing in the top fifteen and getting his card without going to Q. School. He kept pushing and practicing. He wound up grinding himself down to nothing. He had nothing left to draw on and he didn't make it. I'm worried about that happening again."

Robert Szczesny thinks hard about Esteban's game, and he seems to believe that with enough analysis he'll figure out how to, as Robert says, "maximize his potential." He allows that Esteban must work hard. "He isn't a natural golfer. He has to practice, and I understand that," he says. But Robert doesn't understand why his boss can't accept that he performs best when he's relaxed. "In the last month he's stopped joking with the kids in the gallery. He's out in the 95 degree heat hitting ball after ball. It's

like he doesn't understand he has to play well for a full year. He has to pace himself."

Esteban is pushing to make as much money as he can. He seems willing to play in every pro-am event that is offered to him, whether it pays $500 or $2,000. And if there's a $100 bonus paid to players who show up early to schmooze with the amateurs over breakfast, he will do it. "I understand where he's coming from," says Robert. "He never had money, and now he's going to make it when he can. Just getting paid anything to go out and play golf is great.

"I understand that he has a real work ethic. But this is one of those cases where his strength, the thing that has brought him this far, may turn out to be a weakness in the end. A lot of people are like that. I mean, they are real tough, and that helps them succeed, but once they make it they need to change in order to cope with being on top. You might survive without anybody else's help, but it's awfully hard to be the absolute best at anything without a teacher, or someone to help you.

"It's also possible to work yourself into exhaustion. It's not great to be a workaholic if it means you don't get the rest you need, or you are off playing on some course other than the one where the tournament is held. We need to know these courses, to be confident when we tee it up for real."

The scramble for money doesn't bother Robert as much as Esteban's attitude about winning. Though Esteban has always been obsessed with golf, Robert believes he sees a different kind of obsession, especially now that two players who previously trailed him on the money list—J. P.

Hayes and Olin Browne—have suddenly won championships. Ever since they got their victories, says Robert, Esteban has been focused more on winning than on simply playing his best golf.

"Don't get me wrong," he says. "I think if the conditions are right, someday he just might win, especially if he's on fire for four days in a row. But I don't know if he should be going out every week thinking he can win it all. That's going to lead to a lot of frustration pretty quick. Winning is becoming too important. He played a practice round with Keith Nolan the other day and lost $50. He couldn't stand it. It's his choice, but if you ask me, he's got to relax a little bit if he expects to do well out here. You can't force it. That's not the way golf works. Esteban needs to work on some things and wait for his time."

•

This is the paradox of competitive golf. Victory cannot be forced, and consistently good play doesn't necessarily win. On a week-to-week basis, Esteban is performing much better than both Browne and Hayes. He is fifty-eighth in the Tour's "all-around" playing statistic, which takes into account every aspect of play they measure, from driving to putting. Browne is in eighty-second place, even with his victory in Connecticut. Hayes is so far behind he doesn't show up on the official listing, because it includes only 166 names.

The all-around stat is a reasonable index of playing performance, because it takes into account most of the skills needed to beat a golf course. This is why, for example, Vance Veazey shows up among the top ten in driving for distance but is likely to lose his card this year. He's got one trick, not a full bag. When you look at the all-around rankings, there are no Veazeys in the top ten, only Duvals, Woods, Hustons, and Loves. In this ranking, Esteban is ahead of all of the other grinders. He is also ahead of Mark O'Meara, who just happened to win the Masters and British Open this year.

But knowing that his game is good is not enough for Esteban. In his heart lives the kid who was determined to play better than all the members of the Mexicali Country Club, to prove that they were wrong about him. In an unusually unguarded moment, Esteban tells me that he is certain he will make the money he needs to keep his card. His goal is now a victory.

"I know there are some guys who probably think I was lucky in Atlanta, that I'm not that good," he says. "That's why I want to win. And I don't mean like J. P. Hayes did. I don't count that as a real win. I want to win a real, four-day tournament, so there's no question about it. Before, I thought a little bit about winning but mostly about qualifying and making money toward my card. I think that now I know I will keep my card, that I will be out here next year, I should go for it all, go for winning. I've tasted the chocolate, now I want two scoops."

How does winning happen? In most sports, the answer has much to do with physical size, strength, or speed. In golf, the equation is more subtle. Indeed, the difference between the top-ranked golfer in the world and the man ranked 100th is minute. If you doubt this, consider what happened in 1999, at the first tournament in the new World Golf Championship. Every single one of the top-twenty players—including Woods, Duval, and O'Meara—

was defeated, under a format that eliminated each player who lost a match with a sole opponent. The $1 million first prize was eventually won by Jeff Maggert, who began the week ranking twenty-fourth and along the way bested both Woods (number one) and Nick Price (number nine).

Maggert proved that the top players in golf stand on a slippery pedestal and often fall. But this truth does not change the fact that at any given time, a handful of men will be the best. Snead, Nelson, and Hogan dominated their era. Then came Palmer, Nicklaus, and Player. Today about a dozen players—Woods, Duval, O'Meara, Els, Mickelson, etc.—are assumed to be so gifted that they might win any tournament. Below them exist fifty or so regulars who have proven, at least once, that they can do it. No one is surprised when they happen to take first place, but no one in this group ever begins play on Thursday as the favorite. This group includes the likes of Stewart Cink and Jeff Maggert and Bob Estes. J. P. Hayes joined them this year. All of the other members of the PGA Tour, including Esteban Toledo, occupy a place below. They have the talent, perhaps, but they have yet to show they possess the inner qualities to win.

What are these qualities? Ben Hogan believed that it was a Calvinistic commitment to practice. Arnold Palmer believed in daring and nerve. David Duval, who finished second seven times before getting his first win, clearly believed in himself. He told anyone who asked that he expected to win some day, and he did. Many pros speak earnestly of fate, luck, even God. What else could explain why the winner's errant shots always seem to get a lucky bounce? It happened this year when Fred Couples' ball—heading way out of bounds—struck a golf cart and ricocheted back onto the course. This bit of luck helped him win the Bob Hope Chrysler Classic. At the U.S. Open, Lee Janzen was spared a penalty when his lost ball was suddenly blown out of a tree by a friendly breeze. He went on to chip in for par and win the tournament.

Esteban believes in luck, but he also has created his own philosophy of winning drawn from all the golfer traditions. He accepts Hogan's challenge, and practices hard. Like Duval, he believes fervently that his innate talent will one day carry him to a championship. And he is also convinced that a certain spiritual element is involved. "When I am playing, I talk to God, and I talk to my father, not Jon, but my real father, who died. I ask him to help me."

•

In their differing attitudes, Esteban represents the heart's approach to the game, while Robert leads with his head. The distinction is not absolute, of course. Esteban manages the course intelligently. He's analytical, as well as emotional. "I know the holes I should attack and where I need to be careful," he says. But he is convinced that an element of magic is involved in winning. "It's inside of me. I know it. Someday it will come out."

At the tournament following Jackson—the CVS Classic in Sutton, Massachusetts—Esteban feels something stir in his heart. Though he had played terribly there in 1994, his last Tour season, he likes the Pleasant Valley Country Club course and the cool New England climate, especially compared to Mississippi in July. At a little over 7,000 yards, the course is not so long that big-hitters have an excessive advantage. Instead, it challenges players with hilly terrain, tight doglegs, and plenty of trees. Once a forest of mixed hardwoods and pine, Pleasant Valley demands smart play and punishes any lapse in concentration. Hole number 15, for example, confronts players with a stream exactly where a drive would land and a sloping green that rests high atop a hill. It's not unusual for a pro to hit a second shot that falls a few yards short and rolls back, literally, to their feet. Many players, Hogan included, have simply hit two seven irons, so they could stay out of the creek off the tee, and then land their second shots far enough back on the green to save them from rolling off, and back down the hill.

Esteban welcomes the challenge of a narrow and tricky course, but most of all he's pleased by the greens here. They are made of mature bentgrass. This type of grass, grown almost exclusively in the northern half of the country, can be made into a tight, slick surface. It gives under the weight of the rolling ball, providing a smooth trip to the hole. The main benefit of the other type of grass used for greens—Bermuda grass—is that it won't die under the Southern sun. Unfortunately, a putt stroked on a Bermuda green will roll across the tops of the blades. Along the way it is more likely to bump and swerve with the grain. Given the choice, Esteban would never putt on a Bermuda green again.

At the Pleasant Valley Country Club, Esteban also finds a place where the PGA Tour will soon leave behind a longtime partner as it strides into a richer future. The Tour first visited here for the Carling Open in 1965. It was the

richest tournament of the year—the purse was $200,000—
and it was won by Tony Lema. Pleasant Valley went on to
recruit eight different sponsors in thirty-three years. Some
of the greatest players in the modern game have won
here, including Palmer, Billy Casper, Bruce Devlin, and
Ray Floyd. The runners-up have included have Jack Nicklaus, Fuzzy Zoeller, Greg Norman, and Phil Mickelson. As
the nearest tournament site for PGA Tour fans in four
states, Pleasant Valley has always drawn large galleries.
Through it all, the Mingolla family, who owned the club,
ran the tournament with a homey style.

But at the start of year, Tour officials began to hint that
certain tournaments would have to offer more money,
and perhaps accept second-rate dates in order to stay on
the schedule. The CVS drugstore chain was willing to double the small purse at Pleasant Valley to $3 million. But
after three decades of loyal partnership with the Tour, the
Mingolla family wouldn't accept the demand that they
hold their tournament the week before, or the week after
the British Open. There is, perhaps, no worse time to conduct a tournament in the United States. Top players are
either preparing to leave for Great Britain or on their way
home, staggered by jet lag. Few, if any, would go to play in
Massachusetts.

In choosing to end their tournament rather than
diminish it, the Mingollas opened a place on the Tour
schedule that was seized by the Quad City Classic, which
would change its name to the John Deere Classic. The
Mingollas also earned universal praise in New England.
Though the Boston area was losing its only PGA Tour
stop, the press supported the family and painted the Tour

as a villain. The Boston Globe called it The Machine. Many players expressed similar sentiments. Blaine McCallister, winner in 1989, said, "I'm very disappointed in the PGA Tour."

•

When the CVS Classic starts, the competition holds true to expectations. In the absence of the big name players who were recuperating from the British Open, a couple of lesser-known pros, Willie Wood and P. H. Horgan III, share first place with rounds of 64 at the end of the first day of play. Never a winner, Horgan has played on and off the Big Tour since 1989. He is definitely a member of the Tour's lower caste. Wood had dwelt there, too, for thirteen years, before breaking through with a victory in Jackson in 1996.

Nothing in Esteban's play suggests he will be any kind of threat to the leaders. He makes the cut on Friday, but just barely. That day, local favorite Paul Azinger's score of 65, moves him to second, one shot behind Springer. Willie Wood stumbles to third. On Saturday, Esteban's 68 still doesn't move him out the middle ranks. Sunday dawns with Steve Pate, Dave Stockton, Jr., Scott Hoch, and Wood all contending to win. Esteban is forty-third. At this rate he'll earn $5,550. He will inch closer to keeping his card for next year, but after paying taxes, travel expenses, and Robert's salary he will be lucky to net $1,500.

As they prepare for an early tee time that would guarantee they would not appear on the television broadcast, Esteban asks Robert a playful question.

"Should we shoot an 80, or a 64, today?"

"I'd prefer 64," says Robert.

"Alright. Let's do it."

On the front nine, Esteban makes two birdies by knocking the ball close to the hole and one-putting. The other holes he plays at par. It's a nice beginning, but hardly the kind of front nine that suggests he'll get down to 64, especially when you consider that the back nine is much more challenging than the front. But he's starting to hope that he'll play well enough to move up to thirtieth, or maybe twentieth place.

Then on number 12, he rolls in a fifteen-foot putt—the longest he has made all week—for another birdie. He makes an even longer birdie putt on the next hole, and then plays very smart golf on number 15. On this hole, a big hitter might think seriously about trying to drive the green, which is only about 350 yards from the tee. Tiger Woods could do it. So could John Daly and half a dozen others.

But as mentioned, number 15 is a siren that invites a golfer to disaster. Trees shield the flag from the wind. Without the fluttering fabric, players have trouble gauging the prevailing breeze, which blows back at the tee, often strong enough to smother a drive. The wind can blow a ball back as much as forty yards into a bunker or heavy rough.

Refusing to be suckered, Esteban lays up with a three wood and then faces the green from a point 135 yards away. "It's better long," warns Robert, who is worried about bunkers that protect the front of the putting surface. "Get it up there and give yourself a chance to make the putt."

An eight iron carries the ball to the back of the green, where it safely stays put. One putt later, Esteban has another birdie. Coming off the green, his playing partner, Craig Parry, remembers that he was with Esteban in Atlanta for his great finish at the BellSouth Classic. "I guess you like playing with me, don't you?" he jokes.

With three holes to play, Esteban would need three straight birdies for a 64. Making all three seems quite reasonable to him at this moment. For the first time in weeks he's making long putts. Each success is adding to his confidence.

Why this is happening now is a bit of a mystery, even to Esteban. "It's like I know the ball is going to go in when I step up to it," he'll tell me later. "I don't know why my game is working—maybe it's the practice—but I don't know why it's paying off right now. It just is, and it feels great."

The sixteenth hole is a straightforward, 200-yard par-three that offers players a break from the trickery of Pleasant Valley's back nine. Esteban is starting to feel as if his body and mind are capable of landing a golf ball anywhere he pleases. On the tee, he notices a number of reporters and photographers have come out to walk in with him. They had obviously watched the red numbers—red for scores under par—line up beside Esteban's name on the scoreboard in the press room.

Esteban can imagine the four iron that he's holding in his hand sending the ball to the pin. And that's just what it does. He lands it ten yards short and watches it roll within two feet. For a moment he thinks it will go into the hole. It doesn't, but the putt is automatic.

After the round, Robert would tell me, "He got pretty excited on 16. I mean, that's a long way for him to hit a four iron, but he was pumped up. He had a smile on his face like I hadn't seen since Atlanta."

A deceptive and watery par-four, hole number 17 is Pleasant Valley's signature hole. A creek separates the tee from the first cut of fairway. Facing a mild dogleg bend to the right, players must make a second shot over a pond. Forest lines both sides of the narrow fairway. The sheer mass of the woods, especially on the right-hand side, seems to have a magnetic effect on the mind and on golf balls.

"One year, Fuzzy Zoeller hit his driver the first day and went in the woods," recalls Ted Mingolla, owner of Pleasant Valley. "The next day he hit a two iron, to be safe, and that went in too. On the weekend he went down to a three iron and still couldn't keep it out of the trees. He went in on both Saturday and Sunday. It's that kind of hole. Very difficult. The gallery there is huge, and there's always a lot of action."

On this Sunday, the gallery has been watching the name "Toledo" climb up the electronic leader board all day. The players who started the day well ahead of him are just beginning their rounds. They haven't had time to lower their scores further. This means that for the moment, Esteban is in third place, and it looks like he might be in contention to win. He knows this is an illusion. The frontrunners will make their own birdies and pull away, long after he's finished. Nevertheless, the gallery greets Esteban like he's a true contender making a charge. They cheer him after his tee shot—a three wood—floats high and straight, landing about seventy yards short of the pond, left of center.

Up by the clubhouse, Colleen arrives to watch her husband play the finishing hole. She's been away all day, shopping at the local mall for maternity clothes and baby gear. She's shocked to see her husband's name high on the leaderboard.

Standing in the fairway, Bob and Esteban look up at the green. They easily pick Colleen out of the crowd, because she's wearing a red, white, and black dress. For a moment Esteban is distracted, then he focuses on his shot. Before him looms the steep embankment that could send the ball bouncing and then rolling back toward them and into the pond. Esteban decides that a nine iron will plunk the ball safely on the putting surface. Robert is afraid that with this club, the ball won't fly far enough and will tumble back into the drink. He touches the eight iron. Esteban nods, takes it in his hands, and sends the ball onto the green. It lands behind the pin, and spins backward to within ten feet. He makes the birdie putt look too easy. A four on the 583-yard finishing hole yields exactly the score Esteban predicted he would make—a seven-under-par 64.

On the green, Esteban raises his hand to acknowledge the cheer that ends his round. At the end of the day, this marvelous run—five birdies on the final seven holes—will land him in a tie for seventh place. Steve Pate will win, despite hooking three shots in a row into the rough on his finishing hole.

Esteban doesn't know exactly how much he will make at Pleasant Valley, but he's certain he has secured his card. He thinks about his brothers in Mexico, whom he will call from the locker room, and about his sister who needs hearing aids that she cannot afford. He decides that he will send her the money for them right away. "Sometimes my mind just goes to the people I'm from, to that place," he'll explain later. "I can't explain it. It's just the way it is."

The Toledos have tickets on an afternoon flight from Boston to Memphis, the next tournament site, and they are anxious to make it to the plane. After signing his scorecard, Esteban must wade through a crowd of children who want his autograph—no one is refused—and a handful of sports reporters who know very little about him. Pressed to make his flight, Esteban can only answer a few questions. The reporters all want to know how he put together such a great run of birdies.

"I started believing in myself," he says.

Colleen doesn't realize that Esteban has reached his goal—clinching his card for the next year—until they are halfway to Logan airport. That's when they figure out that he will get a $43,650 check, which will move him past the $230,000 mark, and into fifty-third on the money list. There will be no ceremony at greenside to mark this event, no champagne will be uncorked. When they reach Memphis, they will have a nice dinner at a Mexican restaurant. And after Memphis, Esteban will take two weeks off, for a vacation and visit with a friend of Colleen's who lives in Alaska. This will be the sum total of the victory celebration.

Anticlimactic as it seems, this is how it usually happens. Grinders who secure their cards almost always do it gradually, piling one check onto another until they finally cross the threshold. Days after the accomplishment, Esteban reveals a heart that's filled with pride and a just a little macho satisfaction. "I'm getting comfortable around the other players," he says. "When I'm on the first tee, I feel like going toe-to-toe with these guys. C'mon, let's do it!"

This success has also brought Robert a feeling of pride. He measures his progress not in dollars, but in his relationship with his boss. Esteban will never be generous with his praise. So Robert looks for a subtler kind of feedback. He thinks he saw it in Massachusetts. "When I recommended a club, gave him the yardage, or told him what was necessary on a hole, he just didn't question it," he reports. "He has never had a caddie he trusts. Now I think he does, and he knows it."

Robert is also convinced that his counsel is beginning to influence Esteban's temperament. All season long, he's been telling Esteban that bad shots happen to every player, and that he must forget each one. "I started it on the Nike Tour last year," he explains. "I could tell he was a good player, but his body language showed how he was taking every bad break and making it worse in his head. I remind him that before he goes for birdies, he's got to make sure he avoids bogeys. Stay in the right frame of mind, and you can do it. He's got the heart to be there on Sunday and grab the opportunity. But he has to play smart."

Heart and head. The right blend of emotion and intelligence may be the magic ingredient that makes for success on the golf course. The important word here is success, not winning. Knowing the difference is the key to sanity for the vast majority of Tour pros, those who start every Thursday knowing they are not expected to win. In team sport, athletes can expect to win half of the time. Even in tennis, the other major solo game, players can at least enjoy the rush of beating an opponent in the early stages of a tournament. There may be just one champion, but tennis tournaments offer daily opportunities for winning.

This is not true in golf. Depending on the tournament format, every week Esteban knows that eighty, 100, or 160-plus players will lose. Only one will win. In fact, a good many PGA Tour players begin and end their careers without ever winning at all. And everyone on Tour understands that most of the time, the same handful of top competitors are really holding their own tournament-within-a-tournament at the high end of the leaderboard. Week after week it's the same group of names. All the others play in the hope that a brief flash of luck and brilliance will propel them into this group. This is what happened to Esteban in Atlanta.

A Tour caddie, who spoke only on the condition that he would not be named, once told me that this one fact of Tour life—the odds against an average player winning—explains why "most of them are dickheads." He went on to explain that he finds most of the players to be self-centered, arrogant, and socially inept. "I think it's a reaction to feeling impotent on the golf course," he said. "I mean, Tiger and Duval and the other top players are nice and friendly to them, but when they get on the course, everyone knows who really has a chance."

Ironically, the fact that so many PGA Tour golfers will never win it all may also explain why golf fans feel they can relate so directly to the Tour experience. Most play the game themselves and they know how difficult it is. But more important is the fact that winning is just as elusive in real life as it is on the PGA Tour. How many valedictorians are chosen at school? How many corporate managers become presidents of their companies? How many actors become box office stars?

In real life, most of us must find a way to be happy and satisfied—in a word, successful—without ever actually winning a championship. So it is for Tour golfers. They all must at least mouth a commitment to winning. For most, this dream is real. They are competitive men, after all, and the entire premise of the show they put on every week depends on the desire to win. But the players who know, deep down, that they may never hold a trophy on Sunday afternoon must find a way to accept this role. If they do not learn to define success in their own terms, and place their desire to win in the proper context, they will be forever dickheads.

In clinching his Tour card for next year, Esteban has become a success on his own terms. He has proved that he belongs on the Big Tour and that his ascent at Q. School was no fluke. He he has earned an income greater than he could have ever imagined. He has a home, a loving family, and a baby on the way. He likes to talk about winning, and the desire is real. But he knows he is already a success, and this is what make him one of the few down-to-earth men on Tour.

●

Knowing Esteban's philosophy still doesn't prepare me for his final word on the whole matter of winning and success. He reveals this during a late-night talk at yet another look-alike hotel in another in the endless series of Tour

stops. His view is idiosyncratic to the point of being downright romantic. He would make Cervantes proud.

"If I win," he tells me, "I will probably quit right then."

"You mean take some time off?" I say.

"No. I mean quit. Walk away."

"You're not serious."

"Listen, D'Antonio, what is there after winning? I mean,
if I win on the PGA Tour, that means I have beaten the
best. I will know that I can do it. I would be satisfied and
move on."

"Don't you want to stay in it as long as you can? I mean,
think about the money. Everyone else wants to keep
going, to win majors, to be famous, be millionaires."

"I'm not like those guys. Maybe I can't explain it to you.
But you've been to where I came from. You saw how poor
it was, how bad it was. That was not a place where I had
anything. There was no one there to love me. I just took
care of myself. My goal was to get to the PGA Tour, to stay
there and maybe win. If I do that, I think I'd like to maybe
open a driving range so I can go home and be with my
wife every night and raise my children."

"Do other players know this? Does Bob?"

"If I start saying this, people will never understand it.
They don't know the way I feel. I'm a simple guy. I have a
goal. If I get there, that will be enough for me. I would
have my health. People would respect me. I would have
my family and they would be secure. What more could I
want?"

THE SCORECARD

Remaining tournaments	8
Esteban's earnings	$240,758
Rank	53rd

11.

A Tour of His Own ○

While Esteban vacations in Alaska, enjoying a cool reward for reaching his goal, the top Tour players gather at Sahalee Country Club near Seattle for the final major of the year, the PGA Championship. Esteban refuses to torture himself by sitting down in front of a TV to watch, stroke by stroke, as Vijay Singh fends off Steve Stricker, Steve Elkington, Nick Price, and Mark O'Meara to win. Instead he loses himself in his family and the quiet of a country cabin. The most exciting thing he'll see this week is a moose cow and her calf emerging from the nearby woods to graze.

In their very different experiences between August 10 and August 16, Esteban and the PGA Championship contenders exemplify the athlete as independent contractor. Every PGA Tour player makes a solitary journey through the season, following, literally, a Tour of his own. (Probably the last time this wasn't true was in the 1940s and 1950s when some players still drove the tour together in caravans.) So far this year, Esteban has ground through twenty-one PGA Tour events, attended more than a dozen Monday pro-ams, competed in two Nike tournaments and even played once in Mexico to make extra money.

Among the top finishers at Sahalee, none, not even the hard-working Singh, has played as much this year as Esteban. Two of them—Nick Price and Mark O'Meara— have turned up at just fifteen tournaments. It's safe to assume that none of these players has attended a single Monday pro-am, and it's certain they didn't enter a Nike tournament.

As sole practitioners, Tour players also have idiosyncratic lives away from their on-the-course competitions. Friends, family, sponsors, agents, instructors, and others form a tailor-made universe. Tiger Woods leaves the course to attended the opening of the newest All Star Cafe in South Carolina. Steve Elkington rushes off to work on an instructional book for a major publisher.

In the aftermath of his success, Esteban Toledo's little universe is being filled, in part, by Hispanic golf fans and young Mexican-American amateurs who want him to be their Tiger Woods. A few now appear at every tournament, even the Bell Canadian Open, outside Toronto. They crowd around him for autographs and shout at him in Spanish.

The Canadian tournament comes in the second week in September, a time when the hardwood forests outside

Toronto are beginning to turn red and gold, and the cool, dry nights make the fairways at Glen Abbey Golf Club firm and fast. Esteban likes the weather, and he is in good spirits even after an opening round of 76. He has made more than enough money to keep his card, and he's determined to enjoy himself. On Thursday night he shares dinner with fellow grinder Keith Nolan, and then they go to see the movie *Something About Mary.*

On Friday, Esteban is still laughing about some of the more grotesque scenes in the film and still enjoying himself on the golf course, even as the possibility of making the cut slips away. As I watch him move down the fairway, dressed in a white shirt, and black and white checked pants, he seems somehow younger and more alive that he did in midsummer.

Esteban's playing partners, journeymen pros Donnie Hammond and Mike Heinan, are no closer to making the cut and their round together takes on the feeling of a friendly golf outing. On the fifth hole, Hammond listens in as Esteban tells Robert he's going to aim for a little tree 260 yards out because he'll never actually hit it. Of course, he does hit it, and Hammond can't resist a grin, and then a chuckle.

With his chances dwindling, Esteban starts to experiment with his driver. On the ninth hole, a par-four of almost 460 yards, he unleashes one of the longest drives he has hit all year—a wind-assisted 320-yard rocket. It comes to a stop in the rough, which makes it difficult for Esteban to land his second shot softly on the green. He gets it to stick, but it's thirty feet from the hole. Three putts later, he's seen his long soaring drive yield a thor-

oughly unspectacular bogey. As the group makes the clubhouse turn, they are clearly three guys going nowhere.

For most of the back nine, Esteban, Heinan, and
Hammond believe they are already out of the tournament. But on the fifteenth hole they learn that some of
the leaders have slipped, and it looks like the cutline will
be four over par, a relatively high score. Suddenly, they
all realize they could still play for money on the weekend.
Esteban could make it with three birdies, and he decides
to give it his all.

On the sixteenth tee, he hits another drive as hard as he
can. This one also goes about 300 yards. But it drifts right,
into a grove of stubby pines, where it rattles around for a
few seconds before settling beneath the branches. From
where he stands on the tee, it looks like he may be
stymied.

At 516 yards, the par-five number 16 is the second-
longest hole on the course, and the grove of pines
where the ball rests is well over 220 yards from the front
of the green. A few spectators run to the ball and find it
resting on hard, dried, rutted mud. It lies on the far side
of the trees, which are now between the ball and the
green. When Esteban arrives he greets them all cheer-
fully.

"What do you recommend?" he asks a young boy.

"I think you should go for it," he says.

"So do I," he replies.

He asks Bob for the driver and stands to look at the
shot. He's so close to the trees that he cannot go over
them. He'll have to start the ball out very low, perhaps
three feet off the ground, to get through them. Even if he

manages this, the green lies uphill, with bunker all around. He'll have to cut the ball to get it going in the right direction, and hope it rolls, and rolls.

He takes his stance, and then thinks better of trying to hit a driver off the hardpan. He hands the club back to Bob and asks for the five wood. It's got a shorter shaft, which should make it easier for him to clip the ball off this rock-hard piece of earth. He settles in again. But now the five wood doesn't seem right. It has too much loft to make a low shot, and it won't send the ball far enough. So he asks again for the driver.

By this time the crowd has tripled, to about fifteen people, and Esteban is laughing with them about his indecision. Robert, who is not smiling, holds his hand up to ask for quiet.

"Okay, let's do it," says Esteban.

In the silence, he draws the club back and makes a powerful, low move toward the ball. I can almost feel the spectators tense their own muscles, straining to help him. The club strikes cleanly, and the ball flies out under the tree branches. It screams through the air, at shoulder height, for 190 yards. As it gets further from when Esteban stands, the ball becomes a tiny, white dot traveling so fast that when it lands, the slightly left-to-right spin he's put on it is overpowered by the forward velocity. It skips up to the green, curving gently to the right as it slows. When the ball makes it onto the putting surface, it keeps rolling to within about twenty feet of the pin.

The people in the little crowd in the pine groves scream and applaud. They can't make as much noise as a Sunday gallery on the finishing hole, but they loudly acknowledge they have seen something special. Out on the fairway, Donnie Hammond is astonished. Unwilling to wait for Esteban to reach him, he trots over and offers the kind gleeful high five you expect to see on a basketball court.

Looking down at the spot where the ball had once been, I noticed that Esteban had hit it so cleanly that the earth was hardly scratched. Picking the ball off the ground like that with a driver is not easy to do. Then I recalled a little story Jon Minnis had told me about walking with Esteban from the Summit Pointe golf course into the hills and pasture above. Along the way they found a crack driver that someone had hurled into the brush, and half a dozen balls. On the crest of a hill, Jon spotted a fairly fresh cow pie, just crusted over. He challenged Esteban to hit a ball off the crust without splattering what lurked an eighth of an inch below. He did it not once, but six times. "And they were pretty good drives, too," said Jon.

Here at the Canadian Open, Esteban's pick doesn't produce an eagle, but he does score a birdie. In a perfect world, he would score two more on the last two holes, qualify for weekend play, and go on to grab a big paycheck. But one supremely entertaining shot does not a round make. The two finishing holes at Glen Abbey have ruined many front-runners on Sunday, and they show Esteban no mercy on this Friday. A par and a bogie leave him on the wrong side of the cut, along with Hammond and Heinen.

Bob Friend has a much better week in Canada. Friend actually leads the tournament for much of the weekend, only to lose in a dramatic playoff to Billy Andrade. The second-place finish is his best ever on the PGA Tour. It earns him more than $237,000. Without this one perform-ance, Friend would have failed to keep his card.

At dinner on Friday night, Esteban's heart is already on the way home to California for a week with his family in the new home he has barely seen. In the quiet, his mind reverts to a subject—his remarkable journey through life—that always seems to be in his thoughts. "I used to get up at five in the morning to go pick cotton. Now I get up early to go play golf for thousands of dollars and maybe in front of millions of people watching TV." The spectators may marvel when he uses a driver to hit the ball off an impossible lie to a green 200 yards away, but few can appreciate how this man has propelled himself through life.

"You know, the last time I was in Mexico I went into that restaurant where I stole the chicken dinner and then washed dishes to pay for it," he says. "I still remember the way it felt back then. I am still that same Esteban Toledo, not a pro golfer but a person trying to survive. Sometimes I can't believe, myself, what can happen when you just keep trying. I think that's what I can share with people. Not just golf. But I don't know if anyone realizes that. I am the same Esteban Toledo. Just like them."

●

With its huge Mexican-American population, San Anto-nio's interest in a golfer named Toledo runs high. Even before play begins at the Texas Open, the local paper makes sure that the fans there know about Esteban. A fea-ture article describes his long climb to the Tour, and gen-erates enough publicity to draw a big crowd to an exhibition and clinic Esteban will conduct for Hispanic youth. The event has been organized by PAGA, the Pan-American Golf Association, and will be held at a public course in the middle of urban San Antonio. It's called Brackenridge Park Golf Course.

Today, Brackenridge is a scruffy little golf course that sits in a city park in the shadow of a noisy freeway. Hidden among factories, warehouses, and rows of dilapidated little houses, Brackenridge is difficult to find. Once you have, it's difficult to conjure its old glories. The only clue to its illustrious past is the graceful, Tudor-style stone clubhouse, which remains unchanged from when it was built, in 1915.

The "Brack" was the first eighteen-hole, championship-caliber course in Texas, and when it was built it graced a large greenbelt park in the heart of San Antonio. With its many old pecan trees and the San Antonio River slicing through four fairways, Brackenridge was once considered one of the three best public courses in the nation. Designed by A. W. Tillinghast—who also designed Winged Foot, Inverness, and Baltusrol—the 6,185-yard course became the home of the first big-money tournament in golf, the $5,000 Alamo Open. A Scot named Bob MacDonald won the first tournament, Walter Hagen the second. Thus began a tradition that saw the greats of every era through the 1950s play and win here. Most were accompanied by Hispanic caddies. It's doubtful that any of them knew the course had been built by prisoners, most whom were also Mexican-born.

The PGA Tour was last hosted by Brackenridge in 1959, before it moved to longer, lusher pastures. The interstate built in the 1970s carved off portions of several holes, requiring a redesign of the entire layout. The city restricted maintenance, and the course grew shabbier than it had been in its glory days. But it offered local people, and especially youngsters, access to a sport that they otherwise would have never known. It also became the informal home course for PAGA, which operates out of a low-slung little house that sits beside the entrance to the course.

Esteban enters the dark clubhouse bar from the blinding light of the parking lot and needs a moment for his eyes to adjust. Gradually he begins to see a place that is one part bar, one part shrine to golfers with Spanish surnames. Old clubs and trophies are displayed. Pictures of every prominent Hispanic player who ever set foot on a U.S. course hang on the walls.

As Esteban blinks, an old man named Ernie Garcia puts down his longneck beer bottle and rises from his chair to shake his hand. Ernie explains that he was Byron Nelson's caddie for half a dozen Texas Opens. He points to a picture showing him with Byron. Near that picture is a row of photos signed by other beloved visitors to the club: Lee Trevino, Roberto DeVincenzo, Ben Hogan, Jimmy Demeret, Robert Gamez, and now, Esteban Toledo. The club president, Jesse Garza, leads Esteban from table to table, to shake hands with weatherbeaten men who greet him like fond uncles. "I am proud to be here," he tells them. "Thank you."

After he signs a guest book, Esteban is escorted back to Brackenridge. A couple of dozen young players and their parents crowd around him on the putting green. He selects a small child from the crowd, stands him on the grass near the green, and puts a ball down, about two feet from his toes. With the boy giggling and a few onlookers gasping, he takes a wedge and makes a sweeping swing that sends the ball straight up and then over the child's head.

With the crowd warming up, Esteban proceeds to the first tee and demonstrates fades, draws, and low and high shots. He does a remarkable imitation of Lee Trevino's unusual swing and then puts on a little display of power. He loses a bit of his accuracy, but the kids are delighted to see balls fly so far and so high that they lose sight of them.

As he shows what he can do with the golf club, Esteban also tries to motivate the kids with a little inspirational talk. He starts out nervous and overly polite. He introduces everyone from PAGA, his caddie, and even the writer who has tagged along. But then he starts telling his life story, and he begins to relax. He knows the message he wants to deliver. He holds an almost religious belief in the power of dreams and the virtue of hard work. He considers himself proof that the combination is almost unstoppable.

"I am not going to lie. Life is wonderful for me on the PGA Tour," he says, smiling broadly. "But I am more proud of the fact that I came from the other side of the river, the place where they don't have a golf course. That's where I was born, in a place much poorer than you have ever seen. One of the only things I remember from being very young was my father telling me, 'If you want to be somebody, prepare and work hard and you will make it.' It worked. I went from riding my little beat-up bike around

Mexicali to being picked up in a Mercedes Benz. The same thing can happen to you, no matter what kind of dream you have."

The audience listens, but what they really want is golf, so Esteban quickly calls for the two girls who will be his playing partners for three exhibition holes. One of the girls, Christie Cano, lives in the poor neighborhood that surrounds Brackenridge. Not yet a high-school sophomore, she can already drive the ball 225 yards and has managed to post a 64 on this course. She plays in cheap black sneakers and offers only a shy, uncertain smile. But when she hits the ball, Esteban applauds and announces, "She's the next Nancy Lopez."

Esteban is clearly moved by the sight of so many admiring faces. Some of the questions and comments he hears are spoken in Spanish, and he moves fluidly from one language to the other. Far from the pressures of PGA Tour competition, and the bland personalities of most of his fellow pros, Esteban feels as if he's among family. "You know, if I win the trophy, I promise I will leave it here with you guys," he says before departing.

"We love you Esteban, brother," answers a man in the crowd.

•

The love-fest will continue throughout the Texas Open, which is now played at a flashy course called La Cantera. *Telemundo*—a TV network that serves the entire Spanish-speaking world—grabs Esteban for an interview. The local paper publisher an article about the boxer-turned-golfer. And a large group of Mexican-American friends insists on taking Esteban to a homestyle restaurant where they crowd around a table loaded with burritos and quesadillas and overwhelm him with questions.

Some of these men knew Esteban before he became a success. A few even competed against him in minor tournaments. They too had dreamed of a life on the PGA Tour, but their dreams had not come true. In an unguarded moment, one of these men, Tom Garcia, admits that he feels a bit jealous that he lacked Esteban's raw willpower. "I've never been hungry like him," says Garcia, who is American-born. "I was never so driven. I mean, when I was a kid I didn't have to sleep on the golf course to be ready to caddie in the morning. His mentality was like a boxer's. You never think about quitting. I tried, but I didn't give it everything, and then I quit."

For a brief time in the early 1990s, Garcia actually functioned as Esteban's agent. But when the rookie player failed in 1994, the rookie agent did as well. Nevertheless, that experience gave Garcia a perspective on Esteban that few can know. "During that first year on the Tour he was so polite to everyone. He called people 'Sir' and tried to fit in by being extra-nice. On the golf course he was tentative, not confident.

"This time, he's very different," says Garcia. "I mean, he walks around the course like he belongs there with the other pros, and he hits the ball with more confidence. It goes higher, and further. He's much better with his long irons. The confidence shows."

When Esteban hears this kind of admiring talk, he understands it is sometimes tinged with jealousy. All professional athletes—indeed all successful people—must accept the ambivalent reactions of old friends and competitors who fell short of their own dreams. But here, in San Antonio, Esteban is also confronted with the complexities of being an international player connected to another country's golf establishment. The Texas Open is a favorite for Mexican fans and young Mexican pros who are eager to make the jump to the U.S. tour. As usual, half a dozen have either succeeded at qualifying tournaments or received sponsor exemptions to play in the tournament.

In the clubhouse dining room at the La Cantera resort, two of these young Mexicans, Juan Ortega and Alex Quiroz, take pains to show Esteban respect. Quiroz, from Cuernavaca, is the son of a longtime professional golfer. Ortega is a gifted athlete from Mexico City who just took up the game five years ago. They say that Esteban is a controversial figure among Mexican pros. Some admire him and want to follow in his footsteps. Others have trouble understanding how someone from the poor lower class— meaning someone with brown skin and Indian blood— made it in a gentleman's game.

"Golf is very different back home," says Ortega. Though he is a pale, blue-eyed young man who speaks with the Castilian accent of the aristocracy, Ortega is critical of the class barriers in Mexican golf. "It's very, very expensive and there are no public courses or driving ranges. A few people think they really own the game, for themselves. Esteban proves that they don't and it really gets to them. But I love it. It makes me feel like it's possible for me, too."

•

Buoyed by the attention he is receiving, Esteban is more lighthearted with his fellow pros, too. On the first day of play, he's paired with Jim McGovern, one of the few men on Tour who always seems to be smiling. McGovern is grinning by the end of the day, after shooting a 66 and claiming a slice of second place. Mired in 178th place on the Tour money list, with just $94,697 in earnings, McGovern needs to make a lot of money fast if he's going to keep his card. Working alongside him, Esteban cards a more-than-respectable 69 on a course where the thick Bermuda rough demands players keep the ball in the fairway.

After the round, Esteban takes to the practice green where he fools around by hitting a ball against the slope of the green and trying to make it roll back to his feet. McGovern, who is almost giddy with his success, grabs an empty basket from the driving range and tries to catch some of Esteban's pitches. He calls every fellow pro on the green "brother" and brags a bit about being summoned into the media tent for an interview after his round.

McGovern is not the only one who feels a sense of relief on this warm Texas afternoon. The Texas Open is one of those low-purse, late-season events that draws few major competitors and therefore offers an opening to the usual also-rans. Nine of the top ten are skipping it. Their absence means fewer reporters, less pressure, and more laughs.

On the driving range, Esteban practices making left-handed shots by turning his seven iron around. He manages to poke half a dozen shots onto a green that's 100 yards away. Beside him, Tour rookie Keith Nolan, a twenty-six-year-old from Ireland, tees the golf ball on a pencil, takes to his knees, and drives it more than 200 yards. Nolan, a Q.-Schooler who isn't anywhere close to keeping his card, is a pudgy fellow with a boyish face who has put on forty pounds during the Tour season. On his knees, choking up on a driver, he looks like a child in a man's body swinging a sawed-off club. Up and down the range, pros cease what they are doing start laughing.

Nolan needs the relief of such driving range follies. With just four tournaments left in the season, he's so far down on the money list that he needs either to win outright, or grab a couple of top-five finishes to play again next year. (In twenty-two tournaments, he has been cut eighteen times. He has earned less than $22,000 and is ranked at number 246.) But at least for the moment, Nolan can feel happy about his play. He matched Esteban's score, and is well positioned to make the cut. If he does make to Saturday, it will be for the first time in thirteen tournaments.

Mid-September finds about fifty serious competitors— men who have played in more than a dozen tournaments so far—ranked so far below the magic 125 mark that they would need at least a second-place finish to break that barrier. Among them is Iain Steel, who onced offered Bob Szczesny a job but then disappeared to the United Kingdom. While Esteban and Nolan play games on the range, Steel is practicing with a thick rubber strap around his knees. That kind of training aid, at this stage in the Tour season, is a sure sign of desperation. Of course, Steel shot 78 today, which would make any one of these players feel desperate.

Oddly enough, the fourteen Q. School grinders, including Esteban, are evenly split between desperation and satisfaction. Seven—Bob Friend, Jeff Gallagher, J. P. Hayes, Bradley Hughes, Tom Pernice, Lee Porter, and Esteban—have earned so much money that they are certain to keep their cards. And seven—Tim Conley, Lan Gooch, Steve Jurgenson, Tim Loustalot, John Riegger, Vance Veazey, and Mark Wurtz—must be considered long shots at best.

A few of those in the latter group still have a reasonable hope to succeed. Tim Loustalot is in the 141st position and could secure his card with a single showing in the top three. Conley, Jurgenson, and Riegger could do it with a similar performance, and another in the top ten. The remarkable thing about many of the players who dwell on the dark side of the cutline is the amount of effort they've expended for their meager results. John Riegger has played in twenty-three tournaments all over the country to make $113,505. Vance Veazey has gone to twenty-five events to earn $27,208.

And as always, there's Lan Gooch to consider. He's brought his pleasant personality and unreliable game to eighteen different PGA Tour cities and earned a grand total of $3,173. Here in Texas, he makes an 80 on the first day of play. It is his second worst round of the year; his worst was a score of 84 at the Western Open. To his credit, he had followed up that miserable experience with a Friday round of 71. He didn't make the cut, but in the heatwave conditions, and playing on a Cog Hill course that is as tough as any, it was a gritty performance worthy of a Tour pro.

On Friday in San Antonio, Lan is plumb out of grit. His playing partners—Mike Weir and Cameron Beckman—appear for their 9:15 a.m. starting time but Lan does not. Disgusted with his game, and tired of sympathetic looks, he has already left town and will be disqualified for failing to notify tournament officials that he has withdrawn. He will play in two more tournaments before the end of the year, but his game is so bad that he knows his season is over, and he is already groping for a way to think about his year on the PGA Tour. He's trying to decide whether this has been the best season of his life, or the worst.

In golfing terms, Lan Gooch's year on the PGA Tour has given him the equivalent of a graduate school education. "I thought I was pretty good off the tee, but I learned I don't drive the ball nearly well enough," he tells me. "Out here, if you miss the fairway at all, you land in rough that is really unplayable, for me, anyway. These other guys always keep the ball in play."

Lan says that almost everything about the brand of golf played on the PGA Tour is tougher than he knew. All of the golf courses are long and laid out to punish the smallest mistake. Almost all of the greens are fast and so hard that making the ball stick is a challenge every time. The hole positions seem to be selected by sadists. In comparison, the conditions of the courses he played in the past seemed downright forgiving.

"That may be why I hadn't gotten better over the years," he says. "I always played on courses where the par-fours were 380 yards: You could drive it in the rough and still put a sand wedge on the green and make a birdie. At the end of the day you don't think to yourself, 'Boy I've got to work on my driver. You think, 'I made a nice birdie there.' You never realize how poorly you are playing compared with these guys, who are the best."

They are the best, in every way, adds Gooch. Successful

PGA Tour players practice harder, and live more disciplined lives, right down to what they eat and how much they sleep. They are selfish, self-centered, and obsessed, he admits. And their egos won't allow much self-criticism or doubt. "I'm realistic enough to notice that I'm playing really bad, and I have only myself to blame," says Lan. "But maybe that type of realism is bad for a pro golfer. Maybe you have to have a much bigger ego, do everything for yourself, and believe you're always about to win, no matter how badly you are playing. Maybe the problem is I'm too realistic to think like that."

●

While Lan goes home to Mississippi, Keith Nolan falls back to Earth, failing to break par and tumbling out of the tournament. He won't earn a penny this week. Neither will Iain Steel, despite a 69. But five of the grinder desperadoes— Wurtz, Riegger, Loustelot, Jurgenson, and Veazey—will play through the weekend. So will Esteban and McGovern, who lost a stroke to par, but made the cut.

With his hopes still intact, John Riegger seems about as serious as a Sunday morning leader at the Masters. When we bump into each other on the back porch of the clubhouse, he squints in the bright sunlight and insists that he can still leap over forty-five other players on the money list and grab spot number 125 at season's end. "It didn't help that I had the flu last week and the week before," he says. He does look like he's lost weight. "But I can do it. I know I can. Just watch," he says gamely.

Riegger plays well, but not well enough. He finishes the tournament seven shots out of first place and makes a little under $20,000. With two fewer strokes, he would have doubled his money. Nevertheless, he does gain ground in his pursuit of his 1999 Tour Card, jumping ten whole places, to number 160. McGovern makes similar progress, moving from 178, to 169. Both players still have a long way to go.

Esteban plays steadily, shooting 69, 72, 70, 69. He finishes in thirty-seventh place and makes a little more than $7,000. He won't deliver a trophy to the Pan-American Golf Association. (The tournament is won, instead, by Hal Sutton.) But Esteban's play is an improvement over the previous three weeks. And his Mexican-American fan club stays with him to the end. They cheer almost every shot he makes, and whisper curses to hex the other players so their hero can climb higher on the leader board. Their favorite curse is the phrase *sangre de chango,* which means "blood of the monkey." Whispered over and over—"sangre de chango, sangre de chango"—it's supposed to force bad luck on the accursed. At the Texas Open, it leads to a lot of giggling.

Perhaps the only person around Esteban who is not laughing this week is Robert Szczesny. He has worked especially hard this week, because the weather has been warm and La Cantera may be the most difficult course—from a caddie's perspective—on the entire Tour. La Cantera means "the quarry," and the course was carved out of a huge abandoned rock mine. Many of the holes have elevated tees and greens, which require that the caddies tote their loads up and down steep slopes. A prime example is the 125-foot drop in elevation between the number 1 tee and the fairway. Life is made more difficult for the caddies by the fact that getting from the green of one hole to the tee of the next often involves a rather long walk, uphill. The distance between the ninth green and tenth hole is so great that the Tour allows players to be driven in chauffeured golf carts.

Total exhaustion could account, at least in part, for Bob's sober mood. This week his face is showing all of his forty-seven years. His shoulders are drooping a bit more than usual, and his step is slower. But in truth, Robert is more worried than tired. One afternoon after Esteban finishes play at La Cantera, he sits under a shade tree and explains why.

"It all started after the Alaska vacation," he says. Esteban played a round with Paul Stankowski. Stankowski is fourteen spots behind Esteban on the money list, but he drives ball, on average, fifteen yards further. Robert is afraid that Esteban was too much impressed by his playing partner's power.

"Paul had four two-putts for birdies and shot a 65 the day we played with him," recalls Bob. "The very next week, Esteban got a new driver from Taylor Made and tried to hit the hell out of it. He shoots a seventy-four." The following week, in Toronto, Esteban also struggled with the driver, and again missed the cut.

"It used to be that we accepted the fact that we weren't going to reach a lot of those par-fives in two shots," says Robert. "The others guys can do it, but we can't." (In fact, Esteban has made just three eagles on par-five holes all year, 137th on Tour.) "We have to be smart. He's never going to win out here, no matter how hard he works, if he doesn't understand what he can do and what he can't do. I'm worried it's going to get worse before it gets better."

•

Now that September has arrived and the school year has begun, Esteban is not traveling with Colleen and Nicholas. He is free to make his own schedule. On Sunday, in San Antonio, he agrees to play a Monday pro-am in Arkansas and pick up some extra money before heading for Pine Mountain, Georgia, and a tournament called the Buick Challenge. Robert spends the day driving his car, which now has well over 200,000 miles, across the deep South, and fretting about the rain forecast for the Atlantic seaboard and about Esteban making a detour to Arkansas instead of grabbing a practice round at the Pine Mountain course. He's convinced Esteban does not need the money, and that he would benefit more from extra rest and practice.

The rain does come, making the fairways unplayable on Tuesday. Robert walks the course twice, once with a group of caddies checking yardages, and once with Esteban. When play starts for real, he and Esteban soon find themselves in an argument over distance. On the par-five seventh hole, Esteban is convinced that Robert underestimates the distance on his second shot by a good twenty-five yards. The ball lands in the rough, short of the green. Upset, Esteban next hits it into a bunker, and then over the green. He finally makes it onto the putting surface and scores an 8. As bad as things are, they are about to get worse.

"I was trying to stay away from him," Robert would recall later. "I just cleaned the ball and put it in his hand. I didn't know it was cut. he didn't see it, either."

On the green, a cut ball is likely to roll off course, no matter how well it is struck. Noticing this kind of damage is a cardinal rule for caddies. This mistake is too much for Esteban. Once again he feels that he's alone on the golf course without even his caddie for an ally. He two-putts, for a grand total of eight, and stalks to the next tee.

"You know Bob, I can do this myself," he says. And he does. For the next twelve holes, he refuses to say a word to his caddie. He doesn't ask for yardage, advice on the wind, or even a club. He simply waits until the bag is set on the turf, grabs the stick he wants, and goes at it. The result is a score of 75. Things don't get much better on Friday, and he misses the cut. For the third time in four weeks, he won't make a check.

It is ironic that Esteban and Robert would tumble to such a low point so soon after clinching their goal; the 1999 Tour Card. It is also typical of golf. No one stays perfectly happy for very long in this game. So it is with many players and caddies. The relationship requires immense patience. And the caddie must accept that he will be blamed when he is wrong, and when he is not wrong. The player must accept that he truly is alone, at least when he settles over the ball, and that even the best caddies make mistakes. The relationship also requires almost as much communication as a marriage.

In the highly emotional conversation that follows the breakdown at Pine Mountain, Robert insists he was right about the yardage he reported to Esteban, and refuses to back down. The matter of the cut ball is something different. It was a mistake, admits Robert. But he also reminds Esteban that he recently switched to a ball with a softer cover. It's a new product from Titleist, so new that it won't be available to the public for months.

"We never cut a ball all year," says Robert. "I never saw it happen before, so I guess I wasn't checking that carefully."

Before the conversation is finished, Robert seems to quit his job. "I don't want to be responsible for you not attaining your goal," he says. "You should find someone else."

"Bob, I'm not firing you. I'm not asking you to quit. That's not it."

They talk about how all caddies make mistakes. In recent weeks, Tim Herron's caddie failed to show up for Round One of a tournament. Kent Jones's caddie directed him to the wrong ball, which he promptly hit. Even as a rookie, Robert has never made such blatant errors. Gradually emotions cool. Hurt feelings are soothed. They agree that the partnership has worked, and they decide to keep it together. The decision is a relief for both of them, but weeks later, they will both express lingering ambivalence.

Esteban tells me: "He needs to stop getting so excited and scared. If your player is pissed off, you still have to go to him and say, 'I know you're pissed off, but the ball is cut.' I can get a kid from behind the ropes to just carry the bag. I need someone who will do the things that help me win. I'm not here just to make the cut. I'm here to win."

Robert says: "He's got to accept the fact that on some holes, he can't do what other guys can do. I don't think he will ever win unless he accepts who he is and who he is not. I had to do it with my own life. I tried to be more of a ladies' man, more outgoing, but it didn't work. It wasn't me. He's got to be himself, not try to be like anyone else, if he's going to have any chance to win out here."

Though Robert doesn't know it, Esteban is gradually recognizing that he has gone off-course in recent weeks. In a casual conversation, he tells me that switching drivers, and pushing for more distance, may have been a mistake. "It was just stupid of me," he says, in a rare moment of self-criticism. "I've been hitting a lot of drives into the woods."

Stupid, perhaps, but natural. Sprinters always want to go faster. Boxers strive to punch harder. Golfers invariably feel the urge to just hit the ball further. But the ideal swing is a perfect balance of power and control. Adding power almost always diminishes control. It happens to Tiger Woods and it happens to Esteban Toledo.

For his part, Robert is expecting too much if he believes that Esteban can adjust to every one of the challenges of Tour life, and always keep perfect balance in his mind and in his game. Despite the fact that he is a professional golfer at the top of the game, the grinder on Tour is humbled every week when someone else stands on the eighteenth green and accepts the winner's check. Maintaining a healthy ego under such circumstances is almost impossible.

Away from the golf course, the biggest difficulty of Tour life is travel. He has owned his new home now for five months, but Esteban has spent less than a week in it. And though some Tour stops—Hawaii comes to mind—are little visits to paradise, most are business trips to ordinary suburbs, or worse, to places like Mississippi in July. Everything on the road is more difficult than it is at home. By the time a player finds a good hotel and food in these places, it's time to move on.

Finally, Tour players are hard-pressed to maintain any kind of normality in relationships. Family life for the grinder is no easier than it is for a traveling circus performer. Wives can feel neglected whether they come on the road, or stay at home. Children feel the same, and tend to run amok. And simple friendships are complicated by the fact that fellow pros are also competitors, and many outsiders are either sycophants or predators.

Given his strange existence, it is remarkable that Esteban remains as steady as he does. But he does, and two weeks after the blow-up at Pine Mountain, he arrives in Orlando, Florida, prepared to play his brand of golf again. Colleen and Nicholas fly in from California for the Disney National Car Rental Classic, the last tournament of the season. For reasons that include Mickey, Goofy, and Space Mountain, this event is the most popular among the families of touring pros.

The tournament is played on two of Disneyworld's three courses, the Palm and the Magnolia. The Magnolia is more challenging than the Palm Course. Each one has been lengthened by about 500 yards for the pros, which makes them considerably tougher than the layouts used by 120,000 vacationers every year.

•

This year's version of the Esteban Toledo PGA Tour is guaranteed to end on a happy note solely because he is certain of a return engagement next year. The lower-ranked of the Q. School grinders enjoy no such guarantee. Lan Gooch, Mark Wurtz, Vance Veazey, Keith Nolan, and Steve Jurgenson have no chance. They are all so low-ranked they haven't even been invited to play in Orlando.

Tim Conley, Tim Loustalot, and John Riegger are here, and they still have hope. With a top-five finish, any one of them could secure a card.

Of course, the competition for the last few spots on the Tour card money list includes many experienced veterans. Bruce Fleischer, P. H. Horgan II, Larry Rinker, and Mark Brooks are all within $25,000. David Stockton, Jr. enters the tournament holding number 125, and promptly shoots a 77 in the first day of play. His poor play offers an opportunity for all those chasing him. Riegger tries to take advantage with a 69. Conley scores 73, and Loustalot 72. These two are playing themselves right off the Tour.

The mid-way cut—set at a score of even par—is the lowest in the thirty-seven years that this tournament has been played. It is low, in part, because the strong winds that normally blow here in October have been calmed. At the same time, the field is one of the most formidable of the year. It includes David Duval, Vijay Singh, Phil Mickelson, Tiger Woods, Mark O'Meara. Despite the competition, John Riegger begins the weekend in seventh place. Two more rounds of his best golf, and next year's card is his. Tied for forty-third, Tin Conley cannot say the same. Tim Loustalot misses the cut. And there, at the very bottom of the list of survivors, at even par, is Esteban Toledo.

Though he has had to struggle to make the cut, nothing has bothered Esteban this week. In the "Happiest Place on Earth," he is as cheerful as any of the vacationers who gawk at him as he carries his golf bag through the Polynesian Village resort, where he and Colleen and Nicholas are spending the weekend. Colleen is already past the morning sickness stage of her pregnancy. Tests have shown that a baby girl is on the way, and Esteban is already charmed by her. He has trouble keeping his hands off of Colleen's rounding belly, where the kicks seem to grow more powerful every day.

As the last man of the seventy-seven who make the cut, Esteban has the strange fortune to be asked to tee off alone, on Saturday, ahead of the entire field. Solo rounds are not unusual on Tour. Some players enjoy it, while others find it difficult to focus without a someone to compete against or a gallery to please. It's too much like practice. But at 7:30 a.m., as he steps onto the first tee at the Magnolia, Esteban seems like the most relaxed man on Earth. He's wearing matching tan pants and shirt, white shoes and white visor. After hitting a perfectly straight drive of 260 yards, he turns to the tournament volunteers—who are the only audience—and says, "Tell those guys behind me they'll never catch up."

Alone, save for Robert, me, and a middle-aged woman who is the official scorer, Esteban is free to play at his own pace, and the pace is quick. In a little more than an hour, he makes five straight pars. On hole number six, a 195 par-three over a lake, he hits a solid four iron to within five feet of the hole. As Esteban walks to the green, an old man wearing headphones, matching nylon rain jacket and pants, spiked golf shoes, and black rubbers emerges from the woods. With a backpack on his shoulder and a water bottle hooked on his belt, he looks like he's spent the last week in the forest. He stands on the edge of the green as Esteban rolls in his birdie putt. "Muy bonito," says the man from the woods, loud enough for all to hear. He then joins me on the spectator side of the ropes, to double Esteban's gallery.

As we walk together, I discover that Leonard Gaines is a sixty-eight-year-old retired postal worker from south central Los Angeles and perhaps pro golf's most devoted fan. This year alone, he has traveled the country to see eight tournaments in person, from start to finish. He watched every other one on television. He knows the strengths and weaknesses of almost all of the players, even the lesser lights, and he simply adores the game. (He's so obsessed with learning it that he has installed a driving range mat and net in his living room at home.)

Mr. Gaines has much to cheer during the next few holes. On number 7, Esteban hits the flagstick with his second shot. When he gets to the green, Gaines calls out, "It was in and out, baby! In and out!" Esteban grins and says, "That's the name of a hamburger place in California—In and Out Burger." He makes the putt.

On hole number 9, Gaines gets to cry "Good drive, baby!" as Esteban puts a little extra muscle into his swing and hits it 280 yards. Another soft landing, this time within four feet of the hole, leads to a third birdie. Matched with six pars, these scores bring him to three under for the tournament.

Esteban birdies the first hole on the back nine, but suffers a brief setback on number 11. With an eight-foot-long alligator watching from the bank of a pond, he pulls his drive into the rough on the left side of the fairway. His second shot hits a slope leading up to the green and bounces back into a bunker. Though he's one of the best sand players on Tour, Esteban is unable to get up-and-down in two.

"That's alright, baby," says Leonard Gaines. "You'll get it back."

And he does. On the green of the twelfth hole, a par-three, Esteban calls up to the cameraman who is checking his equipment on a little scaffold tower. "Aren't you going to get this on TV?" he says. The cameraman takes the doughnut he has in his hand and jams it in his mouth. He then swivels the camera, pretending to focus on the green. (The camera hasn't even been powered up for the day.) Esteban makes the putt, recovering the shot he lost on number 10, and waves to the camera. "This is for professionals only," jokes Esteban. "Don't try this at home!"

The quiet of the pre-gallery tee time, and the light-hearted feeling of this round, make it seem almost like a victory lap at the end of a long, successful season. Esteban has moved himself from forty-third place on the leader board to fourteenth. Of course, that will likely change as other players turn in their scores, but no matter how anyone else plays today, they will not erase what is shaping up as the best round he has played in nearly three months.

"We need to make eight more good shots," says Bob Szczesny on the tee of hole number 17. "Two pars, and he's got 68 for the day."

He doesn't need all eight to finish. On the final hole, the longest par-four on the course, Esteban hits the ball safely between the bunkers that lie in wait on either side of the fairway 250 yards out. With his ball on the right side, he's in position to attack a green where the only hazards are three big bunkers on the left. His second shot stops ten feet below the hole, a perfect spot for a strong putt

that drops in the center of the cup. "I know I beat someone today," he tells Leonard Gaines after he signs his
scorecard. "I won't play alone tomorrow."

•

The next morning, John Riegger's face is so grim that it's
hard to tell that he's just two shots out of fifth place, two
shots away from becoming the eighth of the Q. School
grinders to clinch a '99 card. After a miserable start to the
year, Riegger has made the cut in sixteen of the last nineteen tournaments. "At least I'm giving myself a chance,"
he tells me. Here in Orlando, he has been under par for
three straight days. And he's ahead of all the other players, including Simpson, Rinker, Brooks, and Horgan, who
are scrambling for spot number 125.

No one could feel more alone this morning than Riegger. With no wife, or children, he's one of the few players
who have come to Disneyworld without a retinue. But like
most everyone else, he has supporters scattered across the
country, who keep up with him via television and the
Internet. Chief among them is his widowed mother, Carolyn. She still lives in his childhood home in little Metropolis, Illinois, on the banks of the Ohio River, ten miles
from where it meets the Mississippi.

With no brothers and sisters, John is, quite literally,
Carolyn Riegger's only family. A worrier by nature, she
frets through every round of every tournament her son
plays, even rushing home at lunchtime from the bank
where she works to check his score by computer. Other
people in Metropolis share an interest in John's play. But
Carolyn reacts sharply to his critics. She tells me that one
longtime friend who couldn't resist a wisecrack about

John always falling "just one shot short" is a friend no longer.

With his mother in Metropolis nervously switching from the computer screen to the television and back, John Riegger struggles to adjust to putting greens that are suddenly slower. So many of the top players had complained about them being too hard and too fast that tournament officials had watered them heavily enough for the likes of Woods and Duval to start attacking pins. Good for them. Bad for Riegger.

Unable to adjust to the greens, Riegger scores bogeys on the second and sixth holes, which ruins his front nine. He rallies toward the end, scoring birdies on numbers 16 and 17 to get back to where he started the day—seven under. On the leader board he can see that Larry Rinker, who barely made the Friday cut, is racing ahead of him. On the final hole, desperation leads to a bogey. As he plucks the ball out of the hole, he knows his PGA Tour membership is lost. Rinker will finish high enough to knock Dave Stockton, Jr.—who missed the cut this week— off the list of 125.

Playing in front of Riegger, Esteban is matched with longtime pro Paul Goydos and fellow Q. School grinder Tom Pernice, who have both secured their spots on the '99 Tour. The day is warm and the sky is bright blue. A huge Sunday gallery is following the leaders—Davis Love II, John Huston, and Tiger Woods. Pernice, Goydos, and Esteban are merely trying to go as low with their scores, and as high in their earnings, as possible. They are also having as much fun as three Sunday amateurs on their best day.

On number 11, a watery par-four of 385 yards, Pernice

hits his drive to the right, landing it on a little strip of grass between a cart path and a pond that runs the length of the fairway. He can't hit the ball without standing on the pavement, so he takes a free drop. The trouble is the embankment that leads from the path down into the water. If he drops the ball, it's bound to land in the drink.

Here Esteban comes to the rescue, volunteering to stand on the incline, with his back to the water, and catch the ball. He climbs down toward the water, and steadies himself. Suddenly, as he stands with his back to the pond and his heels an inch from the water, he remembers the alligator he saw there yesterday.

"Wait a minute!" he shouts in mock terror. "Are there any 'gators behind me?"

Even the Tour officials who have come to oversee the drop start to laugh. After three drops, with Esteban catching each rolling golf ball, Pernice is allowed to place it in play on the fairway and continue. Esteban scrambles back onto level ground.

As I watch Pernice play to an efficient, one-under-par finish, I am reminded of a conversation we had in July. At the time, he had just $87,260 in earnings and was ranked 146th. He didn't know that he would soon earn more than $100,000 in just three tournaments and cement his future, at least for a year. He was, instead, anxiously trying to discover the secret of staying on the Big Tour. He had concluded that it lies in the mind, not the body.

"A lot of us play well enough, but we don't do it at the right times," said Pernice. "The successful players finish well on Sundays. They also truly believe, every week, that they can go out there and win. The way I play sometimes I can't hope to win. I am working on not thinking that way. I'd like to have the true conviction that nobody is going to beat me."

Pernice, who works on his swing with a prominent teacher named Robert Baker, had begun to work on his attitude with the inspirational teacher Tony Robbins. A star of TV infomercials and self-improvement lectures, Robbins works in the tradition of positive-thinking Norman Vincent Peale, but adds modern twists like fire-walking to his seminars. Pernice believes it works. "It clicked with me. I think you do have to visualize yourself having success, not letting anything stand in your way. That's the beginning of making it real."

It is real on this Sunday, as Pernice savors every moment of his final competitive round of the season knowing that he's going to put more money in the bank, and knowing he'll be back in the land of courtesy cars and million-dollar purses next year. He'll end up the season fifty-fifth on the money list, with more than half a million dollars in prize money. This is more than he's earned on the golf course in the entire rest of his career.

Though behind Pernice and Goydos on the money list, Esteban is comfortably their equal today. All three make birdie putts on the fourth green. And by the time he reaches the twelfth tee, Esteban is eight under for the tournament. He's not just having fun. He's moved up to fourteenth place. If he can hold on, he'll make almost $42,000 on a week when he was the last man to escape the cut. He can't hold on, though. Two bogeys on the back nine mean he'll finish even with John Riegger, where the paychecks are a little more than $11,000. Pernice, just one shot better, makes a full $10,000 more.

As Esteban enters the little trailer where he'll sign his scorecard, I walk down the player's runway to the fence where fans queue up for autographs. The season is over for all the Q. School Grinders except J. P. Hayes, whose victory at Westchester allows him to play in next week's Tour Championship.

The season is over for me, as well. I have walked inside the ropes with Esteban for the last time, watching a man who was once a desperate Q. Schooler finish the most relaxed round of the year. When sponsor fees, pro-am checks, and other income is added to his prize money, Esteban Toledo is a good $400,000 richer than he was when I first met him. He is confident, at last, that he belongs on the PGA Tour. He is a father-to-be, and quite possibly the most satisfied man in the Magic Kingdom.

When I spot Leonard Gaines, the super-fan, standing against the fence with a bunch of eager-looking kids, he motions for me to come over. He's waiting to tell Esteban that he has seen him grow into a PGA Tour caliber pro this year. This is high praise from a man who can tell you who won every single tournament this year—on both the men's and women's tours—and by how much.

"I should have been with him today," says Leonard Gaines. "I kept watching him climb up the board. When he got to eight under, I knew he had some holes to play where he could make birdies. He had a chance to go really low this week."

As we talk, Esteban comes out of the scorer's trailer and is mobbed by kids. Hats and programs and golf balls are presented by eager hands. Esteban, who seems more delighted than any of the youngsters, signs each one.

Noticing the crush, Leonard Gaines calls out his congratulations and turns to leave. Then he stops for a moment and turns back to me.

"Tell him he's really made it. Tell him he should feel it deep down inside. Nobody hits the irons sweeter than he does. He's long, and straight, and he lands them soft. If he gets hot with the putter, he's gonna drive them all crazy."

*

Over ten months, the PGA Tour has kept Esteban Toledo on the road for almost 270 days. Though golfers may be babied by tournament officials who give them cars and meals, much of life on Tour is truly mundane. It is ironing tomorrow's shirt at ten o'clock the night before. It is phone calls that just can't replace holding your wife in your arms. It is dragging 200 pounds of luggage through airports. It is driving around Mississippi at midnight looking at "No Vacancy" signs.

The off-season is all of two months long, which explains why most of the pros flee Orlando on Sunday night, eager to put this time into rest or some off-the-course business. But Esteban's blue and white golf bag is not among the dozens that pile up at the bellman's station outside the entrance to Polynesian resort. Esteban is staying to play in a pro-am tournament scheduled for tomorrow.

Robert finds it hard to understand why one of the country's top 100 golfers would reduce his vacation—even by a day—to earn a relatively small amount of money playing with a bunch of amateurs. It might be alright for someone lower in the golf hierarchy—say, John Riegger—but even he didn't accept the offer to play in this event. Even he wants to go home.

On Monday morning, Esteban is hardly ambivalent about his choice. I meet him and Colleen and Nicholas for breakfast at a little fast-food café at their hotel. The place is full of tourist families—toddlers wearing Mickey Mouse ears, mothers toting heavy diaper bags. Esteban gets in the cafeteria line and helps Nicholas get some juice and cereal. While waiting for the cashier, he makes faces at a baby girl who smiles at him over her father's shoulder.

By 8:30 a.m., Esteban is lugging his clubs through the lobby, eager to get to the van that will take him to the pro-am tournament. He doesn't exactly swagger, but he walks proudly, wearing a crisp golf shirt with Toyota emblazoned on the breast and his Tear Drop visor. He looks strong, well rested, happy.

Outside, in the warm Florida morning, a doorman and a bellhop try to take the bag away from him, but Esteban won't let them. The van driver volunteers to put it in the back seat, but still Esteban holds on. When he gets into the van, he rests the bag between his knees, and closes the door.

For a moment, I see the Mexican boy who spent an entire day in a crowded bus clutching a battered old golf bag filled with cast-off clubs. Esteban's first tournament, so long ago, became a dream come true. It started him on the journey along Ouimet's path. This morning, he will be paid money to play golf. He will receive the respect and admiration accorded to a member of the PGA Tour. He will be living proof that the game's highest level still holds a place for outsiders with talent, and, more importantly, character.

"Another beautiful morning," says the van driver as he puts the vehicle in gear.

"Yes, it is," answers Esteban Toledo.

THE SCORECARD	
Remaining tournaments	0
Esteban's earnings	$327,244
Rank (final)	93rd

Epilogue ○

In the brief period between the 1998 and 1999 Tours, Esteban played in the Mexican Open, where he was mobbed by fans who consider him their country's best. He also represented Mexico at the World Cup, in New Zealand. Esteban finished a respectable two over, better than two thirds of the competitors. But his partner shot an embarrassing twenty-five over, destroying the team's chances. To add to the insult, the tournament's organizers never paid his expenses, as they promised, so the privilege of representing his homeland cost Esteban several thousands of dollars more than the $3,700 he got for a twenty-fifth-place finish.

Back in the states, Esteban practiced, got reacquainted with Nicholas and Colleen, and made a point of talking every day to the baby growing in her womb.

In his daily life outside the family, Esteban experienced

his first tastes of being a celebrity, of sorts. Most of them were positive. He was recognized and approached by some admiring fans at the Los Angeles Airport. And at Price Club, he was stopped in the middle of the frozen food aisle by a man who just had to have an autograph. He has also found himself dealing with friends of friends, who wanted to sell him investments, or wanted free tickets to upcoming tournaments. Some people even called up to ask for free golf clubs, as if he had a stash of drivers and irons in his garage.

Life changed for Robert Szczesny, too. He earned enough last year to buy an almost-new car to replace his ten-year-old Grand Prix. He began funding a retirement plan. He spent a couple of weeks resting at his brother's home in Florida, and then took a cross-country trip to visit friends. He stopped at my home in New York, and we invested a few hours in checking Esteban's statistics on the Internet, comparing them with his peers on the Tour.

The numbers showed that the golfers who make the most money on Tour drive the ball straight and far, which puts them in position to make birdies. They also putt well. In 1998, David Duval was second in driving, fifth in putting, and first in sub-par holes. John Huston also ranked in the top ten in all these categories.

Esteban was low on the distance chart—172nd—but made up for it in accuracy, where he ranked fifteenth. Robert figured that increasing his drive from 260 yards to 270, if it could be achieved without much loss in accuracy, would give him a better chance at making birdies and, especially, eagles on par-fives. In this category he was 138th, with just three the entire year.

But as anyone who looks for answers in golf's statistics quickly learns, there are no mathematical absolutes. Some of the big earners on Tour succeeded despite problems with driving distance. Justin Leonard is just one example. Among the top twenty-five money-winners, John Cook's average drive is only 3.8 yards longer than Esteban's. Jesper Parnevik's typical drive is only 4.7 yards longer. But he made more than $1.2 million in 1998 compared with Esteban's $327,000.

As Robert searched for signs that might point the way to better scores, it became obvious that Esteban is much closer to excellence than even his caddie realized. Esteban had ended the year ranked ninety-third on the PGA Tour money list, and 138th in the entire world. His scoring average—fifty-sixth—suggests he's even better than these rankings indicate.

Even more encouraging was the fact that Esteban was at his best under pressure on Saturdays and Sundays, when money is at stake. His average Saturday score—69.94—was thirteenth-best for the entire PGA Tour. In the cold light of the numbers, it was clear to me that a few days of hot putting in any tournament could make him a winner.

•

Esteban began the 1999 PGA Tour with a round worthy of a champion—a 65 at the Sony Open in Hawaii. He did it with seven birdies and two bogeys on a Waialae Country Club course that has been made longer and tougher in response to John Huston's record low score of twenty-eight under par the previous year.

If his play wasn't enough to get the public's attention, Esteban's performance in the press tent afterwards was.

He told reporters what he had told me a few months earlier, that if he won, he was going to retire. At first many in the press thought there must be a language problem here. He must have meant that he would take some time off. But he insisted that he would leave the Tour, and, perhaps, never come back.

"You go to where I've come from," he said. "Take a look around at the way I lived. Then you'll understand that maybe winning once here, and going to be with your family, would be enough."

For the next two days, it looked like Esteban might have the opportunity to prove that he meant what he said. On Friday, as high winds made play more difficult for everyone, a score of 72 kept him in fifth place. On Saturday, he was paired with the reigning PGA Tour Player of the Year, Mark O'Meara, and because of this he got plenty of airtime on the national broadcast of the tournament.

On Saturday at Waialae, the national TV audience saw Esteban at his creative best. On the fourteenth hole, his drive landed behind a tree on the right side of the fairway. One of the broadcast commentators confidently explained why Esteban would have to hit a slicing punch shot to the left of the tree trunk and just hope it ran up to the green. Instead, Esteban hit a towering, right-to-left hook up over the tree and onto the green.

Though his play was outstanding, the TV announcers focused more on Esteban's remarks about retiring after a victory. They insisted his statements were like Michael Jordan's many predictions of his own retirement. Jordan had changed his mind so many times that eventually it was hard to take him seriously. But Esteban was serious. On the telephone he told me, "People think I'm goofy, but I'm just trying to communicate something about what's important. I love being a golfer, but money and being famous are not the most important things in life. When I was growing up, I didn't have the feeling that anyone loved me, or took care of me like a parent should. I am going to do that for my baby. That's what's important in life."

Bob believed that Esteban meant what he said at the moment, but that he was a little baby-crazed. "Besides," he said, "He hasn't won yet, and it may be a long time until he does. By then, I think he will have calmed down a little bit."

Esteban didn't win in Hawaii, but he finished close enough to the top—five shots—that he earned more than $40,000. (If you want to understand the impact of the increased PGA Tour purses, consider that a year earlier the same sixteenth-place finish in Hawaii earned $27,000.) He came back to the mainland high on the possibility that he might soon win a tournament. Then, suddenly, he stopped putting well. Between January 31 and February 21 he was cut from four tournaments in a row. He played one of the worst rounds of his pro career, an 80 at Pebble Beach, and talked so much about his bad putting that Colleen started trying to find a putting instructor who might help him.

It wasn't surprising that during this sour month, Esteban and Robert had their worst falling-out in two years of working together. I learned about it when Robert left a message on my answering machine saying, "Mr. Toledo and I are no longer together. Give me a call at the Tucson Inn." His voice was completely flat, and almost trembling.

After speaking to him, and Esteban, I was able to get a rough idea of what had happened. After a particularly miserable Friday round that led to him being cut at the Nissan Open, Esteban had grumbled something to Robert about needing to shake things up. He even wondered aloud whether a new caddie might help. He asked Robert to call him on Sunday.

Robert was well aware of the increased pressure many Tour caddies felt in 1999. With purses growing, more and more outsiders were beginning to see that caddying could be lucrative and rewarding. At the same time, players were more prepared than ever to blame a caddie for their trouble or to hope that a new one would bring them fortune.

At the time Esteban and Robert had their falling-out, everyone on Tour knew that Tiger Woods was on the verge of firing his caddie, the most famous caddie of all, Mike Cowan. Though Cowan had escorted Woods onto the Tour and helped him win ten tournaments, including the Masters, it wasn't enough for Tiger. In the weeks to come, Jim Furyk and Mark O'Meara would also axe longtime caddies. Robert had heard rumblings of these player-caddie breakups. When it looked like he might lose his job, he grew so anxious that he couldn't wait until Sunday. He called Esteban on Saturday and blurted out a resignation.

"He said something about not wanting to get in the way of my dream," recalled Esteban. "I kept trying to talk to him, but he went so fast and didn't give me a chance to say what I wanted to say."

What Esteban would have said, if he had a chance, was that he wanted to keep their team together. He had no intention of firing Robert. When he got to Tucson, he finally got to have his say. Robert asked for his job back, and he got it, on the condition that he would never walk away again without a real conversation.

After the reunion, Esteban's game picked up. He felt more comfortable during this, his second consecutive year on the Tour. Hotels and restaurants were much easier to locate. Security guards and volunteers at the tournament sites recognized him. And whether it was on the practice tee or in the locker room, all the other players seemed to recognize and accept him. He felt, in every sense, that he was a full-fledged member of the PGA Tour.

Satisfying as it was, this acceptance changed nothing inside Esteban. "I am still the same," he repeated to me early in the season. He was, indeed, the same proud, tough kid from Mexicali with a boxer's instincts. As if to prove it, he nearly got into a fight with one of the itinerant caddies who serve the Tour players. It all started in the morning, when the caddie made a fuss about Esteban supposedly moving on the tee to distract his opponent. By that night, when the two men ran encountered each other in a hotel parking lot, the caddie had worked himself into a rage.

"I was ready to knock him out, I really was," said Esteban. "But I kept remembering what I was there for. I'm a PGA Tour player. I had my business to take care of. He wasn't worth it."

By the middle of March, Esteban would be over the $80,000 mark in earnings, ranked ninety-sixth, and well on his way to another successful year. At the Doral-Ryder Open, he again contended for the lead. And the TV-types started saying his name in the Spanish style, Toe-lay-doh. Johnny Miller, the former Tour great, now a TV commentator, went to great lengths to describe Esteban's recent success as "one of the great stories in golf." When asked to comment about Esteban and his fellow grinders, Ernie Els told reporters at Doral, "These guys have come through the real world . . . they are tough players. . . ."

March also made Esteban the exceedingly proud father of a perfect baby girl, with brown hair and eyes, whom he and Colleen named Eden. Her initials will be E.T., just like her father's. And Esteban would be so taken by the child that he would fight with Colleen so that he would be the one to handle the groggy 4 a.m. feedings.

Eden turned out to be an inspiration. After taking a few weeks off to be a full-time father, Esteban returned to the Tour to play much better golf. After rounds of 69 and 71 at the Shell Houston Open, he found himself in second place on Saturday afternoon, one shot off the lead. His drive on the seventeenth hole at The Woodlands course put him in position to make a birdie and tie the leaders. What happened next would convince anyone that golf is the cruelest game.

From a perfect fairway position, Esteban fired a short iron toward the green, which is protected on the front and left by a quiet little pond shaped like a mitten. The ball cleared the water on the front—the thumb of the mitten—but skittered left along an embankment and trickled down the side and in.

A ball in the water is bad, but no disaster. But what happened next, was. When they reached the spot where the ball had trickled in, Esteban and Robert quickly fell into the routine of dropping a new ball. Robert crouched at the water's edge, with one foot planted on the timbers of a retaining wall, ready to catch it before it rolled into the water. Esteban dropped a ball and watched it settle a foot or so from the wall.

The trouble started when Esteban took his stance. He noticed immediately that his right foot was on top of the beams. Under some circumstances a wall might be a man-made obstruction and he might be allowed to pick up the ball again and drop it elsewhere to get away from the retaining wall. This was not one of those circumstances. The retaining wall at the seventeenth hole at The Wood-lands was considered "in play," not an obstruction. As Esteban bent down to pick up the ball, something inside him said, "This might be wrong." But he did it, anyway.

By the time he plucked up that ball, millions of golf fans around the country were watching. "Oh no, that ball's in play," said the TV announcer. "We've got a prob-lem here."

The nagging voice in Esteban's head got loud enough to persuade him to summon a rules official. After ten min-utes of talking, he was instructed to put the ball back where it was after the original drop. Hit it. And accept a two-stroke penalty. Added to the lost-ball penalty, this meant a triple bogey.

On the next hole, Esteban was so upset that he sent another ball into the water. He almost salvaged his bogey with a thirty-five-foot putt that stopped an inch and a half in front of the cup. The tap-in ended a five-shot swing in just two holes. Esteban dropped from second, to twenty-second.

And here's the worst part. On Sunday, Esteban shot a

steady, even par round. Everyone on the leader board was so tight that scores ballooned. In the end, a score of nine under won the tournament and $450,000. Eight under, the very score Esteban owned standing in the seventeenth fairway on Saturday, was worth $220,000. But because of his debacle, Esteban earned a $53,000 for tenth place. Picking up the ball had cost him $170,000.

•

Esteban also lost money in the slump that began in the golf equipment industry in 1997 and continued into 1999. Early in the year, Callaway cut 700 workers from its payroll, and layoffs were also made at Cobra golf company and Taylor Made. The business crisis had a direct effect on many pros. Taylor Made stopped funding its driver pool and withdrew Esteban's sponsorships. "I guess they don't think I can win," said Esteban. "They're wrong."

Tear Drop, which spent millions acquiring other companies including the iron maker Ram, offered Esteban a deal, but only if he would switch to Ram irons. He was willing to consider the idea, but only if he liked the clubs. Many players have switched clubs in order to get a sponsor's money, only to see their games suffer. Corey Pavin's nosedive in the mid-1990s is the most-cited example of this phenomenon.

When the Ram clubs didn't arrive at his home until the day before he left on Tour, Esteban concluded the company wasn't serious about supporting him and ended the arrangement himself. "I called the president of Tear Drop and thanked him for his support, but said we were finished," recalled Esteban.

The lost income meant that as a fully exempt player

ranked in the top 100, Esteban had less corporate support than he did when he was fresh out of Q. School. This hurt his pride as much as his pocketbook. Indeed, for the first few months of 1999, he endured the embarrassment of using a plain gray golf bag, with no sponsor's message on it. (Plenty of fellow pros teased him about this on the practice ranges.) He wasn't alone, with a blank bag. Payne Stewart used one for awhile. But he felt conspicuous, nonetheless, and was relieved when the Odyssey putter company came along with a modest offer and a label for his bag. If the money from Tear Drop wasn't restored completely, at least his pride was healed.

Of course, every one of the 1998 Q. School grinders who failed to retain their cards would gladly suffer the embarrassment of losing sponsors if it meant getting their exemptions back. None of them made it through 1999 Q. School to regain their cards, but John Riegger came close. He was in fifteenth place going into the next-to-last day of play. Then, on the fifteenth hole, the devil of golf struck.

"It was a par-five and I had aimed for a bunker near the green on purpose. When I got there, the lie wasn't very good. I hit it out, but it went over the green and landed on a cart path. It bounced right up into this hillside that was all rocks. It was unplayable, so I had to put it back in the bunker and start all over again. I made a triple bogey. I felt like someone had just punched me in the stomach. On the next tee I hit the ball right in the water. I knew it was over then. I stopped playing right then, picked up the ball, and went home."

Home is now Las Vegas, where Riegger lives with a fiancée he met last summer, and her two daughters. "I found a woman I play well around," he jokes. "I had to hold on to her." While wintering in Vegas, Riegger talked to some casino operators about a job as a golfing companion for the high rollers. Other former Tour pros, including Dave Stockton and Mark Fowls, have worked corporate outings as a pro-for-hire, but as far as Riegger knows, he would be the only casino pro ever to come from the PGA Tour.

Among the other failed Q. School grinders of '98, Keith Nolan, Tim Conley, Steve Jurgenson, Tim Loustalot, Vance Veazey, and Mark Wurtz played in Nike tournaments or scrambled to get into PGA Tour events through sponsor exemptions, and Monday qualifying. Only Lan Gooch seemed to disappear entirely from pro golf. He retreated to his home in Mississippi, where he decided to take an extended break from tournaments. But even there, the torture continued. Everyone wants to know why he played so poorly. Some local scratch players have even challenged him, and beaten him out of small wagers.

Not surprisingly, Gooch struggled to reconcile his experience. Every week he had been thrilled to lace up his spikes in a locker room shared by the world's best. But he was embarrassed and eventually humiliated as he played the worst golf of his life. "I can remember about one good shot, and that was the first one of the year," he says. "I made a hole in one. But it was at a Nike Tour tournament I played before I got into the field on the PGA Tour. Everything was downhill after that."

A year on the PGA Tour left Lan's ego battered, but not broken. "I played against the best in the world and I didn't measure up," he confesses. "It's what I do best, and I failed. But you know, I've always been a grinder, in golf and in my life. I'll get back into it, and when Q. School comes around I'll throw in my $4,000 and try again. I can't help myself."

●

If the grinders show us all what it takes to compete at a high level, the first ingredient in the formula must be their willingness to make a commitment to a goal, and to persevere despite frequent failures. Lan Gooch could not have been more thoroughly humiliated in his Tour experience, but he is not prepared to give up on himself. He will be back at Q. School one day.

But this one quality—determination—hardly explains why one grinder finally succeeds when others, with roughly equal talents, fail. Even more perplexing is the success of a man who faces every disadvantage, obstacles that defeat everyone around him, and still prevails. The answers to these questions lie in the extraordinary lives of men like Esteban Toledo, who find that the PGA Tour still offers them the opportunity to make dreams come true.

Not long after Eden's birth, Colleen and Esteban put their baby to bed, and retire to the comfortable bedroom on the second floor of their cozy—and mortgage-free—townhouse. In moments such as these, Esteban often reflects on how much his life has changed, and this time, as usual, he was filled with gratitude for Colleen and Nicholas and now, Eden. His mind went back to the clubhouse in Mexicali, to the day the locker room attendant passed a basket and collected 1,000 pesos to send him to that first tournament.

In hindsight, Esteban can see the moments when a

kindness propelled him toward his dream. He was always a resilient person, and he possessed an inner drive to connect with what is good in other people. Esteban can also describe the homemade philosophies that sustained him in his quest. They are his six steps to grinder success:

Never stop dreaming. "My real first dream was to be a boxer, but when they opened me up the second time, I knew I'd have to find another one. I found a new goal. I then created a positive image in my mind of me getting to that goal."

Trust someone. "We all need to follow people who are successful. In golf, I'll go to someone I admire like Peter Jacobsen and ask questions like, 'How do you play under pressure?' In the rest of my life, I look to people who are successful and learn from them. Jon has taught me that the important things are family, your dreams, being honest. Money is not success. The people you love, and your dream, they make you happy."

Learn from failure. "Bad things are always going to happen in life, just like they happen on the golf course. The question is, What do you do after something bad happens? Do you give up, or do you figure out what went wrong and try again? Colleen turned me down five times before she said yes, she would marry me. What if I had not asked the sixth time?"

Be 'people positive.'—"Jon will not say a bad word about anyone, and I have the same attitude. I think that almost every person is really a nice guy inside, and if he's not acting that way it's because he's caught up in a situation that is making life difficult. But even with people like that, if you go to them expecting the best, you're more likely to get it."

Take risks. "On the last hole, if I have a chance to make eagle, I am going to go for it, every time. What's the use of having a dream if you are not going to take the risk of making it come true? And what's worse, trying and failing, or knowing you never really tried?"

Love conquers all. "In 1997, when I went to Asia, a lot of Rita's [Minnis] friends told her I would never make it. When I came back, I could see she was upset. She told me this, and then grabbed my hand and said, 'I know they are wrong, Esteban. You can make it.' I could have listened to the people who didn't care about me, who said I couldn't make it. But I listened to the people who loved me. They said I could succeed, and I believed them."

Of course, there are many more elements in Esteban's method. Some are quite ordinary and practical. For example, at the start of each year, he very deliberately writes down his goals. Committing them to paper makes them more powerful. "This year I wrote down, 'Be a good father. Be a good husband. Win a tournament,' " he told me in 1999.

Other aspects of his approach are more mystical. Esteban believes in God, and has faith that his trust in Him will be rewarded. He also believes in intuition. "I feel it when I'm about to play well," he says. And he believes that life requires a kind of emotional balance. He finds it in his relationship with Jon and Rita Minnis, and in his marriage. Indeed, when you consider Esteban in 1994—when he failed on Tour—and 1998, Colleen's presence is the one big difference.

Although he never explained it just this way, I think that love made the difference in Esteban's golf game. It wasn't required in boxing. There is no love in hitting someone, harder and harder, and taking punishment yourself, until someone falls. But golf requires much more than aggression. It requires inner peace. If you doubt this, consider the supremely talented and supremely tortured John Daly and how his inner demons have thwarted him time and again.

It is a blessing that lost boys who emerge from poverty and loss to be nurtured by kind strangers often feel a debt when they grow up to become happy, successful men. As soon as he reached his own goal, fully aware of the help he received from the Minnises and the strength of character they helped him acquire, Esteban began to think about passing these gifts along. Eden and Nicholas will each receive a share. But on a visit to Mexicali, to show off his family, Esteban began to consider bringing a new player into his story. All around him, in Mexicali, he saw boys and girls whose lives are much like his was before golf. And he began to think seriously about lending some of them a hand. Adoption might even be in the future.

"I know life is hard, and sometimes more bad things happen than good," he said when he returned from Mexicali. "But I also know that dreams come true, and it could happen for one of those kids too. It could happen to anyone with a dream, if they have someone to show them the way and they never give up. I really believe that. If you look at my life, and understand it, you have to believe it too."

If you need any more proof in the value of accepting set-backs and still moving toward your dreams, consider one last story from this ordinary touring pro's extraordinary life. It all began on a Sunday in June of 1999, just prior to the U.S. Open. Esteban was headed from his home in California to Memphis and a one-day qualifying tournament where he hoped to get into the field for his very first Major. But first he had to go to Detroit for a Monday outing on behalf of Toyota. It was part of his sponsorship deal. He got a free Land Cruiser; Toyota got his body at four out of five gigs a year.

According to his contract, Esteban flies first-class to his Toyota outings, but he didn't complain when he was seated in the last row of the coach section next to the toilets. He figured someone made a mistake. No big deal. And he didn't complain when the bathroom malfunctioned, filling the air in the rear of the cabin with a distinct odor.

On Monday, the outing went well. Esteban spent some time chatting in Spanish in the locker room with Lee Trevino (there at the behest of Cadillac) and then he went out and wowed the amateurs with some ball-bending shots.

Then it came time to fly to Memphis, where his Tuesday morning tee time for the U.S. Open qualifying tournament was just after 8 a.m. At the Detroit airport, the first sign of trouble came when he dragged his golf clubs up to the check-in counter. His ticket didn't give him a seat in first class, he was told. In fact, it didn't give him a seat in *any* class. It was a voucher for a free ride, good for standby travel only.

"But go down to gate C-22," he was told. "Wait until the plane is boarded and they'll call your name."

At C-22, Esteban waited, and waited, until they were just about to close the door to the jetway. When he didn't hear his name, he asked the agents. There were seats available, he was told, but the plane was headed for Minneapolis, not Memphis. The Memphis jet was leaving from a different concourse, but if he ran, he might make it.

He ran. He didn't make it. In fact, he got there just in time to see the jet backing out, and rolling away.

It got worse. For the next hour, Esteban tried to find an airplane to Memphis. He was no longer concerned about how his first-class ticket became a nontransferable, zero dollar-value voucher. He wanted to get to Memphis at any price. But nothing was available until 11 p.m. He started calculating the time that remained before must tee up a ball in Memphis and quickly realized that he was bound to be exhausted.

It turned out that the last flight to Memphis was late. It arrived at its destination just before 2 a.m. Esteban got to his hotel at 3 a.m. He undressed, washed, and put his head down on the pillow. It seemed like only minutes passed before the phone was ringing. It was 6:30, and a chauffeur was in the lobby waiting to take him to the golf course. The water he splashed on his eyes stung enough to force them to open wide.

Esteban had never seen the golf course he played that day. But it was short, and tight, and a little scruffy, which suited him well. So well, in fact, that he didn't make a single bogey in thirty-six holes. In muggy, 95-degree heat, he posted scores of 69 and 67. Remarkably, this was not quite good enough. The day's play ended with sixteen men tied for six spots in the open.

Having walked two full rounds on roughly three hours of sleep, Esteban's feet and legs ached. His head was fuzzy and his eyes burned. But on the very first playoff hole, a long-par five, he muscled his drive and a three wood to the back fringe of the green, thirty feet past the pin. A delicate downhill chip stopped five feet above the hole. Trembling with nerves and fatigue, he hit a wobbly put that fell in for birdie. Six other players who also broke par on the hole were then regrouped to continue the playoff. They all knew that one of them would not be going to the Open.

Dusk was falling. On the next two holes, the seven men matched each other, par-for-par. On the fourth hole, Esteban made his par, and joined the others to watch the final group putt. When the last man, P. H. Horgan, stepped up to the ball, it was almost too dark for him to see the hole. Officials declared this would be the last shot. If need be, the competition would be continued the next day. It was a five-footer that Horgan would have normally made. Later he would say that it had been so dark he could not read the green properly. Whatever the reason, he missed. And Esteban, who was so tired he could barely stand, got into his first Major.

●

After surviving the cut at the U.S. Open, Esteban would finish a respectable thirty-fourth in conditions many considered to be unfairly difficult. By the first week in August, he secured his card for the next year with a fourteen-under, seventh-place finish at the Buick Open. In that same week, he actually won an unofficial event—the two-day Erie (Pennsylvania) Classic—with scores of 64 and 66.

He did this all while coping with a downturn in some parts of his game. He was not quite as accurate as last year, not quite as steady in the bunkers. But he still made more money. How? Confidence. Experience had made Esteban confident that he would find a way to succeed. He had truly accepted that he belongs on the Big Tour. As a result, his scoring average got lower and lower, even as he suffered with little hitches in his game. And by the time the 2000 season began, he was a long shot no more.